The Goodheart-Willcox home economics series

Housing Decisions

Evelyn L. Lewis
Professor Emeritus, Home Economics
Northern Arizona University
Flagstaff, Arizona

The Goodheart-Willcox Company, Inc.
South Holland, Illinois

Library of Congress Catalog Card Number 86-19491
International Standard Book Number 0-87006-608-0

123456789-87-543210987

Library of Congress Cataloging in Publication Data

Lewis, Evelyn L.
  Housing decisions.

  (The Goodheart-Willcox home economics series)
  Includes index.
  Summary: Discusses selecting and furnishing a home and career opportunities related to housing.
    1. Housing. 1. Dwellings. 3. Interior decoration.
    [1. Housing. 2. Dwellings. 3. Interior decoration.]
    I. Title. II. Series.
TX301.L46   1987   643   86-19491
ISBN 0-87006-608-0

Introduction

Housing Decisions prepares you to make wise choices concerning your housing. It helps you understand your housing needs, and it shows you how to satisfy those needs. Many housing alternatives are presented throughout the book. You will learn to evaluate them and select the best ones for you.

Housing Decisions gives you a broad understanding and appreciation of the housing field. A logical progression of topics leads you through the decisions you face when selecting and furnishing your home. A chapter describing career opportunities related to housing is included.

Housing Decisions is easy to read and understand. It includes hundreds of illustrations which give you ideas you can adapt to fit your own home. References to the illustrations are made in the copy. They help you link the visual images to the written text.

Each chapter begins by stating objectives which help you set goals for your learning. Following the chapter are a list of key words, questions to help you review the chapter's important points, and suggestions for fun learning activities.

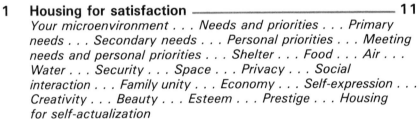

part one

Housing for you

part two
Making housing choices

part three

The inside story

part four
Progress in housing

part 1

Housing for you

Hal and Betty Swanson have lived in their home for twenty years. They moved into the house when their son Keith was three and their other son Mike was a baby. They chose a ranch house with three bedrooms so that each child would have his own space for hobbies and other activities.

Last year, Keith got married and Mike joined the navy. The Swansons decided to convert Keith's room into the den shown here. Since Hal enjoys sailing, they decorated the room with a nautical theme. Betty, who enjoys gardening, added plants to the room. The Swansons use the den mainly for reading and other quiet activities. But they chose a sleeper sofa so that the den could also be used as a guest room.

The Swansons have chosen housing which has satisfied their needs and priorities. They have been able to change their housing to meet their life situations.

How can your housing satisfy your needs and priorities? How can you expect your housing needs to change throughout your life?

9

GEORGE GALE

VENTARAMA SKYLIGHT CORP.

DANY CLEVENGER

DANNY CLEVENGER

GEORGE GALE

Your housing should help satisfy your needs and priorities, regardless of the type of home in which you live.

Housing
for satisfaction

1

After studying this chapter, you will be able to:
- Explain how you interact with your housing.
- Explain how your housing helps you satisfy your needs and your personal priorities.
- Show how you can achieve self-actualization through housing.

Housing, good or poor, has a deep and lasting effect on all of us. Winston Churchill once said, "We shape our buildings, and then they shape us." This is especially true of the buildings in which we live. First, we find a shelter to satisfy our needs. This shelter, in turn, affects the way we feel and act.

Housing, as we will use the word, means the dwelling itself and all that is within it and near it. This includes the furnishings, the neighborhood, and even the community. Throughout our study, we will consider the relationship between people and housing.

Your microenvironment

Housing is your *microenvironment.* It is just one part of your total environment, but it is a very important part. Housing has a great effect on your life-style and your personal development.

Whether you live alone or with other persons, you *interact* with housing. Your housing affects the way you behave and feel. Your style of living affects your housing.

For instance, suppose you live in a small apartment. You would not be able to host a lot of large parties. You would not have enough room, and your neighbors might become angry. In this way, your housing affects your actions.

On the other hand, if you wanted to host large parties, you would probably choose a different kind of housing. A large house that is set apart from others would meet your need. In this way, your life-style affects your housing.

This interaction can also be seen on a smaller scale. Suppose a room in your home is decorated with many expensive works of art. This would give you a feeling of formality and elegance. You would not want to work on your hobbies in this room. However, if hobbies were important to your life-style, you would furnish the room differently. You would adapt your housing to match your way of life.

NEEDS AND PERSONAL PRIORITIES

Your well-being is affected by everything around you. Your microenvironment, in the form of housing, helps fill your needs. It also helps you express your priorities. Human needs and personal priorities, then, are the first concern in a study of housing.

Primary needs

Your needs can be placed in the order of their importance. Some needs are common to all humans. They are physical in nature and have priority over other needs. These are called *primary needs* or basic needs. Food, shelter, clothing, air, and water are some of your primary needs.

Your primary needs must be satisfied before you can think of anything else. As soon as they are satisfied, you become concerned about your needs of lower priority.

Secondary needs

Needs of lower priority are called *secondary needs.* Self-esteem (awareness and appreciation of your own worth) is a secondary need. Another such need is the chance to be successful. These needs are psychological (having to do with the mind) or social (related to other people).

A director of a rescue mission once said that he saw human needs arranged in this order: 1. Soup. 2. Soap. 3. Salvation. When people came to him for help, their primary needs had not yet been satisfied. Hungry people can think only of food. Once they have eaten, their next concern is to be comfortable. Only when their basic needs are fulfilled can persons think of their secondary needs.

Maslow has listed human needs in order of priority as shown in 1-1. The primary needs are at the base of the pyramid. When your primary needs have been fulfilled, you progress up the pyramid, one step at a time. If you can meet the final need of *self-actualization,* you will have developed your full potential as a human being. You will have become the best that you can be. You will be doing those things that you do best. If your talent is writing poetry, you will be the best poet that you can be. If your talent is baseball, you will be playing as well as you can play.

Personal priorities

What is important to you? What do you like? Your answers to these questions tell you what your *personal priorities* are.

Your personal priorities are different than those of anyone else. Perhaps you hold some of the following priorities: friendship, family, money, status, religion, independence, or education. You have formed your set of priorities as a result of the experiences you have had. The people you know, the places you have been, and the things you have done have all influenced your personal priorities.

You use your personal priorities whenever you choose between two or more things. The choice you make depends on which things you desire most. Suppose you had a choice between spending a day by yourself, with your family, or with your friends. Your decision would depend on whether you rank your privacy, your family, or your friends most highly.

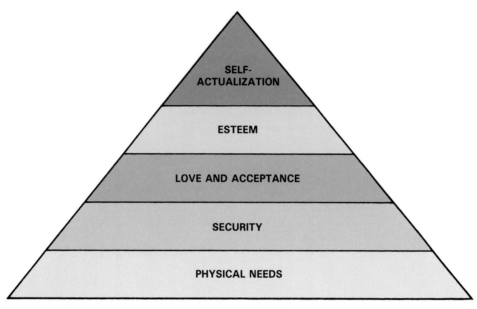

HUMAN NEEDS

1. Physical needs. Your physical needs, such as food, water, shelter and clothing, must be at least partially satisfied before you can think about anything else.
2. Security. Next, you need to feel safe in your surroundings and to know what to expect. You need protection from physical harm and economic disaster.
3. Love and acceptance. At this point, you will do many things to gain affection. You need to be praised and accepted by others. A small failure can make you feel rejected as a person. You need much support, assurance and personal warmth.
4. Esteem. Not only do you want to be liked, you also want to be respected. In this way, you gain confidence and feel necessary in the world.
5. Self-actualization. To reach this level, all other needs must be fulfilled to some degree. Your need is to develop your full potential. You learn because you want to be a "fuller" person. You have pride and self-respect. You can show individuality despite social pressures. You have your own opinions and are able to express them.

1-1 Maslow shows the priority of human needs by arranging them in the shape of a pyramid.

Each time you buy something, you make a priority decision. You decide that you want the item more than the money it costs.

If you share a home with others, you will find that some of your priorities are not like theirs. In this case, the priorities each of you have in common will control the thinking and actions of the group. These shared priorities will influence your housing decisions.

How needs and personal priorities relate

Your needs and priorities are closely related. For example, you need a place to sleep. Sleep is a primary need. A cot in a small room can satisfy this need. But the cot may not meet your priority of comfort. If you have a choice, your priority of comfort will cause you to choose a bed rather than the cot.

You also need space in the small room for activities other than sleeping. Your priorities will determine whether you choose a large, comfortable bed or a small bed which would allow more space for your activities. The beds shown in 1-2 and 1-3 may offer less than your ideal for comfort, but they are more comfortable than a cot. These beds do not take as much space as ordinary beds. But the extra space can be used for activities.

1-2 To save space, the bed in this room is folded to become a sofa during the day.

1-3 Bunk beds leave more floor space for other activities.

MEETING NEEDS AND PERSONAL PRIORITIES

Housing can help to satisfy many of your needs and wants. In fact, housing can be adapted to improve nearly every aspect of life.

Shelter

One of the primary human needs is *shelter*. This need has always been met by a dwelling of some type. The earliest dwellings were in natural settings such as caves and overhanging cliffs. The cliff dwelling in 1-4 was once a shelter for Indians. In 1-5, you can see the entrances to caves that were used for shelter by shepherds 2000 years ago.

The cave and cliff dwellers found their housing to be warm in the winter and cool in the summer. Cold winds and hot sunlight could not reach them.

Later, crude dwellings were built for protection from the weather. People often shared a dwelling with their livestock. In this way, they were all protected from the weather. The body

1-4 This large cliff dwelling called Montezuma Castle is located in central Arizona. Indian farmers probably lived there over 1000 years ago.

1-5 The Qumran Caves shown here are located near the Dead Sea. For centuries, they have given shelter to shepherds and their flocks.

heat of the animals helped keep the shelter warm.

These simple dwellings were built from the handiest materials to be had. Pueblo Indians used adobe (building material of sun-dried earth and straw) and rafters made from native materials. The thick walls and flat roofs in 1-6 provide shelter needed for the climate.

1-6 The Pueblo village of Languna, New Mexico was originally settled in the late seventeenth century. There is now a combination of early dwellings and more recent ones.

Look at the winter and summer dwellings of an Apache Indian family in 1-7. The summer home is built of branches. It offers protection from the scorching sun. Yet the breezes can circulate through the branches. The winter dwelling offers more protection.

Some present-day Bedouins (nomadic or wandering Arabs) still use tents such as the one pictured in 1-8. These simple dwellings can be taken apart and carried from place to place. This is important since the family or group travels continually, searching for food.

Food

The location and form of a dwelling were often related to another primary need—*food*. People built their shelters near sources of food. They also used their dwellings to store food. Many primitive people prepared and ate their food outside their dwellings.

Today, we still like to prepare food and eat outside. Some homes, such as the one in 1-9, are designed with this in mind. Areas within dwellings are also set aside for these purposes. See 1-10 and 1-11 for ways to provide space for cooking and eating.

Air

Your body needs oxygen from the *air* to survive. Every day you breathe about 16,000 quarts (15,142 liters) of air.

Unfortunately, humans pollute the air. The first person to do so was probably the cave

1-8 The Bedouin tent is fashioned from a frame of poles and ropes. These are covered with cloth of goat hair. The tent is divided into separate quarters for men and women. They sit and sleep on cotton quilts.

WESTERN WAYS FEATURES

1-7 The housing of Apache Indians is a clue to their way of life. Here you see a summer home that is under construction. A sturdier winter home is shown in the background.

MARILYN BRANDOM

1-9 This home has a food preparation area in an enclosed patio, making eating outside easier.

16

ALLMILMO CORP.

1-10 For convenience, meal preparation and eating areas are kept close to each other.

ARMSTRONG WORLD INDUSTRIES, INC.

1-11 In many homes, a separate dining room provides a place for eating.

dweller who discovered fire. Wood smoke did not harm the air greatly. However, every new generation has used and abused this discovery. As a result, air pollution has increased. The once thin column of smoke has become a huge, ugly cloud. In 1-12, you can see smoke from this factory polluting the air. Conditions like this exist throughout the United States.

Many people feel uncomfortable unless the air smells fresh and is moving freely. Your own preference for the amount of air circulation may differ from that of other people. Some people do not like a draft, while others do not mind it. You may have a high or a low tolerance (ability to accept or endure) for odors and other pollutants in the air. Can you think of some odors that do not bother you but that irritate your friends? Or do smells offend you more than they offend your friends?

Conditioning the air. You can condition the air in your microenvironment with a climate-control system. In 1-13, a *heat pump* is shown. This type of climate-control system can heat

NEW YORK STATE DEPT., ENVIRONMENTAL CONSERVATION

1-12 Industry is one of the many sources of pollution.

or cool the air in a building. Interest in the heat pump is growing because it uses less fuel than many other types of air conditioners. It can also be used to clean and circulate the air and to control the amount of humidity (moisture) in the air. Look at 1-14 to see how a heat pump works.

ARIZONA PUBLIC SERVICE

1-13 A heat pump with a duct system can heat buildings in winter and cool them in summer.

Electronic air cleaners, as the one in 1-15, clean the air in homes, offices, and other buildings. The air cleaner removes the particles that cause air pollution.

Water

Pure *water* is needed to sustain life. Plumbing systems bring fresh water into buildings and remove it when it has served its purpose.

Wells and community sources supply people with cold water and fulfill their needs for water. But most people prefer the convenience of having both hot and cold water available from faucets. To satisfy this desire, almost all dwellings have a water heater.

The heavy use of water is causing a shortage in some parts of the country. Therefore, recycling water for personal or industrial use has become common.

Controlling humidity. Water that is absorbed into the air as vapor is called humidity. Very high or very low humidity makes people feel uncomfortable.

Some dwellings have been designed with humidity control in mind. In the tropics, many

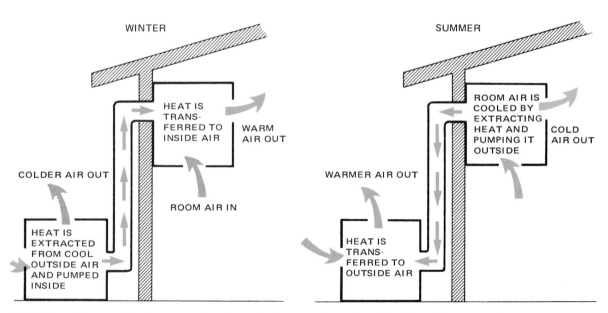

1-14 In winter, a heat pump absorbs solar heat and carries it inside. No matter how cold it is, some solar heat is available. In summer, a heat pump absorbs heat from inside a building and pumps it outside.

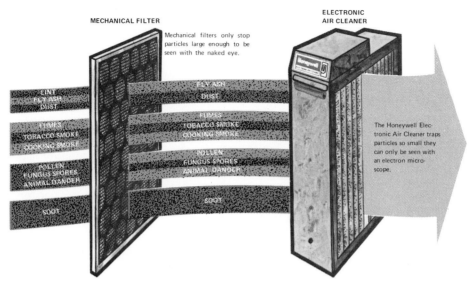

MECHANICAL FILTER

Mechanical filters only stop particles large enough to be seen with the naked eye.

ELECTRONIC AIR CLEANER

The Honeywell Electronic Air Cleaner traps particles so small they can only be seen with an electron microscope.

1-15 The electrostatic method of removing particles found in the air is used in homes, offices, and other enclosed spaces. After the air has passed through the cleaner, it is circulated throughout the area.

dwellings are open to the air and built on stilts. This design allows air to circulate freely under and through the buildings. Good air circulation and breezes help make the high humidity of the region more comfortable.

THE WEST BEND CO.

1-16 This portable humidifier can humidify a seven-room house.

Humidifiers, 1-16, add the desired amount of moisture to the air in a building. *Dehumidifiers* remove excess humidity. Some air conditioning systems include humidity-control features. The heat pump, described earlier in this chapter, is one such system.

Security

Housing should offer *security* from physical danger. It should also help you feel safe and protected from the unknown.

Living in a dwelling that is well-built and in a neighborhood that is free of crime can help you feel secure. However, to satisfy your need for security, you should include some protection devices in your home.

Security from fire. Home fires are one of the most serious types of accidents. They can cause bodily injury or death as well as costly damage to property. *Smoke detectors* give immediate warning if a fire starts. The diagrams in 1-17 suggest good locations for smoke detectors.

Fire extinguishers should be in every home. They are classified according to the type of fire they can stop, 1-18. They should be located where they are easy to use. See 1-19.

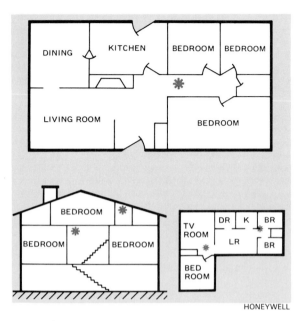

1-17 Smoke detectors should be placed throughout a dwelling.

CLASSES OF FIRES

CLASS A FIRES
Fire in ordinary combustible materials . . . fires involving paper, wood, cloth, and many plastics.

CLASS B FIRES
Fire in flammable liquids, gases and greases . . . a flash fire in your frying pan or oven, or in paint or solvents.

CLASS C FIRES
Fire in electrical appliances and equipment . . . fire caused by faulty wiring, as in a TV.

1-18 Fire extinguishers may stop one or all three classes of fires.

GENERAL SERVICES ADMINISTRATION

1-19 Fire extinguishers should be in plain view and accessible.

Security from burglars. A private residence is burglarized every 15 seconds in the United States. You can take some precautions to prevent this from happening to you. Some of these are listed in 1-20.

You should have a way to see someone at the door without opening it. A peephole or a chain lock permits you to do so. Other security precautions include using outside lighting at every entrance to your home and having secure locks on all doors and windows. You can also install an alarm system. See 1-21.

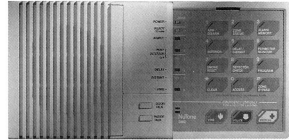

NUTONE/SCOVILLE

1-21 A burglar alarm gives notice when an intruder enters your home.

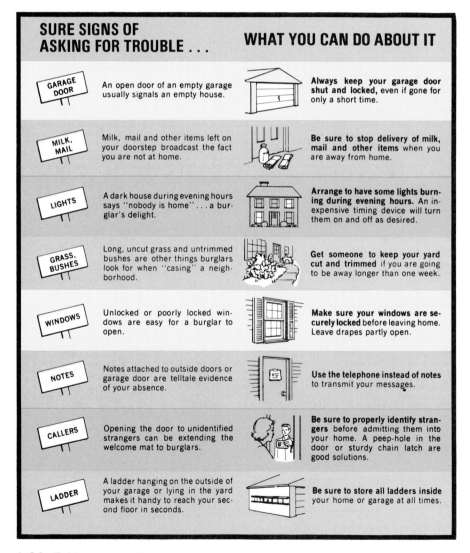

SURE SIGNS OF ASKING FOR TROUBLE . . .

WHAT YOU CAN DO ABOUT IT

GARAGE DOOR	An open door of an empty garage usually signals an empty house.	Always keep your garage door shut and locked, even if gone for only a short time.
MILK, MAIL	Milk, mail and other items left on your doorstep broadcast the fact you are not at home.	Be sure to stop delivery of milk, mail and other items when you are away from home.
LIGHTS	A dark house during evening hours says "nobody is home" . . . a burglar's delight.	Arrange to have some lights burning during evening hours. An inexpensive timing device will turn them on and off as desired.
GRASS, BUSHES	Long, uncut grass and untrimmed bushes are other things burglars look for when "casing" a neighborhood.	Get someone to keep your yard cut and trimmed if you are going to be away longer than one week.
WINDOWS	Unlocked or poorly locked windows are easy for a burglar to open.	Make sure your windows are securely locked before leaving home. Leave drapes partly open.
NOTES	Notes attached to outside doors or garage door are telltale evidence of your absence.	Use the telephone instead of notes to transmit your messages.
CALLERS	Opening the door to unidentified strangers can be extending the welcome mat to burglars.	Be sure to properly identify strangers before admitting them into your home. A peep-hole in the door or sturdy chain latch are good solutions.
LADDER	A ladder hanging on the outside of your garage or lying in the yard makes it handy to reach your second floor in seconds.	Be sure to store all ladders inside your home or garage at all times.

1-20 Taking precautions can help keep your house safe from burglars.

Space

All people have *spatial needs.* That is, they need some amount of physical space around them. They do not like to feel crowded. To gain distance, they create invisible boundaries around themselves. The size of the boundaries varies with each person. It is influenced by many factors. Personal feelings and family backgrounds have a great effect on it. In general, people with a Middle European, Italian, French, or Spanish background tend to need less space than those with an English, Scandinavian, German, or Belgian background.

Hobbies and activities also influence spatial needs. People who like to garden need a large backyard. People who enjoy having many friends near them need more space for entertaining. On the other hand, too much space can make people feel lonely.

Spatial needs are further influenced by the way space is used. In places where space cannot be added or removed, the right furnishings can make the space seem larger or smaller. A room of almost any size can be satisfying if the space is used to its best advantage. By changing the furnishings, a crowded room can become more spacious and airy. Likewise, a large room can become warm and cozy.

Territory. Humans require many kinds of space. Territory is one type of space. It is your "home ground." It offers freedom from trespassers and freedom to roam. Fences and property laws protect your territory. This space gives you a feeling of safety. It becomes part of your identity. It makes you feel secure and "at home."

You also need territory within your home. This is the space within the dwelling that you can call your own. Your territory could be your bedroom, or perhaps just one special part of the room that is for you alone.

When you sit down for dinner, do you always sit in the same chair? If so, that place is another of your territories.

Perhaps your parents have special chairs in some part of the home. The chairs are reserved for their use because everyone else knows the chairs are their territories.

Flight distance. Another type of space is flight distance. A person needs to be free of a feeling of being overcome or threatened by others. When you wish to put distance between yourself and others, you need flight distance. This space gives you room to take defensive action. Have you ever walked on the other side of the street to avoid meeting someone? If you did, you used flight distance.

Social distance. Social distance exists only in your mind. Thus, the distance is imagined, not real.

Your social distance allows you to stay in touch with others. It extends to include everyone with whom you communicate. Thus, if you write to a friend who lives in England, your social distance extends across the Atlantic ocean. At the same time, it may not even extend across the street if you do not communicate with neighbors.

Personal distance. Each person is enclosed in an invisible "bubble" called personal distance. This is the normal space you keep between yourself and others.

The size and shape of your personal distance "bubble" change constantly. The occasion and the people who are with you affect the amount of space you need. Sometimes you want to be far away from other people. At other times, you want to be near them and to touch them.

LA MARR HUBBS

1-22 This house on a riverbank provides privacy for its occupants.

22

To see how much personal distance you need for a normal conversation, try this test with a classmate. Stand across the room from each other, and begin a conversation. Slowly walk toward each other as you talk. Notice how your feelings change as you come closer together. At what distance do you begin to feel uncomfortable?

Privacy

You need *privacy* to maintain good mental health. Sometimes you need to be completely alone. You need to be where others cannot see or hear what you are doing, and where you cannot see or hear others. At other times, you just need to be able to think, daydream, read, or study without being disturbed.

Since your need for privacy varies, it can be satisfied in many ways. One of the most extreme ways to achieve privacy is to live alone in a dwelling that is set apart from other buildings, 1-22. Another way is to have a private room or some other place where people enter only when they are invited, 1-23.

You may not be able to live alone or to have a private room. You can still fulfill your need for privacy. Doing a task that must be done alone, such as mowing the lawn, provides some privacy. Driving alone in a car isolates you from others. A chair that is set apart from other furnishings in a room can be a private place for you. Hobbies that require you to concentrate, such as woodworking or playing a piano, can free you from other thoughts. Even the sound of a vacuum cleaner can give you some degree of privacy by isolating you from all other sounds.

Social interaction

Sometimes you need privacy, but sometimes you need to be with others. Since humans are social by nature, you have a need to be close to and involved with other humans. You need *social interaction*. This need began at birth and will continue until you die.

Your housing serves as a background for social interaction. Your neighborhood and community influence the way you interact with others. Even the layout of the lots or sites in

1-23 When this boy reaches his tree house, he can pull the rope up after him. He will have privacy since others cannot enter.

your neighborhood affects interaction. The layout affects the opportunities you have to meet and visit with your neighbors.

Some areas within a dwelling are designed to encourage social interaction. Most living rooms, family rooms, and patios provide a relaxing atmosphere which sets the stage for interaction. The furniture in these areas is arranged so that persons can talk to one another without shouting, as in 1-24. Since mealtime is often a social time, most eating areas are also designed to make conversation easy.

Family unity

You want *family unity* if you consider the health and well-being of your family as a whole to be important. A "tightly knit" family wants family unity. Decisions in this kind of family are made to benefit all family members, not just one.

When family unity is a priority, several areas of the home are designed for group living. The home may include a family room where the whole family can take part in activities. Other families may have an outside area for recreation, 1-25. However, even a chair can provide a place to meet the priority of family unity. See 1-26.

Economy

People who place a special emphasis on cost have a priority of *economy*. Cost can be in terms of either money or effort.

Housing costs *money* whether you rent or buy a home. Space inside a home costs money. The furnishings and equipment you put into a home cost money. Utilities such as electricity, gas, and water cost money. Caring for the home costs still more money in the form of maintenance and repair bills.

1-25 A place for outdoor family recreation provides a chance for family unity.

1-24 The furniture in this room is placed closely together to encourage social interaction.

1-26 Family unity can even be obtained by sitting in a big chair.

If you place economy high among priorities, you will choose a dwelling with only as much space as you really need, 1-27. You will buy only the furnishings and equipment you need. You will use conservation methods such as turning off lights in empty rooms and setting thermostats at moderate temperatures to reduce your utility bills. You will try to keep your home in good shape since maintenance bills almost always cost less than repair or re- placement bills. You may also make your own home repairs.

Effort costs in housing are high, since everything you do takes some amount of effort. Washing dishes, making beds, scrubbing floors, dusting furniture, washing windows, painting walls, and mowing grass are only a few of the many home tasks that require effort.

Although the tasks cannot be eliminated, effort can be economized. Dwellings can be designed for efficient use of effort. For max- imum efficiency, dishes should be stored near the sink or dishwasher. The linen closet should be near the bedrooms and the bathrooms. A coat closet should be located near an entry. The equipment needed for scrubbing floors should be stored in or near the rooms with floors that need to be scrubbed. The list could be con- tinued, but you can see that efficiency and orderliness can save effort.

Self-expression

Showing your true personality and taste is called *self-expression*. Do you enjoy collecting special things such as rocks or coins? If so, you are careful to choose just the right ones. You polish them until they shine. You may want to arrange them in some order and show them to your friends. All of these activities are ways you express yourself and your interests.

Your housing gives you an outlet for self-expression. For instance, the colors you use to decorate your home can be a clue to your personality. If you have an outgoing, vibrant personality, you can show it by using bright, bold colors inside your home. If you have a

1-27 People who consider economy a high priority may choose to live in a home with only as much space as they really need. Instead of a separate dining room, they may have a roll-out table like this in their kitchen.

Housing for satisfaction   25

quiet, subdued personality, you can show it by using pale, soft colors, 1-28. Furnishings can also help you express yourself.

Creativity

Creativity is having new ideas. You show creativity when you express your new ideas to others.

Primitive people showed creativity when they carved pictures in cave walls to tell stories. People still create pictures, stories, and poems. Today, many pictures are made using cameras, while others are made using oil paints, watercolors, or charcoal, 1-29. Some of the new stories and poems are published in books. Others are set to music and recorded on tapes or discs.

Pictures, stories, and poems are only a few of the countless ways you can show creativity. Playing musical instruments is another way to show creativity, 1-30. Or you may enjoy working with flowers. You can arrange the plants so that your flower garden has a special design. Or you may want to make flower arrangements.

WESTERN WAYS FEATURES

1-29 Artist Ted Degrazia displays his creativity by painting murals.

Beauty

Self-expression and creativity can help you add beauty to your microenvironment. *Beauty* is a quality that makes things pleasing to the eye. Another word for beauty is *aesthetics*.

Beautiful surroundings, as shown in 1-31, can make you feel good and release you from tensions. This is why beauty is an important factor in housing.

Your concept of beauty is unique. The things that appear beautiful to you may not appear beautiful to someone else. In fact, they may not even appear beautiful to you after a while. Your concept of beauty changes as you grow and develop. Do you and your close friends see beauty in the same objects? Do your family members agree?

Esteem

You need to be *esteemed* by others. When you are esteemed, you are respected, admired, and held in high regard. Your housing tells other people something about you and can help you gain esteem. A home that is clean, neat, and attractive will gain the approval and esteem of others.

You also need *self-esteem;* you must think well of yourself, 1-32. Your self-esteem is

SUN LAKES DEVELOPMENT CO.

1-28 Quiet, subdued people may show their personalities by decorating with soft, pale colors.

26

JOHN RUNNING

1-30 Having a piano in your home gives you a chance to express your creativity by playing it.

SUN LAKES DEVELOPMENT CO.

1-31 Beauty in a room can help you feel happy, content, and peaceful.

affected by the way you feel about your housing. A pleasant, satisfying home in which you enjoy living can help you gain self-esteem and confidence.

Prestige

Prestige means having a favorable position in the eyes of others. Prestige is closely related to esteem, but prestige is a more powerful term. It is associated with fame, influence, prominence, and authority.

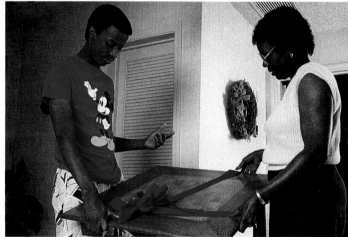

JOHN RUNNING

1-32 As this son gives his mother a table that he made, both of them gain self-esteem.

Housing can give you prestige. It can help you show that your status (rank or position) in society is high. If you consider prestige a priority, you will want others to recognize your home as being something special.

A word of caution is needed in regard to prestige and housing. You should be careful not to make too many assumptions based on the appearance of the housing of others. You may get the wrong impression since your personal priorities are different than those of other people. For instance, something that others view as giving them prestige may seem very insignificant to you. On the other hand, something that is simply a source of comfort to others may seem very prestigious to you.

Look again at 1-8. The tent that provides shelter also tells the status of the Bedouins who live there. A large number of long poles shows prosperity and is a sign of prestige. Bedouins who are very prosperous also have highly decorated curtains or tent coverings. In the United States, a swimming pool helps many people satisfy their priority of prestige, 1-33. Long poles and swimming pools may seem very different, but both show prestige.

HOUSING FOR SELF-ACTUALIZATION

Housing can help you satisfy many of your primary needs, secondary needs, and priorities. It can offer opportunities for you to satisfy your ultimate need of self-actualization.

1-33 An inside exercise pool helps some people feel a sense of prestige.

However, satisfaction through housing does not occur by mere chance. You need to think about it, plan for it, and act to achieve it.

The following true story shows how events and planning can go together to allow for self-actualization:

Two young women found jobs in a new community. When they met each other at work, each learned that the other was hunting for a place to live. The housing shortage and the unfamiliarity of the area caused them to set out on their search together.

They rented a summer cottage that was vacant for the winter. It stood in a forest a few miles from the city in which they worked.

The forest setting appealed to both of them, so when a nearby piece of land was offered for sale, one of the women bought it. Then they bought an old house in the city that was about to be torn down to make room for expanding businesses. They had the 50-year-old house moved to the newly-acquired site. See 1-34.

The two women got along well because they had similar interests. One of the interests they shared was antiques, so they decided to restore the old house and refurnish it with antiques. They paid frequent visits to second-hand stores, garage sales, and antique shops.

They spent hours refinishing woodwork and floors. They cleaned and refinished old trunks, chests, and bedsteads. They also came up with many creative decorating ideas. One idea was to use fabric instead of wallpaper on the walls of a bedroom.

The women did all their cooking on a wood-burning range. Wood-burning heaters, and a fireplace in the living room gave warmth to the home.

The outside of the dwelling provided more opportunities for satisfaction. They spent a great deal of time outdoors cutting firewood, taking long walks, and

1-34 This house was moved from a city location and restored.

enjoying the scenery. They built bird houses and animal feeders near their house, inviting the forest dwellers to visit them.

The women also took advantage of the beautiful mountain peaks in the distance. When they moved their house to the forest setting, they were careful to place it so they would have a good view of the mountains. See 1-35.

Restoring and furnishing the old house took much thought, planning, and effort. It gave these women a chance to do what they enjoyed. They did the very best job they could. Their decision to tackle the job of restoration provided the opportunity for self-actualization.

As you read the story about the two women, did you notice how many of their needs and priorities were satisfied by their housing? Would a similar housing situation satisfy your needs and personal priorities? If not, what kind of housing situation would satisfy them?

What opportunities for self-actualization does your present housing provide? Does it give you the freedom you need to develop your interests and to do the things you enjoy doing? If you had the chance, how would you change your housing to better meet your needs and priorities?

1-35 A huge bedroom window provides a fantastic view of the mountains.

Housing for satisfaction 29

to Know

aesthetics . . . economy . . .
electronic air cleaner . . . esteem . . .
family unity . . . flight distance . . .
heat pump . . . housing . . . humidifier . . .
microenvironment . . . personal distance . . .
personal priorities . . . prestige . . .
primary needs . . . privacy . . .
secondary needs . . . security . . .
self-actualization . . . self-expression . . .
shelter . . . smoke detector . . . social distance . . .
social interaction . . . spatial needs . . . territory

to Review

Write your answers on a separate sheet of paper.
1. The word housing refers to the dwelling and what is _____ and _____.
2. Housing is your:
   a. Microenvironment.
   b. Macroenvironment.
   c. Total environment.
3. Name four primary needs for people.
4. Secondary needs are generally _____ or _____ in nature.
5. Describe persons who have satisfied their need of self-actualization.
6. Explain the term personal priority.
7. List three factors that influence spatial needs.
8. Describe five ways to achieve privacy.
9. People who place a special emphasis on cost have a personal priority of:
   a. Esteem.
   b. Self-expression.
   c. Prestige.
   d. Economy.
10. Give three examples of ways housing can let you show your creativity.
11. If you are held in high regard, you are _____.
12. Give an example of how housing can help you satisfy your need or personal priority of:
   a. Security.
   b. Social interaction.
   c. Self-expression.

13. Given the chance, how would you change your housing to better satisfy your need of self-actualization?

to Do

1. Work with other members of your class to make a bulletin board display. Draw a large pyramid like the one in 1-1. Find or draw pictures that show how housing can meet the different kinds of needs.
2. List in order of importance your needs and personal priorities that are satisfied by your housing.
3. Make a collage showing various types of dwellings used throughout the United States.
4. Use the "ice cube test" to determine whether or not your classroom or a room in your home needs humidification. (The room should not be the kitchen, since cooking vapors may give an increased humidity level.) Room temperature should be 72 to 75 deg. F (22.2 to 23.9 deg. C) for the experiment. Drop three ice cubes into a glass, add water and stir. If moisture does not form on the outside of the glass in three minutes, humidification is needed.
5. Find out how to use a fire extinguisher.
6. To study how persons react to changes in their microenvironment, try these experiments:
   a. Change the climate conditions of a room by heating pans of water, opening or closing windows, using fans, raising or lowering temperatures.
   b. Change the amount of space per person in a room. First crowd the people together; then give them a lot of space. (One way is to place chairs closely together, then place them far apart.)
7. If you have permission, rearrange furniture in some part of your house or yard so that someone has more privacy. Report to the class about your actions and the results.
8. Have a class discussion about ways housing can encourage social interaction.
9. Divide into small groups. Make a list of the ways housing can help meet the priority of prestige. Compare your list with those of other groups.

Housing and life situations

After studying this chapter, you will be able to:

■ Explain how your housing is affected by the people with whom you live.

■ Show how housing changes in different stages of a life cycle.

■ Explain how your life-style, your socioeconomic status, and your physical condition affect your housing.

Countless circumstances affect you and the way you live. These circumstances are called *life situations*. They are related to every aspect of your life. They set the stage for the way you interact with other people and with your housing.

Living units

Persons who share the same living quarters are called a *living unit*. The size of a living unit can vary from a single person to hundreds of persons.

The one-person living unit may be someone who has never married. Or it may be someone whose marriage has ended because of the loss of a husband or wife through death, desertion, or divorce.

Although some single people live alone, others are part of larger living units. A college residence hall, 2-1, houses a large living unit of single people. Nursing homes house large living units of elderly singles.

Many adults are the heads of *one-parent families.* In some of these families, one parent has died or left the home. Other one-parent families consist of an adult who has never married and one or more children. A one-parent family may be a separate living unit, or they may share housing with others and become part of a larger living unit.

A common living unit is the *nuclear family.* It includes a husband and wife and their children, 2-2. A married couple, even if childless, is considered a nuclear family.

A living unit is sometimes an *extended family.* This happens when relatives share a dwelling with a nuclear family. There are two kinds of extended families. One kind consists of several generations of a family. For instance, children, parents, and grandparents make an extended family. The other kind of extended family consists of many persons of the same generation. Perhaps you know of extended families in which aunts, uncles, and cousins all live together. Some families may extend in both ways to include grandparents, parents, children, in-laws, aunts, uncles, and cousins, 2-3.

EUGENE BALZER

2-1 Students who live in a residence hall form one type of living unit.

JOHN RUNNING

2-2 The nuclear family consists of parents and their children.

LIFE CYCLES

As you grow, you pass through different stages of life. Each of these stages is a part of your *life cycle.* In each stage, you have new opportunities and face new challenges. You develop new needs and priorities. These changes have a great effect on your housing.

Individual life cycles

Each person follows a pattern of development called an *individual life cycle.* It is divided into four stages according to age groups:
1. Infancy.
2. Childhood.
3. Youth.
4. Adulthood.

Each stage can be divided into substages. For instance, the substages of youth are:
1. Preteens.
2. Early teens.
3. Middle teens.
4. Late teens.

In which substage do you belong? Do you have brothers and sisters in other substages or in other stages?

Eric Erikson, who is well-known for his studies of human development, views a person's development in another way. He says that humans go through eight stages of life which he calls *critical periods.* In each critical period, personalities develop and change. He relates

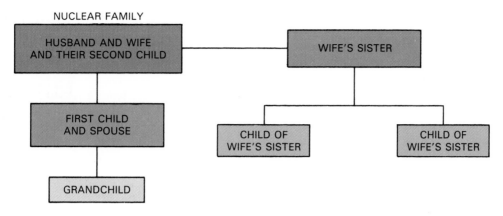

NUCLEAR FAMILY

HUSBAND AND WIFE AND THEIR SECOND CHILD

WIFE'S SISTER

FIRST CHILD AND SPOUSE

CHILD OF WIFE'S SISTER

CHILD OF WIFE'S SISTER

GRANDCHILD

2-3 Some families are extended in more than one direction.

CRITICAL PERIOD	AGE	DESCRIPTION	POSITIVE OUTCOME	NEGATIVE OUTCOME
1	Birth to 18 months	Children develop trust, or lack of it, in themselves, other people, and their environ-ment. Degree of trust developed depends on the quality of care they receive. If children cannot trust those who care for them, they can trust no one.	Trust	Mistrust
2	18 months to 3 years	Children want to do things for themselves. This makes them feel they are in control of themselves and their environment. They learn skills needed for survival in society. Those around them must give encouragement.	Autonomy	Shame and doubt
3	4 and 5 years	Children initiate activities on their own. Freedom to do things and to start activities help them in this stage.	Initiative	Guilt
4	6 to 11 years	Children are allowed to plan, undertake, and complete projects and activities. They develop their sense of industry at school as well as at home. Praise for their efforts help them.	Industry	Inferiority
5	About 12 to 18 years	Adolescents have new feelings and desires. They develop values—new ways of looking at life and thinking about the world. They seek to learn who they are. They take pride in achievement. Peer relationships develop.	Identity	Role confusion
6	Young Adulthood	Young adults develop the ability to share with and care about others. A close relationship with friends and/or a marriage partner develops.	Intimacy	Isolation
7	Young adult to mature adult	Adults are concerned about others outside the family. There is a special concern for children and youth.	Genera-tivity	Self-absorption
8	Mature adult	As persons become older they can look back on their lives with satisfaction. They continue to enjoy life.	Integrity	Despair

2-4 Erikson recognizes eight critical periods in the development of humans.

these developments and changes to the environment. For positive development, a positive setting or environment must be present. In contrast, a negative environment produces negative development. Study 2-4 to learn about the eight critical periods of development.

Family life cycles

Just as you have a place in an individual life cycle and in the eight critical periods of development, your family has its place in a *family life cycle*. A family life cycle has three stages:

1. Founding family stage.
2. Expanding family stage.
3. Contracting family stage.

The family life cycle has substages that fit into these three stages. See 2-5.

The *founding family stage* is the time the married couple is on its own. The husband and wife make adjustments to married life and to each other.

The *expanding family stage* is the time the family is growing. It includes the childbearing periods, the years of caring for young children, and the school years for children and teens.

The *contracting family stage* is the time the family becomes smaller. The first substage is

DORIS KIMBROUGH

2-6 These two people have just been launched and are starting a new family life cycle.

the launching period. This is when the children become adults and leave their parents' home. They may leave to go to college, to begin a career, or to get married, 2-6.

FOUNDING FAMILY STAGE	EXPANDING FAMILY STAGE	CONTRACTING FAMILY STAGE
	SUBSTAGES	
Married couple	Childbearing Preschool children School-age children Teenagers	Launching Middle years Later years

2-5 The family life cycle includes both stages and substages.

34

2-7 As an infant grows, he or she needs more space for sleeping. A crib provides this space.

The second substage of the contracting family is the middle years, sometimes called the "empty-nest" period. This is when all the children have been launched. The married couple is again on its own.

The final substage is the later years. During this time, either the husband or wife is usually found living alone after the death of the other. As people live longer, this stage increases in time.

Family groups usually include more than one substage. In some cases, the substages overlap. For instance, when a family has both a teenager and a school-age child, the family is in overlapping substages.

Other families may have gaps between the substages in their life cycles. An example would be a family with a school-age child in which the mother is pregnant.

Life cycles and housing needs

As you move from one stage or substage of your life cycles to another, your housing needs change. Therefore, your place in your life cycles should be considered as you plan your housing. If you think about both your present and future needs, your housing can help you live the kind of life you want.

One good example of a changing need is the need for space. How much space do you need for sleeping? When you were a baby, you probably slept in something that took up very little space.

As you grew, you needed more sleeping space. You may have slept in a crib like the one shown in 2-7. Later, you may have moved to a twin-size bed, or a bunk bed, 2-8. Bunk beds provide the same amount of sleeping space as twin beds without taking up as much floor space. Finally, you may have moved to a full-size bed.

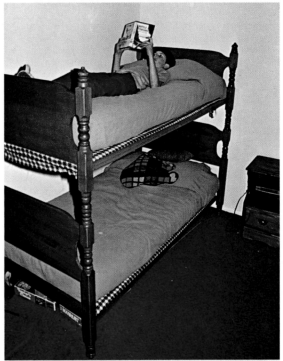

2-8 When a child outgrows a crib, a twin, bunk, or full-size bed may be used.

You also need space for your activities and space for storage. These needs for space change throughout a family's life cycle. The young married couple in the founding family stage may not need very much space. But once they enter the expanding family stage, their needs for space increase greatly. During this stage, the number, the ages, and the activities of their children will affect their space needs. See 2-9.

Each new family member requires additional space, 2-10, and as each member grows, he or she requires even more space. Teenagers need space for studying and entertaining friends as well as storage space for sporting equipment, stereo equipment, and clothes.

As a family moves into the contracting stage, it needs less and less space. When family members are launched, they take many of their belongings with them, leaving more space for the rest of the family. The married couple may have more room than they can use when all the children have been launched.

JOHN OEHLER

2-10 An expanding family must realize that each new member needs space.

LIFE-STYLES

Life-style means a living pattern or way of life. Every living unit and every person has a life-style. To a degree, all life-styles are alike. That is, they must all satisfy the primary needs of humans. Beyond this point, life-styles take many different directions.

Your life-style is an extension of you. It is influenced by your secondary needs, personal priorities, and life cycle. It reflects your experiences, personality, and goals.

The people who live in the home pictured in 2-11 like having a beautiful house with expensive furnishings. Their life-style includes hosting formal dinner parties.

The cartoon in 2-12 illustrates the point that many people enjoy "roughing it." Camping may be part of their life-style. However, a family that goes camping often may have to change its life-style for a while during the childbearing substage of its life cycle.

Look at 2-13. Can you guess what type of life-style the family in that home has?

Some specific life-styles are described on the following pages. You may find that one type seems to "fit" your situation. You may see your life-style as a combination of two or more types. Or you may have a life-style that is not described in this section. Whatever life-style you have, the right kind of housing can help you make the most of it.

BRUNSWICK CORP.

2-9 As children grow and take on new activities, their needs for space increase.

2-11 The formal dining room is a clue to the life-style of the people who live in this house.

Individualistic life-style

If you prefer to "do your own thing," you have an *individualistic* life-style. You do what you want to do. You are not concerned about what others may think. If you wanted to live in a purple house, you would paint your house purple. If you wanted to travel, you would find a way to do it, even if it meant quitting your job and selling your house.

The first owner of the Winchester Mystery House, 2-14, was a very individualistic person. Sarah Winchester was a widow who lived alone in the huge dwelling. She believed that no harm could come to her as long as work continued on the house. So 16 people worked around the clock every day of the year. The house grew until it had 160 rooms, 10,000 windows and 44 stairways.

2-12 Some people have a greater appreciation of the outdoors than others.

2-13 This home is in a subdivision designed for those who own light aircraft. On the other side of the hangar is a two-car garage.

Persons with an individualistic life-style are not all eccentric. They simply follow their inner desires and feelings without considering the praise or scorn they may receive from others.

Influential life-style

If you like to influence (have some control over) people and events, you prefer an *influential life-style.* You are highly motivated and have a strong desire to reach goals.

2-14 Most windows in the Winchester Mystery House have 13 panes; stairways have 13 steps.

2-15 A home office is needed by many people who work at home.

Your roles include leadership. You use your resources of talent, energy, and money to create and support projects. These projects may be to promote religious, civic, or political activities.

Your housing should let you and your associates perform your activities in comfort. You may need a private work place or a room where committee meetings could be held. See 2-15. If you host large parties or receptions for your organizations, a large outdoor area would be an asset, 2-16.

If you have an active life-style, you need housing that allows you to be efficient. You want to devote all your spare time and energy to the activities that are important to you. The kitchen shown in 2-17 was planned for convenience as well as attractiveness. Food can be prepared quickly, or even in advance, so all family members have time for their jobs, volunteer work, or social activities.

2-16 A big outdoor area offers plenty of room for large groups of guests to circulate freely as well as room for children to play.

Supportive life-style

You have a *supportive life-style* if you like to help others. You may help family members, or you may work away from home helping others. You may combine the roles of a helper at home and a wage earner outside the home. Your housing should let you support others whether your support is psychological, financial, or physical.

The storage closet shown in 2-18 can easily be changed into a home computer center. Both young and older family members can use the computer to play video games and to help them learn or organize information.

2-17 Much counter space, easy access to appliances, and two ovens make food preparation easier.

40

2-18 This built-in storage closet also serves as a home computer center.

2-19 The person who built this playhouse was supportive of the children who enjoy it.

2-20 Installing tile to reduce the noise level in the home could be considered a supportive activity.

A supportive person built the playhouse in 2-19. Look at 2-20 and 2-21. The persons pictured have supportive life-styles. They work to improve the lives of other people.

Community life-style

If you enjoy doing things with a group, you may like group living and a *community life-style*.

2-21 The people who prepare meals are being supportive of the living unit.

Housing and life situations   41

Communities or "communes" vary widely. In some, members differ in age, sex, and background. In others, members are very much alike. Some communities are small. They consist of only one living unit. Others are as large as a village or town.

In every community, the members have at least one aspect of their lives in common. They may share the same religious beliefs, the same theory of life, the same career goal, or the same substage of the life cycle.

Frank Lloyd Wright's Taliesin in Wisconsin and Taliesin West in Arizona are types of communities. Their members are students of the Frank Lloyd Wright School of Architecture. The students live on campus and share the responsibilities of operating and caring for the school. On Saturday, students can be seen doing various chores, 2-22. Their community lifestyle permits them to combine their education with work and daily living.

Planned retirement communities are another type of community. The members are senior citizens who have much leisure time. Many of them have similar interests and hobbies.

A typical layout of a retirement city is shown in 2-23. It has homes, shopping centers, and recreational facilities close together. Many leisure activities are provided in this type of community, 2-24.

DEL E. WEBB DEVELOPMENT CO.

2-23 Designed for retired people, this community combines housing, shopping, and recreational areas.

WESTERN WAYS FEATURES

2-22 This architectural school offers the chance for a community life-style. All students share the chores of cooking, cleaning, and maintenance.

Basic life-style

Living simply and without many modern conveniences is called a *basic life-style*. Concern about the effects of pollution and the depletion of natural resources has caused some people to try this way of life.

The move to a basic life-style has called attention to new building designs and new ways of using resources. These ideas are illustrated in the work of Paolo Soleri. Soleri is an architect and philosopher who studied under Frank Lloyd Wright. In the late 1960s, he began designing, building, and living in simple dwellings. By 1970, he had begun work in a

2-24 Parties are frequently held in many retirement communities.

remote area of Arizona on a place he calls Arcosanti. "Arcosanti" is a combination of the words "architecture" and "cosanti." Cosanti is an Italian word meaning "before things."

Native rock, sand, and stone are used as building materials at Arcosanti. All the structures are placed closely together to conserve land. They are designed to use the sun for warmth and light. When the work is done, water will be recycled, and waste products will be converted into energy.

Arcosanti is shown in 2-25. It was one of the chosen sites for the 1976 bicentennial celebration of the United States.

Sometimes a basic life-style is forced upon a living unit. In 2-26, you can see how one couple met its primary housing needs after its home burned. At first, the husband and wife used the "temporary" dwelling because they could not afford other housing. Later, they chose to stay in the dwelling. They spent the money they could have used for better housing to travel.

QUALITY OF LIFE

Quality of life is the degree of satisfaction obtained from life. Good housing provides people with satisfying surroundings and can improve the quality of their lives.

Quality of life is important to you as an individual. Just as you are unique, your concept of quality of life is unique. The things you

2-25 Structures at Arcosanti are made in different sizes and shapes. Native building materials, such as concrete that is made with local sand and stone, are used.

think improve the quality of your life may not appeal to someone else.

Your housing environment affects your individual quality of life. If your housing helps you meet your needs and priorities, it is adding satisfaction to your life. Thus, it is improving the quality of your life.

Quality of life is also important to you as a member of a living unit. Your living unit, whether it is your family or some other group, is one part of your life situations. Its members play a part in shaping your secondary needs, priorities, and attitudes. In turn, the combined needs, priorities, and attitudes of the members determine the type of housing environment in which you live. If all the members are concerned about the well-being of the group as a whole, the quality of life for the living unit will be high.

Quality of life for society

The future of a society depends on individuals and groups who work to make life better for all. Some of the work is social in nature. This means that groups of people must cooperate with each other to reach the common goal of improving the society's quality of life. All people cannot make equal contributions toward reaching that goal. Some degree of "give and take" is required. However, if everyone considers the well-being of the society as a whole, the quality of everyone's life can be improved.

The physical aspects of the society also need attention. Again, the concept of interaction between people and their housing becomes important. Beautiful surroundings such as well-kept buildings and natural landscapes satisfy many needs of people. In turn, people must be willing to use their resources of time, money, and energy to care for their surroundings—to maintain buildings, to landscape lawns, to support public parks, and to control pollution.

Human ecology is the study of humans and their environment. Much research is being done in this area. People are becoming aware of the problems caused by pollution. For instance, waste water from homes and factories, if not treated properly, dumps bacteria and other pollutants into streams, lakes, and underground water supplies. Burning fuel for heat and power adds harmful elements to the air.

Instead of wishing for "the good old days," people must move ahead to find ways of solving such problems as noise, air pollution, traffic congestion, and waste of natural resources. Solving these problems will improve the quality of life for society.

SOCIOECONOMIC STATUS

Socioeconomic status is a term used to describe both the *social class* and the *economic level* of an individual or group. Both are conditions that affect the life situations of a living unit.

Social class

People are born into a social class or level in society. They tend to stay in the same class as their parents. However, they can move up or down the *social ladder*, 2-27. An adult's social class depends largely on his or her family background, occupation, and level of education.

In the United States, the three main social classes are:
1. Lower class.
2. Middle class.
3. Upper class.

2-26 This converted goat shed is the home of one couple who has a basic life-style. A hammock (right) provides a place to sleep.

These may be further divided as shown in the social ladder.

Economic level

Economic level is determined by the amount of money an individual or a family has to spend. The economic level of an adult is determined mainly by his or her family background, occupation, and education. These are the same factors that influence social class, so you can see the economic level and social class are closely related.

The three main categories of economic level are:

1. Low-income group.
2. Middle-income group.
3. High-income group.

Socioeconomic status and housing

An individual's or family's housing is greatly affected by socioeconomic status. When you are looking for housing, you have to make the following decisions:

- Where will the dwelling be located?
- How large will the dwelling be?
- Shall I live in an apartment or a house?
- Shall I buy or rent?

All of these housing decisions are influenced by your social class and economic level.

Housing for low-income, lower-class people. A "low-income family" has an income which is not more than 80 percent of the median income in a certain geographic area. A "very low-income family" is one with an income of 50 percent of the median income or less. (Median means the midpoint.) See 2-28 for examples of median incomes.

People in the low-income group or lower class often have difficulty finding adequate

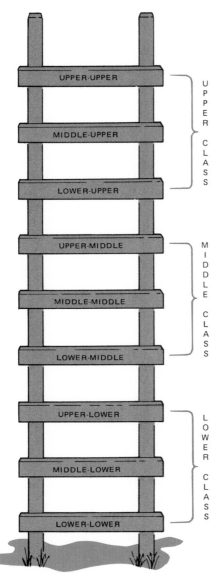

2-27 Steps of a ladder are used to represent social classes in the United States. The middle class is the largest class.

EXAMPLES OF MEDIAN INCOMES
OF TWO GEOGRAPHIC AREAS

AREA A		AREA B
9,000		
12,000		65,000
15,000		70,000
18,000		73,000
20,000	median incomes	75,000
22,000		78,000
25,000		80,000
27,000		82,000
30,000		

2-28 Within a given area, a certain number of people earn more than the median income. The same number of people earn less than the median income.

housing, 2-29. Many of them live on *fixed incomes* such as Social Security or welfare benefits. Their incomes remain the same regardless of other economic changes such as inflation. A growing group of low income people is made up of the aging, especially older women.

Federal, state, and local governments are trying to improve the housing of low-income people. These governments have passed many acts to try to improve the situation. The acts have several goals. Two major goals are to eliminate slums and to promote integration. Another goal is to provide community service centers such as commercial areas and recreational areas. Yet another goal is to improve old housing and build new housing, 2-30.

2-30 Government housing projects can help improve the housing of people with limited incomes.

2-29 Families in the lower class live in the least desirable parts of communities.

When concerned individuals work with the government, housing for those with limited incomes can be improved. One example of this is found in a midwest city. Of its 70,000 people, most are of minority groups and many are jobless.

Good housing was hard to find in the city. Then the community found a leader who understood the needs of the people. Funds from a federal grant were obtained. Churches began working on projects to improve housing. Consultants from a nearby university worked with the community leaders and an architect.

They talked to residents to find their likes and dislikes in housing.

After overcoming many hurdles, the development was completed. It contains 64 town house units. The residents pay one-fourth of their income for rent which includes utilities and maintenance. The state cooperative extension service is teaching the residents home management and repair.

The success of this project encouraged people in the nearby areas to act. People became concerned and committed themselves to work for better housing. They began improving their run-down neighborhoods.

Does your community have government-sponsored housing for people with limited incomes? If so, are the people living their pleased with it?

Housing for middle-income, middle-class people. The group of middle-income, middle-class people is the largest group in the United States. Therefore, it receives the most attention. The mass media focus on the middle class. Most occupations fit the middle-income level. Most dwellings are designed for middle-class families. Most furniture is made for middle-class homes.

The stereotype of a typical, middle-class family is one that lives in a comfortable house in a good neighborhood, 2-31. Although that is often true, not all middle-class people of today fit that description. Changing life-styles have revised the entire concept of families and

2-32 A scenic setting like this lake makes housing more desirable and more costly.

family life. In addition, housing patterns are changing. Alternatives to the typical, single-family dwelling are being found. Apartments, condominiums, and town houses are now the homes of many middle-income, middle-class people.

This trend will probably continue. In fact, today's "average" family may have difficulty buying a house. The incomes of families are not growing as quickly as the prices of houses. A basic economic formula says that a family should spend no more than 2 1/2 times its annual income for a home. But the average home in the United States is priced much higher than this figure. The average family has had to pay up to four times its income to purchase an average home.

Since the prices of dwellings have risen faster than incomes, the middle-income, middle-class people have faced and will continue to face some major changes in their housing and way of life.

Housing for upper-income, upper-class people. Since money is usually not an obstacle for upper-income people, they are able to live in the most desirable locations. These include elegant, downtown apartments; waterfront dwellings, 2-32; and large houses surrounded by acres of land, 2-33. The older mansion shown in 2-34 stands on the edge of a well-known golf course.

2-33 People with high incomes can afford to live in large houses with spacious grounds.

2-31 A nice house in a nice neighborhood is typical of middle-class families.

2-34 Older homes of good quality and in good locations are usually owned by people of the upper class.

Housing and life situations 47

Those in the upper class often have more than one home. The homes may be located in various cities where the people work or meet with business associates. Additional homes may also be used as vacation sites, as the one shown in 2-35.

HOUSING AND PHYSICAL CONDITION

Physical condition affects life situations and housing needs. Someone who is handicapped has special needs according to the type of handicap. A birth defect or an accident can leave a person crippled, blind, or deaf.

The elderly often have some physical weakness or handicap. Partial loss of hearing or sight is the most frequent condition that limits the elderly. Most older persons are also more sensitive to heat and cold.

Housing can be built or adapted to better satisfy the needs of handicapped and elderly persons.

Housing for the handicapped

Millions of disabled Americans need special housing. They have many different handicaps. Some are blind. Some have difficulty moving and may be confined to wheelchairs. Others are mentally retarded.

The history of care for the handicapped is not pleasant to study. The United States has had places for the disabled for over 100 years. However, they were not begun as an effort to give the disabled the best of care. Instead, there were places to put handicapped people so they would not interfere with the rest of society. The needs and personal priorities of the handicapped were not considered.

Handicapped people need more than a place where they can "mark time." They need an environment that gives them a chance for positive development and self-actualization. Like everyone else, handicapped persons should be allowed to become all that they can be. They need the opportunity to learn to care for themselves. They need to be involved with life and to help others.

Most states now have special housing for disabled people. The types of special housing

JIM WALTER CORP.

2-35 Vacation homes vary widely. Some are in wooded areas, some are near ski resorts, and some are along a beach.

are varied. Some are still in the experimental stage.

Nebraska has a state program providing small group homes. From five to 15 persons live in each home. The advantage of this type of housing rather than an institution is that persons can live more normal lives and have more privacy.

Connecticut has similar small group homes that house 12 adults. Other states, such as Texas and Arizona, have group homes in rural areas. The rural setting provides work opportunities that are not available in cities. The disabled may garden, care for animals, or complete other chores that are a part of operating the home.

National organizations have taken steps to improve housing for the disabled. As long ago as the 1950s, organizations were working together on such projects. The National Society for Crippled Children and Adults and the President's Committee on Employment of the Physically Handicapped developed a set of standards for buildings. The standards were developed to make buildings usable by the physically handicapped.

The New York Society of the Deaf recently built the Tanya Towers. Part of the building contains individual apartments for those who have learned to care for themselves. One entire floor of apartments is leased to the United Cerebral Palsy Association. People with cerebral palsy who need only minimal care live there.

Other housing projects for the handicapped are held in "halfway houses." Those enrolled in the programs are "halfway" ready to care for themselves. Skills are learned under expert supervision. When they are ready, the handicapped persons go out to live independently.

The Veteran's Administration has developed standards for specially adapted houses. Their designs for people confined to wheelchairs include ramps, wide doors, "wheel-in" shower stalls and kitchen and bathroom facilities at the right height, 2-36.

With the help of a cooperative landlord, rented apartments can also be adapted to fit the needs of a handicapped person. In one instance, a nurse studied what changes were needed for a multiple sclerosis patient. By making only six minor changes, the patient was able to live independently in an apartment. The changes were:

1. Moving the telephone, doorlatch, and heat controls so they could be reached from a wheelchair.
2. Installing a built-up toilet seat.
3. Placing grab bars on the bathtub, and putting a straight chair in the tub.
4. Lubricating the windows so they would be easy to open.
5. Lowering a clothes rack.
6. Trading a gas range for an electric range.

Not all disabled persons can benefit from changes like these. But those who can appreciate being able to care for themselves and to make their own housing decisions.

Housing for the elderly

The number of elderly people is increasing because people are living longer. During recent years, the population of those over age 65 has increased more than 20 percent. Any population that shows such rapid growth demands attention. Thus, housing for the elderly has become a national concern.

The eldery are often uncomfortable in housing that satisfied them when they were younger. Their energy level is lower, and their health is usually on the decline. Even simple, everyday activities are sometimes difficult. Climbing stairs and opening a garage door may be heavy chores.

Home ownership among the elderly is higher than among the general population. However, many find their homes difficult to maintain. The dwelling becomes run-down. Adding to this problem is the fact that retirement income is often low. It does not allow for the costs of maintaining a home.

Some elderly persons find that living in their old neighborhoods is inconvenient. They are often far from shopping centers and community centers where they can be with other people, 2-37. If they have difficulty driving, they may not be able to leave home very often. This leads to loneliness, especially if they live alone.

The elderly need housing in which household routines can be done easily and little maintenance is required. They also need to have access to other facilities.

Planned retirement communities, discussed earlier in this chapter, are one solution to the needs of the elderly. On a smaller scale, retirement apartments or rest homes offer similar solutions, 2-38.

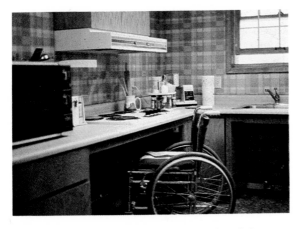

2-36 Kitchen counters must be the right height for work. They must also provide access for a wheelchair.

U.S. DEPT. OF AGRICULTURE

2-37 The elderly enjoy getting together in a center for senior citizens.

GEORGE GALE

2-38 Rest homes satisfy the housing needs of many elderly people.

to Know

basic life-style . . . community life-style . . . contracting family . . . economic level . . . eight critical periods . . . expanding family . . . extended family . . . family life cycle . . . fixed income . . . founding family . . . human ecology . . . individual life cycle . . . individualistic life-style . . . influential life-style . . . launching . . . life cycle . . . life situations . . . life-style . . . living unit . . . nuclear family . . . one-parent family . . . quality of life . . . social class . . .socioeconomic status . . . supportive life-style

to Review

Write your answers on a separate sheet of paper.
1. Define the term life situations.
2. List five circumstances that influence your life situations.
3. Persons who share the same living quarters are called a _____.
4. List the four main stages of the individual life cycle.
5. Give an example of the way housing needs change as a family moves from one stage of its life cycle to another.
6. Describe two ways a family expands and two ways it contracts.
7. Define the term life-style.
8. Make a list of descriptive terms for each of the following types of life-styles:
    a. Individualistic.
    b. Influential.
    c. Supportive.
    d. Community.
    e. Basic.
9. Give two examples of how the quality of life for society can be improved.
10. An adult's social class depends largely on his or her:
    a. Family background.
    b. Occupation.
    c. Level of education.
    d. All of the above.

50

11. The social class and the economic level of a living unit determine the unit's _____.

12. Describe two kinds of housing programs designed for handicapped persons.

to Do

1. List the circumstances that determine the life situations of your living unit. Then list some of the housing needs your living unit has because of these life situations.

2. Survey your classmates to find out how many types of living units they represent.

3. List some housing needs for each of the four main stages of the individual life cycle. Consider privacy, recreation, and clothing storage. Compare your list with that of a classmate.

4. Consider a specific housing need (such as space) and explain how it changes during each stage of the family life cycle.

5. Find information and pictures of various types of housing from around the world. Discuss the life-styles that go with each type of housing.

6. Develop a survey form. Then survey members of your class, school, or neighborhood to find out about their various life-styles. Make a list of those things that are alike in their life-styles.

7. Hand in a written report explaining how Frank Lloyd Wright influenced housing.

8. Find housing advertisements that suggest an improved quality of life, and indicate if you think the ads are true or misleading.

9. Write a paper about the handicapped and their housing needs.

Rest homes are the solution to the housing problems of some senior citizens.

part 2

Making housing choices

Yolanda and Robert Jackson have just moved into this house near a large city. When the Jacksons first got married, they decided to rent an apartment. Since Yolanda was still going to college, they wanted to wait until their income was higher to buy a house. Also, they wanted the ability to move to a new area without having to sell a house.

After Yolanda graduated, she became a loan officer at a suburban savings and loan. The city marketing firm where Robert worked had just given Robert a promotion. Robert and Yolanda felt that they could afford the kind of house they wanted to buy. But they had many decisions to make before they bought a house.

Although the city would have been a convenient location for Robert, the Jacksons were not sure that they wanted to live in the city. They were thinking about starting a family, and they wanted to have a spacious house with a large yard. Besides, a suburban location would be better for Yolanda.

The Jacksons decided to build this new house in a new development. The neighborhood has schools and a shopping center nearby. Commuter lines are nearby also.

You may face the same types of decisions about housing in the future. What options will be available to you? How will you decide which option is best for you?

You will face many decisions during your lifetime. One of them may be the selection of a house. Would the house you select be like either of these?

3

Decision-making skills

After studying this chapter, you will be able to:
- Define the different types of decisions.
- List some of your human and nonhuman resources.
- Explain the three main categories of housing decisions.
- Discuss the steps of the decision-making process and make wise decisions.

In the first two chapters of this book, you have read that many decisions affect housing. These decisions are related to your needs, personal priorities, and life situations. Since these factors change continually, you continually face new decisions. By making these decisions wisely, you and your living unit will have the chance to grow and develop into better persons.

TYPES OF DECISIONS

Decisions are not all alike. Learning to recognize the different types of decisions will help you develop decision-making skills.

Decisions can be classified into two groups. One group consists of those which vary according to the thought and care used in making them. See 3-1. Another group classifies decisions by their relationship to other decisions.

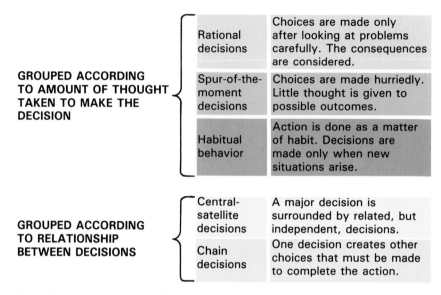

GROUPED ACCORDING TO AMOUNT OF THOUGHT TAKEN TO MAKE THE DECISION	Rational decisions	Choices are made only after looking at problems carefully. The consequences are considered.
	Spur-of-the-moment decisions	Choices are made hurriedly. Little thought is given to possible outcomes.
	Habitual behavior	Action is done as a matter of habit. Decisions are made only when new situations arise.
GROUPED ACCORDING TO RELATIONSHIP BETWEEN DECISIONS	Central-satellite decisions	A major decision is surrounded by related, but independent, decisions.
	Chain decisions	One decision creates other choices that must be made to complete the action.

3-1 Decisions are classified by the amount of thought devoted to them or by their relationship to other decisions.

Decisions according to thought and care

The three types of decisions that vary according to the amount of thought used to make them are *rational, spur-of-the-moment,* and *habitual.*

Suppose you had your own bedroom and you wanted an upholstered chair in it. If you shopped until you found a chair that looked good with what you already had in your room, you would have made a *rational decision.*

If you bought the first chair that appealed to you without a thought about how it would look in your room, your decision would have been a *spur-of-the-moment* one.

Habitual behavior does not call for a decision unless there is something new in the situation. Turning on the faucet in your bathroom is a habit. You do not have to make a decision unless water fails to come out of the faucet when you turn it on.

Interrelated decisions

Some decisions can be described by their relationship to other decisions. *Central-satellite decisions* and *chain decisions* are examples.

The concept of *central-satellite decisions* is illustrated in 3-2. The central decision is the big one. The satellite decisions are related to it, but they do not depend on it.

In a *chain decision,* one decision triggers others. Once you have made one decision, you must make each succeeding decision. If you fail to make any one of them, the action stops. See 3-3 for a diagram of a chain decision related to housing.

Suppose some of the grass in your yard is dying. Long ago, you had planted a certain variety of grass because it was attractive. Now the backyard is used as a playground by children and pets, 3-4. It is also used as a path from one part of the yard to another. The heavy traffic prevents the grass from growing.

You may choose to remove this grass and replace it with a hardier variety. The new variety will withstand the traffic and will look more attractive. It will also require less care.

The decision to replace part of the grass is the first decision in a chain. The second "link" is the decision to replace only the grass in the backyard. The next is to decide which variety

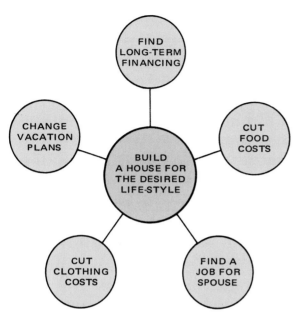

3-2 The central decision is to build a house; the others are satellite decisions. They are related to the central one, but they are not dependent on it.

JOHN OEHLER

3-4 Children and pets need clean, safe areas where they can play.

of grass to use. Other "links" include deciding where you will get the grass, whether you will do the work yourself or have someone else do it, when it will be done, and how you will pay for it. Each of these decisions must be made before the grass can be replaced.

Now suppose that you have decided not to replace the grass. Instead, you want to protect the grass from heavy use. In this case, the decision to keep the same grass becomes a central decision. Satellite decisions are needed. You

may decide to shift some of the play activities to a patio since some play activities are better suited to hard-surfaced areas, 3-5. Other activities could be moved to another part of the yard. In 3-6, older children play catch on the front lawn while younger children use their wheeled toys on the sidewalk.

Another satellite decision may be to set up traffic barriers. Careful placement of lawn furniture or flower beds can force people to walk around the grassy area instead of through it.

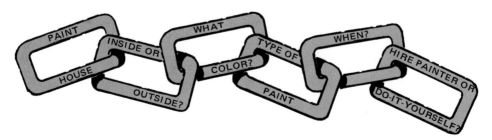

3-3 In chain decisions, additional decisions are needed to complete the action of the first one.

3-5 Wheeled toys, such as skateboards, work best on concrete or asphalt surfaces.

GEORGE GALE

3-6 A sidewalk or a surfaced driveway can satisfy the need for a play area. Ball practice can take place on the lawn.

RESOURCES FOR HOUSING DECISIONS

Resources are sources of supply or support. You need resources to carry out any type of decision you make. They are available to you in many forms.

Human resources

When you use your ability, knowledge, or energy, you are using a *human resource*. Even your health and your attitude toward a problem are human resources. See 3-7.

Someone with the ability to make home repairs has skill as a human resource. Someone who is willing to learn how has attitude as a resource. When these resources are developed and used, decisions can be made, and results can be achieved.

If you are a person with a high energy level, you may spend time after school and on weekends doing extras to improve your housing. If you have a low energy level, you may choose to hire someone to do what is needed to keep your house in shape. You can rest while they work.

You will seldom use only one resource at a time. They are all closely related. To develop a new skill, you will need a good attitude, knowledge, and time.

Time is sometimes called a human resource. How you use time is really what counts. You have 24 hours a day, 365 days a year, just as everyone else has. Time is the only resource that all people have in the same quantity. Other resources come in different quantities for different people. You will even have them in different quantities at different times during your lifetime. For instance, you may have more energy now than you will have when you are 30 years older. On the other hand, you are likely to have more money to spend then than you have now.

Some older people are short of both money and energy. To make their resources meet their needs, they must know how to use their wisdom and experience to save money and energy.

You have a choice of which resources you wish to spend and which ones you wish to save. Suppose that you owned a house that needed

INVENTORY OF HUMAN RESOURCES

PERSON	HUMAN RESOURCE	Physical health	Energy	Knowledge and information	Ability or skill	Attitude	Other (specify)
Husband/Father:							
Wife/Mother:							
Teenagers: (1)							
(2)							
Children: (1)							
(2)							
Others: (1)							
(2)							

3-7 Human resources are the help you can get from people. To make an inventory of the human resources in your living unit, make a similar chart on a separate sheet of paper. Rate members on a scale from 0 to 5.

painting. You could paint it yourself. That would take a lot of your time which you may prefer spending in some other way. In that case, you might decide to buy someone else's time to get the house painted. You could hire a painter or a friend.

Some of your human resources are depleted as you use them. Others increase with use. You may use up all of your energy and time, but you can increase your skills as you use them.

Nonhuman resources

Nonhuman resources include property, money, goods, and useful community help. These are shown in 3-8.

Consider how the resource of money is used in housing. Everyone has some housing expenses. Money is needed to buy or rent a place to live. Additional money is needed for furnishings, equipment, utilities, and repairs. You must decide what you can afford to spend

for these things. That amount will be determined by a number of factors such as:
- The income you are making.
- The amount of money you have saved for housing.
- Your life-style.
- Your other property.

The property you acquire and the way you use it are related to your housing decisions. Property resources include such things as land, buildings, and furnishings. The housing you can afford is partly determined by choices you have made about other property. Perhaps you are willing to drive a less expensive car so that you can have new furniture. If you choose a better car, the furniture or some other feature of your housing may have to wait. You may decide to reupholster or repair older furniture rather than replace it.

Community resources. Community resources are often taken for granted, but they can play an important part in your housing decisions. One such resource is a public library. You can study the books in the library to prepare for a better job or to do your homework. You can also read books for recreation. In addition to books, libraries offer statistical records, government documents, maps, magazines, and newspapers.

A city park with a playground and a picnic area is another community resource, 3-9. If you know that a park is nearby, you may decide to choose a site or lot with a small yard.

Special classes for self-improvement are also community resources. By taking advantage of these classes, you could learn such skills as furniture refinishing, upholstery, and home maintenance. Then you could complete some do-it-yourself projects like the one shown in 3-10.

Other community resources include hospitals, fire stations, police departments, schools, shopping centers, and recreational facilities. What community resources are available where you live?

STEPS IN DECISION-MAKING

To make a wise decision, you must know your goal or problem. Then you can determine the best way to reach the goal or to solve the problem. Thus, the first step in the decision-making process is called *problem identification*.

3-8 Books, land, buildings, money, and tools are a few examples of nonhuman resources.

SUN LAKES DEVELOPMENT CO.

3-9 Community recreational resources are sometimes clustered.

It includes:
- Defining the problem.
- Finding the cause.
- Considering the effects of the problem on the people involved.

In step two, you find different ways to solve the problem. This is called *seeking alternate solutions.* Each possible solution is studied. At this time, the following questions must be answered:
- What resources are needed?
- What will happen as a result of each solution?
- Will the outcome give lasting satisfaction?
- Will everyone involved be satisfied?
- What other decisions need to be made?

The third step is *choosing one of the alternatives and taking action.* Hopefully, you will have chosen the best alternative. But in many cases, you will have to change your decision. You will have to go back to the second step and look at the alternate solutions again. You may even find that you have not accurately identified the problem.

Some decisions have to be changed because you could not foresee the outcome. Suppose you had decided to use the money you had earned by mowing lawns to buy a pet rabbit. If the outcome was that your whole family became angry with you, you might have to change your decision. Other decisions must be changed because the necessary resources are not available. Suppose you had decided to barbecue

JOHN RUNNING

3-10 This wall hanging has been assembled by a creative person. Friends share in enjoying the results.

Decision-making skills 61

steaks for dinner. If you had forgotten to buy charcoal and lighter fluid, you would have to change your decision. You would have to cook indoors instead.

Going through the steps

One way to learn about the decision-making process is to consider one housing problem and think through all the steps needed to make a decision about it.

Suppose you are a member of a family that is expanding. Your grandmother is coming to spend a winter with you. As a result, the housing needs and priorities of your family will change. How will your new needs and personal priorities be met? How will your grandmother's needs and priorities be met?

Step one: Problem identification. The problem is to find a way to satisfy the needs and personal priorities of all members of the new, larger living unit.

Determine the causes of the problem.
- Grandmother needs to spend the winter in a milder climate.
- Grandmother cannot afford to pay a separate rental price.
- Your family enjoys Grandmother and wants her to come for the winter.

Consider the effects of the problem.
- Some or all members of the living unit will be more crowded.
- The life-style of the living unit will change.
- Extra money may be needed to provide housing for Grandmother.

Step two: Seeking alternate solutions. One solution is to have Grandmother occupy the room that the family uses as both a home office and a guest room.

Determine what additional resources are needed.
- Another office area.
- A place for guests.
- Money to make the needed changes.
- Time to reorganize the room.

Consider the consequences.
- Items may be stored in places where they are hard to find and use.
- There will be less chance for use of the home office unless it is moved.

- Members of the living unit will need to "double up" when there are guests.
- Less money will be spent on some things—perhaps recreation.
- Leisure time will be given up by one or more members of the living unit to get the room ready.
- There will be more use of the shared facilities such as laundry equipment and the bathroom.
- The arrangement is temporary (for the winter) and may not provide lasting satisfaction for Grandmother.
- Members of the family may not be satisfied with their changed life-style.

Other decisions must also be made.
- Where will things be stored?
- Will there continue to be a home office?
- Where will guests sleep?
- How will the extra money be obtained?
- Who will get the room ready?
- What will Grandmother do next summer?

A second solution is to add a room with a bath to the house. What resources will be needed to carry out this alternative? What are the possible consequences? What other decisions will need to be made? Can you think of other solutions to the problem?

Step three: Choosing one of the alternatives and taking action. The choice is that Grandmother will occupy the dual-purpose room. (You may make a different choice.)

Take the necessary action.
- Make the other decisions listed and carry them out in the order that seems best.
- Check to see if the outcome is satisfactory for all involved.
- Change some of the minor decisions for more satisfaction, if necessary.

Going through the decision-making process takes time and thought. It helps you make rational and wise decisions.

If you review this example of Grandmother's visit, you will see that the decisions can be classified not only as rational decisions, but also as central-satellite decisions. The central decision is that Grandmother is coming to stay with the family for the winter. The other decisions are satellite decisions.

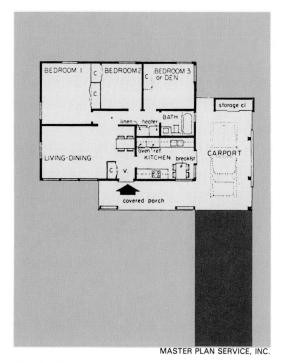

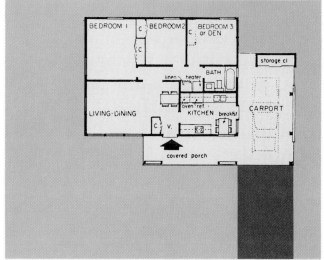

MASTER PLAN SERVICE, INC.

3-11 The location of a dwelling on a lot will determine the size of the yard space around it.

CATEGORIES OF HOUSING DECISIONS

Most housing decisions fit into one of three major categories: location, form, or acquisition.

Location

Every part of housing has a *location* or place. Some things are located outside a dwelling; others are within it.

The dwelling itself is located on a site or lot. Its location affects the size and shape of the yard. Compare the three locations of the dwelling pictured in 3-11. Each tree, shrub, fence, and sandbox also has a location outside the dwelling.

Inside a home, every room, door, chair, appliance, and picture has its own place.

Someone has made a decision about the location of everything. It may be a major decision such as choosing a site for a new building. Or it may be a minor decision like choosing a place for a toothbrush.

You may think that the location of your toothbrush is not important and should not be considered a housing decision. Finding your toothbrush every morning may be a habitual behavior for you. But when you first moved into your home, someone decided that the bathroom was the best place for storing toothbrushes.

Form

Form refers to the physical shape of objects. There is form to all that is within and without a dwelling. Trees, buildings, furniture, and lamps all have form. Your toothbrush has a form that makes it easy to handle and to use.

Decision-making skills   63

The form of a dwelling can be a high-rise apartment building, a town house, a small house, or a mansion. Beds can be twin, full, queen, or king-size. Doors can swing, slide, or fold open. A chair can be in the form of a kitchen chair, a rocker, or a reclining chair. Even objects that are used for the same purpose can have different forms. The chairs shown in 3-12 are both dining chairs, but their forms or shapes are different.

Acquisition

Acquisition is the act of getting something. Acquiring or getting housing is divided into two parts: process and cost.

Process. Process is the way you do things. In housing, process is the way you acquire housing. How did your living unit acquire the dwelling in which you live? Did they build it, or was it built by someone else? Did they buy it? If so, was it new or used? Did they pay cash for it, or are they making monthly payments? Perhaps they acquired the dwelling by renting it, receiving it as a gift or borrowing it from a friend.

After the initial (first) acquisition, additional processes are needed to maintain a household. You make arrangements to have the electricity and water turned on. You pay your utility bills by check, money order, or cash. You deliver the payments either in person or through the mail.

Cost. Cost is the amount of your resources you spend to acquire housing. The money you spend for rent or mortgage payments, utilities, and home maintenance is part of what you pay for housing. The other resources you spend, such as time, energy, and skills, add to your housing costs.

Suppose you have chosen to pay for your utilities by mail. You write checks to cover the amount of the bills and mail them to the utility companies. What do you spend to pay for your utilities? You spend the amount of money charged for the utilities. You pay for stamps, and you may pay a small amount to the bank for your checks.

Paying bills also costs time and energy. You can save both of these resources by mailing the

3-12 These two dining chairs have different forms or shapes.

payments rather than delivering the payments in person.

When decisions about location, form, and acquisition of housing are rationally made, they are more likely to satisfy the living unit.

to Know

acquisition . . . central-satellite decisions . . . chain decisions . . . community resources . . . cost . . . decision-making . . . form . . . habitual behavior . . . human resources . . . location . . . nonhuman resources . . . process . . . rational decisions . . . resources . . . spur-of-the-moment decisions

to Review

Write your answers on a separate sheet of paper.

1. A _____ decision is one that is made after thinking carefully about a problem or goal.

2. When you make a decision in a hurry, with little or no thought given to the possible outcomes, it is called a _____ decision.

3. (True or False) Closing the door as you leave your home is called a habitual behavior.

4. When one decision requires other decisions

to carry it out, the decisions are called:
  a. Central-satellite.
  b. Chain.
5. Describe five community resources.
6. List the three major steps in the decision-making process.
7. Give an example for each of the following categories of housing decisions:
  a. Location.
  b. Form.
  c. Acquisition.

to Do

1. Set up three columns on a separate sheet of paper. Label the first column "Degree of satisfaction;" the second, "Decision;" and the third, "Type of decision."

   In the center column, list some housing decisions that have been made by members of your living unit. In the right-hand column, list the type of decision (rational, spur-of-the-moment or habitual behavior).

   Write a (+ +) in the left-hand column if there was a great deal of satisfaction from the outcome. Write a (+) if there was some satisfaction and a (−) if there was no satisfaction.

2. Have a class debate about this statement: Rational decisions give more satisfaction than spur-of-the-moment decisions.

3. In a small group, write and present a skit to the class showing how resources can be decreased and increased at the same time.

4. Read the following case study, and complete the suggested activities.

   Andy and Jane are students in a community college. They plan to be married in June. Both are working at part-time jobs and will continue in school after their wedding.

   They will both graduate after another year. Andy plans to work in an auto repair and welding shop. Jane wants to continue her part-time job in the college library. In four or five years, they plan to start a family. They want two children.

   Jane likes music and wants a piano. Andy likes to fish and garden.
  a. Identify a major housing decision this couple will face.
  b. What resources will be available to them? What are the alternatives they may consider? What are the possible outcomes of each alternative? What other related decisions will they have to make?
  c. Which alternative would you choose as a solution? Give reasons for your choice.

Finding a satisfying place to live involves making decisions about the
region, community, neighborhood, site, and home.

4

A place to live

After studying this chapter, you will be able to:
- Describe different regions in which people live.
- List factors people consider when choosing a community or neighborhood.
- Discuss decisions about a home and its site involved in choosing a place to live.

Once you decide you need a new place to live, you will have many other decisions to make. Some of those decisions will concern location. In fact, you will face five major decisions when choosing a place to live. These are:

1. The *region* or area of the world, country, or state.
2. The *community*—country, suburbs, or city.
3. The *neighborhood* or section of the community.
4. The *site* or *lot* within the neighborhood.
5. The specific *home*.

REGION

The specific part of the world, country, or state in which you live is your region. Reasons for choosing a certain region are varied. You may like the scenery. See 4-1, 4-2, and 4-3.

4-1 A desert region is noted for mild winters but very hot summers.

4-2 Mountainous regions offer cool summers and very cold winters.

4-3 Along the New England coast, the weather is affected by the ocean. This spot is near the site of the first Pilgrim landing at Plymouth Rock.

Perhaps the climate is important to you. People with asthma or arthritis often choose to settle in a dry climate. Such a climate is found in the southwestern part of the United States. Look at 4-4 to learn about the different climates in this country.

You may choose a certain region in order to be close to family members or friends. The chance for employment may also lead you to a certain region. Jobs are usually easier to find in regions with large cities.

Several things to consider when you are choosing a region are listed in 4-5. Which ones would you like to find in your ideal region?

COMMUNITY

A region is divided into communities. A community may be a large city, a small village, or a rural area.

Cities are high-density areas. Many people live close together. If you enjoy being in contact with people most of the time, you are a *contact person.* You may enjoy city life.

Rural areas and the outskirts of towns and cities are low-density areas. If you enjoy being alone most of the time, you are a *noncontact person.* You may choose to live in a community of this type.

Some communities are designed for specific groups of people. For instance, some are built especially for retired persons. University communities consist of large groups of students and professors. Some communities are developed by businesses for their employees and their families.

Before choosing a community, you should consider more than just its size and social aspects. The number and type of services offered in a community should also be studied.

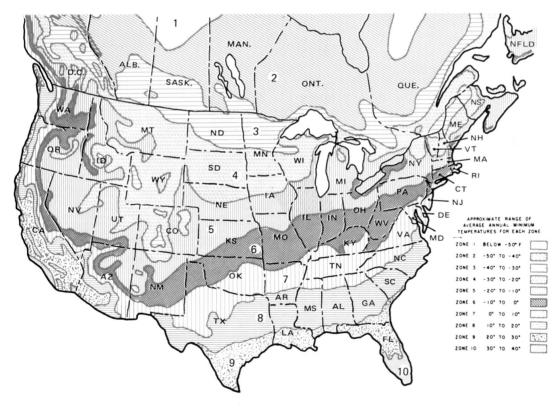

4-4 This map shows the annual range of temperatures in regions of the United States and Canada. Your choice of a region could depend on the kind of weather you prefer.

DECISIONS	RANGE OF AVAILABLE CHOICES		
General Climate	Hot	to	Cold
	Dry	to	Wet
	Constant temperature	to	Varying temperature
Topography (Prairie, lakes, mountains, etc.)	Flat	to	Mountainous
	Desert	to	Forest
	Low altitude	to	High altitude
Employment Opportunities	Limited in type	to	Varied
	Limited in number	to	Plentiful
	Low-paying	to	High-paying
	Seasonal	to	Steady
Cost of Living	High	to	Low
People	Family and friends	to	No acquaintances
Value System (A set of values that seems to dominate the thinking and actions of people)	All people equal	to	Class conscious
	Conservative	to	Liberal

4-5 These are some of the choices that will influence your selection of a region in which to live.

What kinds of stores are in the community? Is the school system good? Does your religious group have a meeting place? Are good medical facilities located in the community? Will you have good fire and police protection? Are resources available for self-improvement? What recreational facilities are offered? Are jobs easy to find? If some of these services are not available in the community, how far away are they? What kinds of transportation are offered?

The chart in 4-6 can serve as a guide for evaluating a community. Which factors apply to your present community? Which ones would you like in your ideal community?

NEIGHBORHOOD

Regions are divided into communities, and communities are divided into neighborhoods. A neighborhood consists of a group of homes and people. The buildings in any one neighborhood are usually similar in age, design, and cost. The people in a neighborhood usually have some similarities too.

Physical neighborhood

The physical neighborhood is determined by the way the land and buildings are used. Some neighborhoods are all *residential*. That is, they are all occupied by living units. *Commercial* neighborhoods include stores and businesses. Shopping centers are a kind of commercial neighborhood. *Industrial* neighborhoods include businesses, factories, warehouses, and industrial plants.

Some neighborhoods combine residential, commercial and industrial buildings, and land. For instance, when a local grocery is surrounded by homes, the neighborhood is a combination of residential and commercial buildings.

Zoning rules and other restrictions

Some neighborhoods have *zoning rules* which require that the land and buildings can be used for only one purpose. The rules are made by local or state governments. A neighborhood may be zoned for either residential, commercial, or industrial use, or for a combination of uses.

Housing developers can set additional limits which are called *restrictions*. (Developers are those who build houses. They develop a plot of land into a neighborhood. Sometimes the developed plot is called a subdivision.) These restrictions may control the design of the buildings that can be constructed. They may also limit the kind and number of animals that can be kept in a neighborhood. In 4-7, you can see a set of restrictions drawn up for a subdivision.

A *planned neighborhood* is usually in a zoned area with restrictions. Before anything is built, the size and layout of the individual lots are determined. This creates the shape of the neighborhood. Three ways of arranging lots are shown in 4-8, 4-9, and 4-10.

All homes built in this type of neighborhood must fit into the overall plan. Some planned neighborhoods have only single-family homes. Some have only apartment buildings. Other planned neighborhoods are for only mobile homes.

The quality of construction and the type of design are sometimes controlled in a planned neighborhood. This assures the residents that the neighborhood will not become run-down.

Many planned neighborhoods include recreational facilities. Parks, 4-11, and playgrounds,

THE COMMUNITY

DECISIONS		RANGE OF AVAILABLE CHOICES		
Type		Rural Industrial Commercial Commuter (suburb)		
Size		Single dwelling (farm) Village Town City Metropolis Megalopolis		
Density of Population		Sparse	to	Dense
Cost of Living		Low	to	High
Population Composition Age Religion Income Ethnic group Occupation Interests		Homogenous (similar)	to	Heterogenous (varied)
Community Facilities Educational Environmental protection Recreational Transportation Medical Fire and police protection Shopping Banking Job opportunities Religious organizations		Few	to	Many
Value System (A set of values that seems to dominate the thinking and actions of the people)		Prejudiced	to	Free from prejudices

4-6 When you look for a community in which to live, these factors may be considered.

DECLARATION OF RESTRICTIONS FOR SWISS MANOR SUBDIVISION

1. All of said lots in Swiss Manor Subdivision shall be known and designated as residential lots and shall not be used for any business purpose whatsoever.
2. No structure whatsoever other than one private dwelling, together with a private garage or carport, for not more than three cars, shall be erected, placed or allowed to remain on any of the lots.
3. No dwelling house shall be erected which contains less than 1200 square feet of liveable space, exclusive of attached garage, porches, patios and breezeways. No residence shall be built which exceeds the height of 2 1/2 stories or 30 feet from the curb level. All structures on said lots shall be of new construction and no building shall be moved from any other location on to any of said lots.
4. There shall be no trailer houses, or homes built around or incorporating trailer homes. All camper trailers, campers or boats shall be stored behind the dwelling house, or be stored within the garage.
5. There shall be no unused automobiles, machinery or equipment allowed on these premises outside of enclosed garages. All driveways or parking areas used for parking vehicles shall be constructed of concrete.
6. All clothes lines, equipment, service yards, woodpiles or storage piles shall be kept screened by adequate planting or fencing to conceal them from view of neighboring lots or street. All rubbish, trash or garbage shall be removed from the lots and shall not be allowed to accumulate thereon. All yards shall be kept mowed and all weeds shall be cut. Garbage and refuse containers may be brought to the street not more than 12 hours before collection time and must be removed within 12 hours after collection time.
7. No animals, livestock, or poultry of any kind shall be raised, bred or kept on any lot, except for dogs, cats and other household pets may be kept provided that they are not kept, bred or maintained for commercial purposes, and so long as applicable laws in respect to restraining or controlling animals are observed.
8. No lot may be subdivided, or a portion sold unless it becomes a part of the adjacent property.
9. No solid wall, hedge or fence over 2 1/2 feet high shall be constructed or maintained past the front wall line of the house. No side or rear fence shall be constructed more than 6 feet in height.
10. All utility lines must be brought underground to the dwelling house.
11. No structure shall be built nearer than 25 feet to the front property line. No living areas shall be located nearer than 10% of the lot widths to any side property line and no carport or garage closer than 5 feet.
12. No billboards, signs, or advertising devices, except suitable "For Sale" or "For Rent" signs shall be maintained.
13. Before construction of the initial structure of any building, plans and specifications and materials must be approved by the Developer or its successor.
14. Construction of homes must be started within one year after purchase of lot and must be completed within one year after commencement of construction.
15. No property owner shall in any way divert the drainage water in such a way that it will encroach upon a neighbor's property.
16. These declarations shall constitute covenants to run with the land, as provided by law, and shall be binding on all parties and all persons claiming under them, and are for the benefit of and shall be limitations upon all future owners in said Swiss Manor Subdivision.

4-7 This list of restrictions was made by the developers of a subdivision. Its purpose is to assure that all owners will maintain a certain style of living.

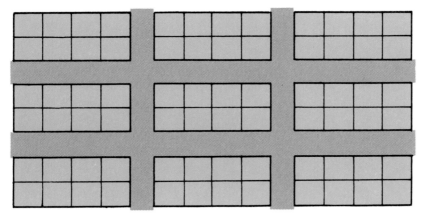

4-8 In a traditional "gridiron" arrangement, all of the lots are the same size and shape.

4-9 The contour shape of streets and lots adds variety and interest to these neighborhoods.

4-10 The cluster layout of lots places fewer homes together in groups with less traffic on the streets.

4-11 Parks beautify a neighborhood and provide space for recreation.

4-12 Playgrounds are a part of many planned neighborhoods.

4-12, are built in locations that are convenient to the people living in the neighborhood. A clubhouse, like the one shown in 4-13, is often built as a place for meetings and social activities.

Social neighborhood

The type of people in any one neighborhood may be quite varied. Then the neighborhood is *heterogenous*. If the people are very similar to each other, the neighborhood is *homogenous*. Sometimes neighborhoods or whole communities are made up of people who are similar in age, ethnic background, income level, or occupation. These patterns occur in both rural and urban settings.

Another factor involved with social neighborhood is population density. A low-density neighborhood has more space for each individual than a high-density one has. Generally, low-density neighborhoods have prestige, but this rule has many exceptions.

SUN LAKES DEVELOPMENT CO.

4-13 A clubhouse offers space for social activities.

Smaller homes, smaller lots, and more people in less space create high-density neighborhoods. Mobile home parks, 4-14, and apartment buildings fit this category.

Which kind of neighborhood would you choose? What are your reasons for making that choice? The factors listed in 4-15 can help you make a decision.

SITE

A location within a neighborhood is called a site or lot. It is the piece of land on which the home is built. It extends as far as the property lines.

Each site has its own characteristics—size, shape, contour (hills and curves), and soil type. These characteristics should be considered before you choose a site for your home, 4-16.

Certain sites are considered more prestigious than others. Sites that allow for privacy, that have a nice view, and that offer plenty of space

4-14 This mobile trailer park has a high density.

A place to live   75

are likely to be in great demand. They are also more costly than other sites. What kind of site would be your ideal? Would you like to be close to your neighbors, or would you prefer to have more privacy? Would you like to have your home on a hill or on flat land? What kind of view would you like?

If you are buying a house that someone else built or if you are renting an apartment, you should look carefully at the placement of the home on the site. It will have a great effect on your microenvironment. It will determine the views, the amount of sunlight and the amount of protection from wind you will have.

If you are building a house, you can choose the site and the type of house you want. You can place the house where you want it on the site. This gives you the chance to make the house and the site work together to form a satisfying microenvironment.

Natural restraints

Careful planning is needed to make the most of your site. You will meet many *restraints* or obstacles. Some will be natural, and some will be legal.

One kind of natural restraint is the *topography* of a site. Topography is the slope or lay of the land. Sites that are flat make the job of mowing grass easy. Flat lawns are also good places for children's games and lawn furniture. See 4-17.

Hilly sites are more difficult to maintain, but they are often very attractive. Some houses (such as split-level houses) look best on hilly sites.

Sites with extremely steep slopes have some disadvantages. A home built at the top of a slope may be difficult to reach, especially in winter. Also, soil may wash away and cause land erosion.

THE NEIGHBORHOOD

DECISIONS	RANGE OF AVAILABLE CHOICES		
Physical	Residential Commercial Industrial Combination Zoned	to	Unzoned
Organization of Lots	Attractive	to	Unattractive
	Much street traffic	to	Little street traffic
	Park and play areas	to	No park or play areas
Type of Structures	Single-family Multifamily Mixed		
Location in Community	Edge	to	Center
Density of Population	Sparse	to	Crowded
Population Composition Age Occupation Income Religion Interests Ethnic group	Homogenous (similar)	to	Heterogenous (varied)
Value System (A set of values that seem to dominate the thinking and actions of the people)	Agrees with own values	to	Does not agree with own values

4-15 Which of these factors would you include in your ideal neighborhood?

DECISIONS	RANGE OF AVAILABLE CHOICES
Location in Neighborhood	Edge to Center

Orientation to Environment
   Sun   Prevailing wind
   Water   Erosion
   View   Pollution
	Takes advantage
	of features to Ignores features

Physical Characteristics
   Size
   Shape
   Contour of the land
   Soil characteristics
	Large to Small
	Regular to Irregular
	Level, Gentle slope, Steep slope
	Sand, Gravel, Rock, Clay

4-16 Before you choose a site, you should consider all your choices.

Landscaping can be done to change the topography of a site. Small hills can be built to make the site more attractive, as shown in 4-18. Landscaping also includes the addition of trees, shrubs, and gardens.

Soil and water. Soil conditions affect both the site and the home. Poorly drained soils freeze and expand. This can cause sidewalks and driveways to crack and bulge. Plants have difficulty growing in shallow or nonporous topsoils.

High water levels can cause swampy yards, wet basements, and poor plant growth.

Orientation to the sun. Homes with southern and western exposures will have much sunlight. They may need protection from the intense

GEORGE GALE

4-17 The topography of this site is very flat. It is a good place for running games.

SUN LAKES DEVELOPMENT CO.

4-18 Landscaping adds greatly to the beauty of this site.

A place to live 77

summer sun. Some homes are shaded by trees. Shade can also be provided by built-in features such as roof overhangs.

In regions where sunlight is almost always welcome, houses are often built with large amounts of glass, 4-19. Glass allows sunlight to bring light and warmth into the dwellings.

4-19 The abundant use of glass permits sunlight to enter this home.

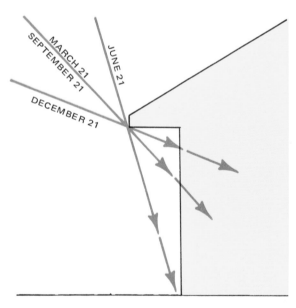

4-20 The sun shines at different angles on the south side of a home at different times of the year. By knowing this angle, architects can plan a proper roof overhang.

The width of the overhang on a roof affects the amount of sunlight that enters a building. Wider overhangs block out more sunlight. The time of year also affects the amount of sunlight received, 4-20. Because of the earth's changing position in relation to the sun, more sunlight reaches the northern hemisphere during the summer.

Orientation to the wind. Homes can be located so that they are protected from strong winds. Windbreaks are used to provide some of this protection. Trees and shrubs are natural windbreaks. Walls and fences of stone or wood, as shown in 4-21, are also windbreaks. A garage placed on the north side of a home will usually eliminate drafts from cold winter winds and reduce heating costs.

In most regions, the prevailing (most frequent) wind changes direction with the season. This should be taken into consideration when planning for protection from the wind. The illustration in 4-22 shows a home that is well-oriented to both the sun and wind.

Orientation to scenery. A pleasant view is desirable, but it is not always provided by nature. If necessary, you can create a nice view. Landscapers use gardens, shrubs, and

WESTERN WOOD PRODUCTS ASSOC.

4-21 Windbreaks are used to protect the private areas of this house.

decorative fences to change the scenery. See 4-23 for an example of a landscaped view.

Legal restraints

Legal restraints affecting sites may be federal, state, or local laws. They are established for your protection.

The *minimum property standards (MPS)* are an example of a federal law. These standards regulate the sizes of lots. They are set by the Federal Housing Administration (FHA).

GEORGE GALE

4-23 Terraces and plantings on a lakeshore have changed the view in this microenvironment.

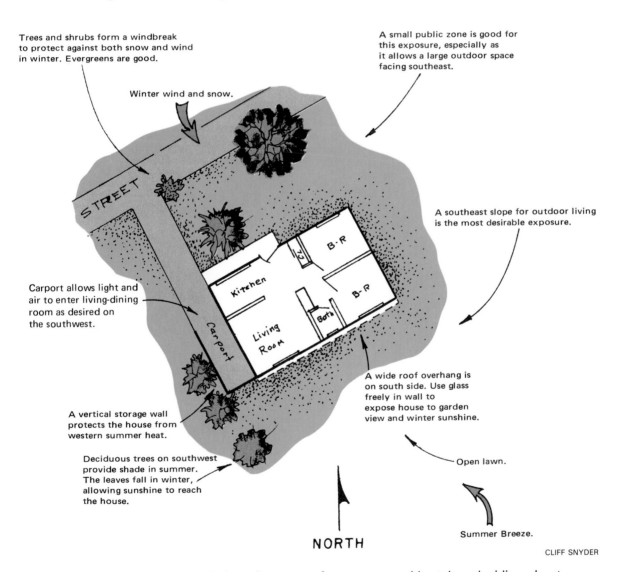

Trees and shrubs form a windbreak to protect against both snow and wind in winter. Evergreens are good.

Winter wind and snow.

A small public zone is good for this exposure, especially as it allows a large outdoor space facing southeast.

STREET

A southeast slope for outdoor living is the most desirable exposure.

B-R

B-R

Kitchen

Carport allows light and air to enter living-dining room as desired on the southwest.

Carport

Living Room

Bath

A wide roof overhang is on south side. Use glass freely in wall to expose house to garden view and winter sunshine.

A vertical storage wall protects the house from western summer heat.

Deciduous trees on southwest provide shade in summer. The leaves fall in winter, allowing sunshine to reach the house.

Open lawn.

NORTH

Summer Breeze.

CLIFF SNYDER

4-22 Orientation to sun and wind are important factors to consider when deciding about the location of a home on a site.

MPS vary according to the shape and location of a site. In some cases, the minimum size of a lot is 65 ft. (19.8 meters) wide and 130 ft. (39.6 meters) from the front to the back. Look at 4-24 to see a plan for a lot that meets these MPS.

Higher standards than the MPS may be set by the local government or by the developer. State and local authorities also establish limits and standards for the quality of construction, for water supplies, and for disposal of wastes. Do you have a housing authority office in your community? If so, what legal restraints do they enforce?

Zones within the site

The part of the site that is not covered by the home can be divided into three zones:

1. Public zone.
2. Service zone.
3. Private zone.

The *public zone* is the part of the site that can be seen from the street. It is usually in front of the house. If the house is on a corner lot, the public zone is L-shaped. It includes the front and one side of the lot. Since the public zone is seen more often than any other part of the site or home, people work hard to make it attractive, 4-25. They use pebbles, flagstone, trees, shrubs, and gardens to create an interesting and beautiful microenvironment.

If the house is as far forward on the lot as the law permits, the public zone is small. Many people want small public zones because they are easier to maintain.

The *service zone* includes sidewalks, driveways, and storage areas for such things as trash, tools, lawn equipment, and cars. A service zone may also include a clothesline for drying laundry. In this zone, convenience is most important.

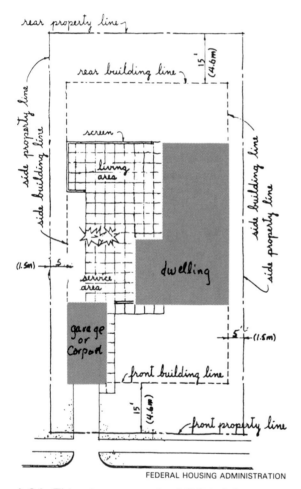

FEDERAL HOUSING ADMINISTRATION

4-24 This plan meets the MPS (minimum property standards) for a rectangular lot in the middle of a block.

4-25 Many materials are used to make this public zone attractive.

4-26 Sidewalks and driveways are parts of the service zone that can be seen by others. The garage door hides the inside of the garage, which is also part of the service zone.

At least a part of the service zone can usually be seen by others, 4-26. However, many people choose to have as much of it screened from view as possible.

The *private zone* is for recreation and relaxation, 4-27. It provides a place where children and pets can play. Private zones can be separated from public ones by using shrubs, hedges, screens, fences, or walls.

Many living units want a large private zone. In it, they can place yard accessories such as outdoor furniture and barbeque equipment. Yard games and swimming pools are also found in the private zones of some dwellings.

Other living units prefer a small private zone so they can care for it easily. Some want a home without a private zone; they want all the available space inside the home.

In 4-28, you can see how two different houses are placed on sites to provide all three zones—public, service, and private.

HOMES

After choosing a region, a community, a neighborhood, and a site, your next decision is to choose a home. The two major groups of homes are *multifamily* and *single-family*. Within each group are several variations.

Multifamily homes

Multifamily homes are a type of housing designed for more than one living unit. Each living unit within the home has its own distinct living quarters.

Today, life-styles are changing, and the demand for multifamily housing is increasing. Single persons, young married couples, and retired persons have always been the living units most interested in this kind of housing. Now, in addition to these, more nuclear families, one-parent families, and other living units are

4-27 Both children and adults can relax and have fun in this private zone.

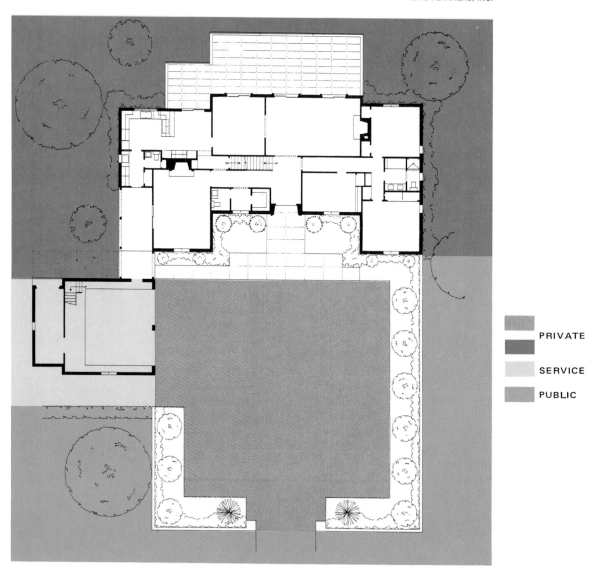

PRIVATE

SERVICE

PUBLIC

4-28 The house shown above has a huge private zone. In the plan shown below it, you can see that the public and service zones are much smaller.

turning to multifamily units. They are usually less costly and easier to maintain than single-family homes.

Almost all *rental, cooperative,* and *condominium* units are multifamily homes. (A few are single-family homes.) Some of these units are in high-rise buildings, 4-29. Others are in low-spread buildings as shown in 4-30. They may be huge, or they may be just duplexes (with two living units) or quadraplexes (with four living units).

Rental apartments range from the tenement house to the exclusive penthouse. (A penthouse is an expensive suite located at the top of a luxury apartment building.) They also vary in the number and type of facilities offered. Many

4-30 Low-spread apartment buildings require larger lots per living unit than high-rise ones.

ROLOC

4-29 The Marina Towers are high-rise buildings in Chicago where several hundred families live.

apartment buildings have washing machines and dryers, tennis courts, and swimming pools for the residents. Some huge, high-rise buildings are like a small city. They include business offices, schools, stores, and recreational facilities.

Cooperative apartments or *co-ops* are not very common. The entire building is owned by a nonprofit corporation. The people who live in the building are the stockholders in that corporation. Therefore, when people move into a co-op, they "buy" their apartment by purchasing shares in the corporation.

Residents of a co-op have a voice in how the corporation is run. They even get the chance to select their neighbors. If a living unit wants to move into the co-op, the corporation votes on it. If the vote does not pass, the living unit cannot move into the apartment.

Another advantage of living in a co-op is that neighbors meet each other and work together to create a pleasant housing environment. A disadvantage is that if they disagree with the others on an issue, they will be forced to go along with the decision of the majority.

Condominium units (sometimes called condos) are somewhat like cooperative units. Both are owned by the people who live in them, and both are usually multifamily homes. The difference is in the type of ownership. Instead of buying stock in a corporation, condominium buyers purchase the homes as if they were separate houses. At the same time, the buyers receive a portion of the common areas. They share the ownership of the lot, parking areas, recreational facilities, and hallways with the other condominium owners.

The terms cooperative and condominium describe types of ownership. They do not refer to building designs. You cannot tell if a building has rental, cooperative, or condominium units by looking at it, 4-31.

Single-family homes

In spite of the rising trend for multifamily homes, the most desired type of housing today is still the single-family dwelling. It is designed to house one family or living unit.

Attached homes. Some single-family homes are attached. That is, they are designed for one living unit, but they share a common wall with the homes on each side. *Town houses* and *row houses* are names for these homes. Usually, entire sidewalls of homes are shared, but there are variations, as shown in 4-32.

The owners of an attached, single-family home or a town house own the home itself and the land on which it is located. They have their own entrance and yard area.

Free-standing homes. When single-family homes are not connected to another unit, they are called free-standing. They vary in size, design, color, features, and cost.

The most individualistic type of house is one that is *custom-designed* and *custom-built*. An architect considers the needs, personal priorities, and life situations of a living unit and then designs a house to "fit" them. A contractor then builds the house according to the architect's plans and living unit's wishes. This kind of house is "a dream house." It is very expensive and takes a long time to plan and build.

Some houses are *custom-built from stock plans.* In these cases, persons go to a contractor and look at house plans. They choose the plan that they want, and the contractor builds a house for them on their site.

Owner-built houses are for those with lots of skill, time, and energy. They can be less

GEORGE GALE

4-31 These town houses could be rentals, co-ops, or condominiums. You can't tell by looking at them.

costly in terms of money than other types of housing. Sometimes a contractor is hired to put up the house shell, and the living unit does the interior work. In other cases, the living unit does it all. Building a house can be a great experience for a family if they have the necessary human resources.

Examples of *tract* houses are shown in 4-33. They are built by a developer who builds an entire neighborhood at once. The houses are built before they are sold to living units. One or two sets of plans are used over and over to

DANNY CLEVENGER

4-32 These town houses share only part of their sidewalls.

84

GEORGE GALE

4-33 Tract houses look very much alike.

MARLETTE

4-35 Manufactured housing often looks as if it were built right on the site.

save money. Because few variations are made, the houses lack individuality, but they are less expensive to buy than custom-built houses.

Manufactured housing is built in factories and then moved in modular sections to the sites. See 4-34. Today's manufactured housing has improved so much in appearance and quality that you often cannot tell a manufactured house from a house that was built on the site piece-by-piece. See 4-35. Modular sections are sometimes used in multifamily homes too.

Kit houses are another type of manufactured housing. The shell of a kit house is finished at a factory. It is then moved to the site and completed on the inside according to the buyer's wishes. A kit house is pictured in 4-36.

Like other manufactured housing, the quality of kit houses is improving. This type of

TOM KIRBY ADVERTISING FOR BULLOCK CO.

TOM KIRBY ADVERTISING FOR BULLOCK CO.

4-34 Walls are assembled to the floor system of a modular house. Then trusses and roof are added to complete the sections. Completed sections are then transported to the building site by truck.

dwelling is less costly than most others. The total cost is influenced by several factors. Some of these factors include the size of the house, the style of the house, and the distance from the factory to the site. Another factor is whether all the materials and labor for the house are purchased with the kit or separately.

Mobile homes are still another kind of manufactured single-family home. Most homes are "fixed." That is, they are attached to a foundation which is anchored to the ground. Mobile homes are an exception. They can be moved by attaching wheels to them. (Mobile homes should not be confused with *motor homes* which are automotive vehicles equipped as a home, 4-37.)

Moving a mobile home is not as easy as it sounds. Each state has laws that must be followed when moving a mobile home. Some local governments have passed additional rules. The zoning laws of some neighborhoods and communities prohibit the placement of mobile homes in certain areas.

Small mobile homes, like the one shown in 4-38, can be moved by the owners as long as all laws are followed. Larger mobile homes are more difficult to move. For instance, the one in 4-39 would have to be moved in parts. A company that specializes in such moving could handle the job, but most large units are set permanently on a site.

GENE BALZER

4-37 Motor homes, also called recreational vehicles (RV's), are a good type of home for people who travel a great deal.

More decisions

Other considerations when choosing a dwelling include its condition if it is not new, the price, the size, the design, and the way it looks on the site. The chart in 4-40 can guide you as you make decisions about a home.

MOVING TO A NEW LOCATION

How many times have you and members of your living unit moved from one place to another? How do you compare to the average American family which moves once every five years?

NATIONAL HOMES CORP.

4-36 This kit house is a single-family dwelling.

MARLETTE

4-38 Mobile homes no more than 14 ft. wide can usually be moved by the owners.

4-39 To move double-width mobile homes, they must be split into two sections.

THE DWELLING

DECISIONS	RANGE OF AVAILABLE CHOICES		
Ownership	Rental Cooperative Condominium Private		
Form			
Multifamily	High rise Few units Few extra facilities	to to to	Low spread Many units Many extra facilities
Single-family	Custom-designed and custom-built Custom-built from stock plans Owner-built Tract house Modular dwelling Kit house Mobile home		
Landscaping	Dwelling "fits" site Many trees and shrubs	to to	Dwelling looks out of place No trees or shrubs
Outside Zones Public Service Private	Large	to	Small
Structural Quality	High Standard Deteriorating Deteriorated		
Price	High Affordable Low		
Size	Huge Adequate Too small		

4-40 Many options are possible when you choose a home.

Many moves made by living units are from one home to another within the same neighborhood or community. Short moves may be expected as a living unit ends one stage of its life cycle and enters another. Changes in lifestyle, occupation, socioeconomic status, or other life situations also cause people to move.

If you decide to move, how will you do it? You have a number of alternatives. You may hire a moving company. They will move everything for you if you desire. They will even do the packing for you. See 4-41. Ask them for an estimate of their fee before you make a decision. The distance between homes and the amount of work required determine the cost.

This method of moving is the most costly in terms of money, but it saves you time and energy.

About two-thirds of all moves are do-it-yourself efforts. If you do not own a truck or trailer, you can rent one and move yourself, 4-42. In this case, you will need someone to help load heavy items. Family and friends often help when the move is only a short distance.

Another alternative would be to sell all of your household goods and buy replacements when you reach your new location. This might be a wise choice if you were planning to go abroad for a few years. Can you think of other times this would be a good decision?

4-41 Movers and packers can help make moving easier.

UNITED VAN LINES

UNITED VAN LINES

4-42 Rental trucks and trailers come in many sizes. You can use them to move your belongings.

U-HAUL RENTAL SYSTEM

U-HAUL RENTAL SYSTEM

to Know

architect . . . attached home . . . community . . .
condominium units . . . contractor . . .
cooperative units . . .
custom-designed and custom built . . .
developer . . . fixed home . . .
free-standing home . . . kit house . . .
landscaping . . . manufactured housing . . .
minimum property standards . . .
mobile home . . . multifamily home . . .
neighborhood . . . owner-built . . .
physical neighborhood . . .
planned neighborhood . . . private zone . . .
public zone . . . region . . . rental units . . .
restrictions . . . service zone . . .
single-family home . . . site . . .
social neighborhood . . . subdivision . . .
topography . . . tract house . . . zoning rules

to Review

Write your answers on a separate sheet of paper.

1. List the five major decisions concerning the location of housing.
2. Give three reasons you might have for living in a certain region.
3. Regions are divided into communities and communities are divided into _____.
4. Neighborhoods in which all buildings are occupied by living units are called:
   a. Residential.
   b. Commercial.
   c. Industrial.
5. Explain the meaning of the following:
   a. FHA.
   b. MPS.
6. List two natural and two legal restraints that affect sites.
7. Name and describe the three zones within the site.
8. What are the differences among rental, cooperative, and condominium units?

9. A fixed home is one that:
   a. Shares a common wall with the home on each side.
   b. Is not connected to another building.
   c. Is attached to a foundation which is anchored to the ground.
10. An architect _____ the home and the contractor _____ it.
11. How does a tract house differ from one that was custom-built from stock plans?
12. Describe three forms of manufactured homes.

to Do

1. Choose a region other than your own in which you would enjoy living. Study an atlas and encyclopedia to find out more about the area.
2. Make a list of advantages of living in your own community.
3. Choose another community in which you would like to live. Write to its Chamber of Commerce to find out the advantages of living there.
4. With a small group of classmates, prepare a brochure on your neighborhood.
5. Find magazine and newspaper articles about planned communities.
6. At your public library, check the zoning regulations and building codes of your community to find out what control they exercise over housing.
7. Make drawings of homes on sites showing the three zones of a site.
8. Look at the classified advertising section of a newspaper. Compare the facts given for single-family homes with those given for multifamily homes. Which type is most often listed for sale? For rent?
9. Brainstorm in small groups and make lists of things to check when choosing a place to live.
10. Describe your ideal region, community, neighborhood, site, and home.

Should you rent or buy housing? Should you build a new house or move into one that is already built? These are questions you must answer as you seek to acquire housing.

5

Acquiring housing

After studying this chapter, you will be able to:
■ Discuss the advantages and disadvantages of renting and buying homes.
■ List several items to check before signing a lease.
■ Explain the steps in buying a home.
■ Define many legal and financial terms related to acquiring housing.
■ Describe condominium and cooperative ownership.

Do you remember the three major categories of housing decisions? Location and form are two of them. The other one is *acquisition*. Regardless of where your home is located or what form it has, you will make choices about acquiring or getting it. Acquisition involves two basic aspects—process and cost.

Process

Process is the method you use to accomplish something. Thus, process in housing refers to the method you use to acquire any part of your housing. See 5-1.

Getting something that you have not had before is called *initial acquisition*. Buying your first lawn mower or your first sofa is an initial acquisition.

Process also includes repairing or replacing any part of housing. It may mean replacing your home because it has burned. It may mean finding a different home in a new area because you have changed jobs. Or it may mean something as simple as replacing a worn-out washer in a leaky water faucet.

Another part of process is the operating and maintaining of housing. Who operates the lawn mower at your house? Does the same person maintain it?

The way you pay for your housing is also included in process. You can pay for things in several different ways:

- Full amount paid with cash, check or debit card.
- Payment deferred by use of a credit card.
- Down payment made, and the balance paid over a period of months or years. This is called *installment buying.*

Cost

When you think of *cost,* no doubt you think of money. In addition to the spending of money, cost also means the spending of other resources, 5-2.

Shopping for a new television set costs time and effort. Buying it costs money. This is the initial monetary cost (the first cost in terms of money). Operation also costs money. If the television does not work well, it will have to be repaired or replaced. These costs can demand even more of your resources of money, time, and energy.

Consider what is involved in replacing the plumbing in a home. You would first have the cost of getting materials to replace the old lines. Additional costs would be the time and energy you would spend removing the old plumbing. If you did not have the time, energy, and knowledge, you would have to pay someone else for using their resources.

Process is related to cost

Process and cost are sometimes so closely related that they must be considered together. You have read about the processes for buying things. When you pay the full amount with cash, you pay only what the item is worth.

If you pay by check or debit card, you may have some banking costs. Some banks charge for checks and for providing checking and debit card services. (Paying by debit card is like paying by check except a debit card is used in place of a check.)

Credit cards are often used to buy things. The cost of using credit cards varies. You must pay a fee just to get some credit cards; others are free. You can use some credit cards without extra cost if you pay the full amount you owe by the date listed on the bill. This may be within 30, 60, or 90 days, depending on the company.

THE PROCESS OF ACQUISITION

DECISIONS		RANGE OF AVAILABLE CHOICES
Possessing	Own	Buy Build Own to rent
	Rent	Privately owned Publicly owned Company owned
Financing	Cash	Currency Check
	Terms	Short term Long term
	Sources	Current income Savings Private loans Commercial loans Governmental loans
Operating		Furnish Maintain Repair
Replacing		Sell Trade Abandon
Adapting		Remodel Refinish Redecorate

5-1 When acquiring housing, you will want to consider all available choices.

If you pay only a part of what you owe by that date, finance charges will be added to the rest of the amount you owe. The credit card company is required by law to tell you exactly how much extra you will be charged. To determine the cost of a credit card, ask the following questions:

- Is there an annual fee?
- What is the interest rate?
- Is interest charged beginning with the time of purchase?
- Is the amount due paid in full?

Using the process of installment buying costs you the most money. This is because part of the money you are using belongs to someone else. That person, company, or bank is *financing* you. They have paid your bill and are willing to wait for you to pay them back. But in the meantime, you must pay extra for the privilege of using their money. This extra amount is called a *finance charge*. It includes the interest as well as any carrying charges. *Interest* is the price paid for the use of the money. It is stated as an annual percentage rate of the amount borrowed. *Carrying charges* are the amounts other than interest that are added to the price of something when it is bought by the installment buying process.

You can pay back the money you borrowed over a short or long period of time. The longer you take, the more interest you will pay. Most homes are purchased with *long-term financing*. You can take as long as 30 years to pay back the money you borrowed for a house. In the end, the interest may cost more than the house itself.

ACQUIRING A HOME

Should you rent or buy? Home ownership is valued highly by some. To others, it is not important. They prefer to rent their homes. Some people would like to own their living space, but for various reasons, they do not. They may not have the cash or credit that is needed to buy a house. Or perhaps they are not sure how long they will be located in one place.

At some time, you will have to decide how to spend the money you allow for housing. You will need to use rational decision-making to choose between renting and purchasing a home. Your choice will depend on your life-style, your stage of the life cycle, and your other life situations.

A PLACE TO RENT

About one-third of all Americans rent their housing. The majority of these are single persons, young married couples, and senior citizens. Many are people with low incomes. They are known as *renters, lessees,* or *tenants.*

Renters pay for their housing in monthly installments. When they first move into a building, the landlord or lessor usually requests a *security deposit* in addition to the first month's rent. The security deposit insures the landlord against financial loss in case the renter fails to pay the rent or damages the building. The amount of the security deposit commonly includes one month's rent. It may include an additional amount.

Renting housing has a number of advantages. Renters are free to move as they desire. They need not worry about the value of property going up or down or about buying and selling. They have a clear idea of what housing will cost them. They have no hidden costs—like a new roof—that come with ownership. Since they do not own the house they can save money that would be spent on improvements.

Any type of housing can be rented, but the most common rental units are multifamily dwellings. Duplexes, triplexes, and apartment buildings are usually occupied by renters. Single-family houses can be rented too, as well as vacation and travel houses.

Before you move into any rental unit, examine it closely. Take a checklist like the one in 5-2 with you. Ask the landlord questions like those listed in 5-3. Be sure that you can answer each question and that you are happy with the answers. You want your housing to bring satisfaction, not frustration.

The written lease

Rental agreements can be on a month-to-month basis or for a specific length of time such

RENTERS' CHECKLIST

Laundry facilities

_____ How many washers and dryers are available?
(A good ratio is one washer and dryer for every ten apartments.)

_____ Are washers and dryers in good working order?

Building lobby

_____ Is the lobby clean and well lit?

_____ Is the main entrance locked so that only residents can enter?

_____ Is a security guard provided? If so, what hours?

Entrance, exit, and halls

_____ Are elevators provided? If so, are they in good working order?

_____ Are the stairs soundly constructed and well lit?

_____ Are fire exits provided?

_____ Is there a fire alarm or other warning system?

_____ Are halls clean, well lit, and soundly constructed?

Bathroom(s)

_____ Do all plumbing fixtures work? Are they clean?

_____ Does the hot water supply seem adequate?

_____ Do floors and walls around fixtures seem damp, rotted, or moldy?

Kitchen

_____ Is the sink working and clean? Does it have drain stoppers?

_____ Is there an exhaust fan above the range?

_____ Is the refrigerator working properly? Does it have a separate freezer compartment?

_____ If there is a dishwasher, does it work properly?

Air conditioning

_____ Is the building centrally air conditioned or are separate units present for each apartment?

_____ Does the air conditioning unit work properly?

Heating

_____ What type of heat is provided (gas, electric)?

_____ Does the heating system work properly?

_____ Is there a fireplace? If so, are there smoke stains or any other signs that it has not worked properly?

Wiring

_____ Are there enough electrical outlets? (There should be at least three to a room.)

_____ Do all switches and outlets work?

_____ Are there enough circuits in the fuse box or circuit breaker panel to handle all of your electrical equipment?

5-2 Check apartments carefully as you search for a place to rent.

Lighting

_____ Are there enough fixtures for adequate light? Are the fixtures in good working order?

_____ Does the apartment get a good amount of natural light from windows?

Windows

_____ Are any windows broken or difficult to open and close?

_____ Are windows arranged to provide good ventilation?

_____ Are screens provided?

_____ Are there drafts around the window frame?

_____ In high-rise buildings, does the landlord arrange for the outside of the windows to be cleaned? If so, how often?

Floors

_____ Are floors clean and free of gouges?

_____ Do floors have any water stains indicating previous leaks?

Ceilings

_____ Are ceilings clean and free of cracks and peeling?

_____ Are there any water stains indicating previous leaks?

Walls

_____ Are walls clean and free of cracks and peeling?

_____ Does the paint run or smear when rubbed with a damp cloth?

Soundproofing

_____ When you thump the walls, do they seem hollow or solid?

_____ Can you hear neighbors downstairs, upstairs, or on either side of you?

Telephone

_____ Are phone jacks already installed?

_____ Are phone jacks in convenient locations?

Television

_____ Is an outside antenna connection provided?

_____ Is a cable TV connection provided?

Storage space

_____ Is there adequate closet space?

_____ Are there enough kitchen and bathroom cabinets?

_____ Is additional storage space provided for tenants?

Outdoor play space

_____ Are outdoor facilities provided? If so, are the facilities well maintained?

5-2 (continued).

as one or two years. They can be either written or oral. The most common rental agreement is a *written lease,* 5-4. It is a legal document spelling out the conditions under which the tenant rents the property. It lists the rights and responsibilities of both the lessor (landlord) and the lessee (tenant).

A written lease should include:
1. Address and specific apartment number.
2. Date signed.
3. Signatures of lessee(s) and lessor.
4. Date of occupation and length of lease.
5. Cost of rent; when and where it should be paid.
6. Statement on lease renewal. Is it automatic? See 5-5.
7. Allotment of specific responsibilities (snow-shoveling, lawn-cutting, repairing, painting, etc.).
8. An entry clause allowing the landlord to enter the apartment for specific reasons with notice or in an emergency.
9. A clause concerning who is responsible for water, electricity, gas, oil, or other bills.
10. A statement concerning the security deposit: the amount, the conditions which must be met before it is returned, and when it will be returned.
11. A clause on assigning and subletting.

Check for any restrictions. (See Assigning and subletting a lease.)
12. A clause that states the final inspection of the premises will be made in the tenant's presence.
13. A statement that the lease can be changed only upon written approval of both the lessor and lessee.
14. If the tenant desires particular provisions to be included in the lease, the tenant should request to have them written down and added to the original lease. Such provisions might include necessary repairs, additional furniture, or the installation of appliances. A specific date should be included by which time all changes are to be fulfilled. Signatures of both parties should be obtained.

Leases vary a great deal. Some of them include restrictions about guests, pets, excessive noise, and the installment of extra locks. Be sure you are aware of any special restrictions in a lease before you sign it.

Suggestions for lessees or renters can often be secured from a renter's association in your community or state. Sometimes the terms and words in a legal agreement are hard to understand. A member of the renter's association will be glad to explain them. *Do not sign a lease until you understand each statement in it.*

QUESTIONS FOR LANDLORDS

Before you sign a lease, be sure to ask the landlord these questions:

- What is the rent per month? How and when is it to be paid?
- Is a security deposit required? If so, how much is it? Under what conditions will it be returned?
- Does the lease say that rent can be increased if real estate taxes or other expenses to the landlord are raised?
- What expenses are there in addition to rent? (These may include utilities, storage space, air conditioning, parking space, master TV antenna connections, use of recreational areas such as a pool or party house, installation of special appliances, and late payment of rent.)
- How are deliveries of packages handled?
- Is loud noise prohibited at certain hours?

Read the lease carefully. Mark any provisions that you do not like. Try to have them removed from the lease. If there are any provisions that you would like to have added (such as a sublet clause) ask the landlord if they can be added.

5-3 Ask a landlord these questions to make sure you understand the conditions of your lease.

APARTMENT LEASE
UNFURNISHED

DATE OF LEASE	TERM OF LEASE		MONTHLY RENT	SECURITY DEPOSIT*
	BEGINNING	ENDING		

IF NONE, WRITE "NONE". Paragraph 2 of this Lease then INAPPLICABLE.

LESSEE

NAME •

APT. NO. •

ADDRESS OF • PREMISES

LESSOR

NAME •

BUSINESS • ADDRESS

In consideration of the mutual covenants and agreements herein stated, Lessor hereby leases to Lessee and Lessee hereby leases from Lessor for a private dwelling the apartment designated above (the "Premises"), together with the appurtenances thereto, for the above Term.

ADDITIONAL COVENANTS AND AGREEMENTS *(if any)*

LEASE COVENANTS AND AGREEMENTS

RENT

SECURITY DEPOSIT

CONDITION OF PREMISES; REDELIVERY TO LESSOR

LIMITATION OF LIABILITY

1. Lessee shall pay Lessor or Lessor's agent as rent for the Premises the sum stated above, monthly in advance, until termination of this lease, at Lessor's address stated above or such other address as Lessor may designate in writing.

2. Lessee has deposited with Lessor the Security Deposit stated above for the performance of all covenants and agreements of Lessee hereunder. Lessor may apply all or any portion thereof in payment of any amounts due Lessor from Lessee, and upon Lessor's demand Lessee shall in such case during the term of the lease promptly deposit with Lessor such additional amounts as may then be required to bring the Security Deposit up to the full amount stated above. Upon termination of the lease and full performance of all matters and payment of all amounts due by Lessee, so much of the Security Deposit as remains unapplied shall be returned to Lessee. This deposit does not bear interest unless and except as required by law. Where all or a portion of the Security Deposit is applied by Lessor as compensation for property damage, Lessor when and as required by law shall provide to Lessee an itemized statement of such damage and of the estimated or actual cost of repairing same.

3. Lessee has examined and knows the condition of Premises and has received the same in good order and repair except as herein otherwise specified, and no representations as to the condition or repair thereof have been made by Lessor or his agent prior to, or at the execution of this lease, that are not herein expressed or endorsed hereon; and upon the termination of this lease in any way, Lessee will immediately yield up Premises to Lessor in as good condition as when the same were entered upon by Lessee, ordinary wear and tear only excepted, and shall then return all keys to Lessor.

4. Except as provided by Illinois statute, Lessor shall not be liable for any damage occasioned by failure to keep Premises in repair, and shall not be liable for any damage done or occasioned by or from plumbing, gas, water, steam or other pipes, or sewerage, or the bursting, leaking or running of any cistern, tank, wash-stand, water-closet or waste-pipe, in, above, upon or about said building or Premises, nor for damage occasioned by water, snow or ice being upon or coming through the roof, sky-light, trap-door or otherwise, nor for damages to Lessee or others claiming through Lessee for any loss or damage of or to property wherever located in or about said building or Premises, nor for any damage arising from acts or neglect of co-tenants or other occupants of the same building, or of any owners or occupants of adjacent or contiguous property.

5-4 Responsibilities of the landlord (lessor) and the tenant (lessee) are clearly stated in the lease.

USE; **SUBLET;** **ASSIGNMENT**	5. Lessee will not allow Premises to be used for any purpose that will increase the rate of insurance thereon, nor for any purpose other than that hereinbefore specified, nor to be occupied in whole or in part by any other persons, and will not sublet the same, nor any part thereof, nor assign this lease, without in each case the written consent of the Lessor first had, and will not permit any transfer, by operation of law, of the interest in Premises acquired through this lease, and will not permit Premises to be used for any unlawful purpose, or purpose that will injure the reputation of the same or of the building of which they are part or disturb the tenants of such building or the neighborhood.
USE AND **REPAIR**	6. Lessee will take good care of the apartment demised and the fixtures therein, and will commit and suffer no waste therein; no changes or alterations of the Premises shall be made, nor partitions erected, nor walls papered, nor locks on doors installed or changed, without the consent in writing of Lessor; Lessee will make all repairs required to the walls, ceilings, paint, plastering, plumbing work, pipes and fixtures belonging to Premises, whenever damage or injury to the same shall have resulted from misuse or neglect; no furniture filled or to be filled wholly or partially with liquids shall be placed in the Premises without the consent in writing of Lessor; the Premises shall not be used as a "boarding" or "lodging" house, nor for a school, nor to give instructions in music, dancing or singing, and none of the rooms shall be offered for lease by placing notices on any door, window or wall of the building, nor by advertising the same directly or indirectly, in any newspaper or otherwise, nor shall any signs be exhibited on or at any windows or exterior portions of the Premises or of the building without the consent in writing of Lessor; there shall be no lounging, sitting upon, or unnecessary tarrying in or upon the front steps, the sidewalk, railing, stairways, halls, landing or other public places of the said building by Lessee, members of the family or other persons connected with the occupancy of Premises; no provisions, milk, ice, marketing, groceries, furniture, packages or merchandise shall be taken into the Premises through the front door of said building except where there is no rear or service entrance; cooking shall be done only in the kitchen and in no event on porches or other exterior appurtenances; Lessee, and those occupying under Lessee, shall not interfere with the heating apparatus, or with the lights, electricity, gas, water or other utilities of said building which are not within the apartment hereby demised, nor with the control of any of the public portions of said building; use of any master television antenna hookup shall be strictly in accordance with regulations of Lessor or Lessor's agent; Lessee and those occupying under Lessee shall comply with and conform to all reasonable rules and regulations that Lessor or Lessor's agent may make for the protection of the building or the general welfare and the comfort of the occupants thereof, and shall also comply with and conform to all applicable laws and governmental rules and regulations affecting the Premises and the use and occupancy thereof.
ACCESS	7. Lessee will allow Lessor free access to the Premises at all reasonable hours for the purpose of examining or exhibiting the same, or to make any needful repairs on the Premises which Lessor may deem fit to make; also Lessee will allow Lessor to have placed upon the Premises, at all times, notice of "For Sale" and "To Rent", and will not interfere with the same.
RIGHT TO **RELET**	8. If Lessee shall abandon or vacate the Premises, the same may be re-let by Lessor for such rent and upon such terms as Lessor may see fit; and if a sufficient sum shall not thus be realized, after paying the expenses of such reletting and collecting, to satisfy the rent hereby reserved, Lessee agrees to satisfy and pay all deficiency.
HOLDING **OVER**	9. If the Lessee retains possession of the Premises or any part thereof after the termination of the term by lapse of time or otherwise, then the Lessor may at Lessor's option within thirty days after the termination of the term serve written notice upon Lessee that such holding over constitutes either (a) renewal of this lease for one year, and from year to year thereafter, at double the rental specified under Section 1 for such period, or (b) creation of a month to month tenancy, upon the terms of this lease except at double the monthly rental specified under Section 1, or (c) creation of a tenancy at sufferance, at a rental of _____ dollars per day for the time Lessee remains in possession. If no such written notice is served then a tenancy at sufferance with rental as stated at (c) shall have been created, and in such case if specific per diem rental shall not have been inserted herein at (c), such per diem rental shall be one-fifteenth of the monthly rental specified under Section 1 of this lease. Lessee shall also pay to Lessor all damages sustained by Lessor resulting from retention of possession by Lessee.
RESTRICTIONS **ON USE**	10. Lessee will not permit anything to be thrown out of the windows, or down the courts or light shafts in said building; nothing shall be hung from the outside of the windows or placed on the outside window sills of any window in the building; no parrot, dog or other animal shall be kept within or about said apartment; the front halls and stairways and the back porches shall not be used for the storage of carriages, furniture or other articles.
WATER AND **HEAT**	11. The provisions of subsection (a) only hereof shall be applicable and shall form a part of this lease unless this lease is made on an unheated basis and that fact is so indicated on the first page of this lease, in which case the provisions of subsection (b) only hereof shall be applicable and form a part of this lease. (a) Lessor will supply hot and cold water to the Premises for the use of Lessee at all faucets and fixtures provided by Lessor therefor. Lessor will also supply heat, by means of the heating system and fixtures provided by Lessor, in reasonable amounts and at reasonable hours, when necessary, from October 1 to April 30, or otherwise as required by applicable municipal ordinance. Lessor shall not be liable or responsible to Lessee for failure to furnish water or heat when such failure shall result from causes beyond Lessor's control, nor during periods when the water and heating systems in the building or any portion thereof are under repair. (b) Lessor will supply cold water to the Premises for the use of Lessee at all faucets and fixtures provided by Lessor therefor. Lessor shall not be liable or responsible to Lessee for failure to furnish water when such failure shall result from causes beyond Lessor's control, nor during periods when the water system in the building or any portion thereof is under repair. All water heating and all heating of the Premises shall be at the sole expense of Lessee. Any equipment provided by Lessee therefor shall comply with applicable municipal ordinances.
STORE ROOM	12. Lessor shall not be liable for any loss or damage of or to any property placed in any store room or any storage place in the building, such store room or storage place being furnished gratuitously and not as part of the obligations of this lease.

5-4 (continued).

FORCIBLE DETAINER	13. If default be made in the payment above reserved or any part thereof, or in any of the covenants or agreements herein contained, to be kept by Lessee, it shall be lawful for Lessor or his legal representatives, at his or their election, to declare said term ended, to re-enter the Premises or any part thereof and to expel, remove or put out the Lessee or any other person or persons occupying the same, using such force as he may deem necessary in so doing, and again to repossess and enjoy the Premises as in his first estate; and in order to enforce a forfeiture of this lease for default in any of its conditions it shall not be necessary to make demand or to serve notice on Lessee and Lessee hereby expressly waives all right to any demand or notice from Lessor of his election to declare this lease at an end on declaring it so to be; but the fact of the non-performance of any of the covenants of this lease shall in itself, at the election of Lessor, without notice or demand constitute a forfeiture of said lease, and at any and all times, after such default, the Lessee shall be deemed guilty of a forcible detainer of the Premises.
CONFESSION OF JUDGMENT	14. Lessee hereby irrevocably constitutes any attorney of any court of record of this state to enter Lessee's appearance in such court, waive process and service thereof, and confess judgment from time to time, for any rent which may be due to Lessor or his assignees by the terms of this lease, with costs and reasonable attorney's fees, and to waive all errors and right of appeal from said judgment and to file a consent in writing that a proper writ of execution may be issued immediately.
RENT AFTER NOTICE OR SUIT	15. It is further agreed, by the parties hereto, that after the service of notice, or the commencement of a suit or after final judgment for possession of the Premises, Lessor may receive and collect any rent due, and the payment of said rent shall not waive or affect said notice, said suit, or said judgment.
PAYMENT OF COSTS	16. Lessee will pay and discharge all reasonable costs, attorney's fees and expenses that shall be made and incurred by Lessor in enforcing the covenants and agreements of this lease.
RIGHTS CUMULATIVE	17. The rights and remedies of Lessor under this lease are cumulative. The exercise or use of any one or more thereof shall not bar Lessor from exercise or use of any other right or remedy provided herein or otherwise provided by law, nor shall exercise nor use of any right or remedy by Lessor waive any other right or remedy.
FIRE AND CASUALTY	18. In case the Premises shall be rendered untenantable during the term of this lease by fire or other casualty, Lessor at his option may terminate the lease or repair the Premises within 60 days thereafter. If Lessor elects to repair, this lease shall remain in effect provided such repairs are completed within said time. If Lessor shall not have repaired the Premises within said time, then at the end of such time the term hereby created shall terminate. If this lease is terminated by reason of fire or casualty as herein specified, rent shall be apportioned and paid to the day of such fire or other casualty.
PLURALS; SUCCESSORS	19. The words "Lessor" and "Lessee" wherever herein occurring and used shall be construed to mean "Lessors" and "Lessees" in case more than one person constitutes either party to this lease; and all the covenants and agreements herein contained shall be binding upon, and inure to, their respective successors, heirs, executors, administrators and assigns and be exercised by his or their attorney or agent.
SEVERABILITY	20. If any clause, phrase, provision or portion of this lease or the application thereof to any person or circumstance shall be invalid or unenforceable under applicable law, such event shall not affect, impair or render invalid or unenforceable the remainder of this lease nor any other clause, phrase, provision or portion hereof, nor shall it affect the application of any clause, phrase, provision or portion hereof to other persons or circumstances.

WITNESS the hands and seals of the parties hereto, as of the Date of Lease stated above.

LESSEE: LESSOR:

_____ (seal)   _____ (seal)

_____ (seal)   _____ (seal)

ASSIGNMENT BY LESSOR

On this _____ , 19_____ , for value received, Lessor hereby transfers, assigns and sets over to

_____ , all right, title and interest in and to the above lease and the rent thereby reserved,

except rent due and payable prior to _____ , 19_____ .

_____ (seal)

_____ (seal)

GUARANTEE

On this _____ , 19_____ , in consideration of Ten Dollars ($10.00) and other good and valuable consideration, the receipt and sufficiency of which is hereby acknowledged, the undersigned Guarantor hereby guarantees the payment of rent and performance by Lessee, Lessee's heirs, executors, administrators, successors or assigns of all covenants and agrements of the above lease.

_____ (seal)

_____ (seal)

5-4 (continued).

```
NOTICE TO TERMINATE TENANCY*

TO: Name _____

    Address _____

    City _____ State _____


You are hereby notified that I (we) shall be terminating my (our) tenancy of —

Apartment _____ at _____ Street _____


State of _____ on _____ day of _____ , 19 _____ .


Dated: _____ , 19 _____ .


                                    Name _____

                                    Address _____

                                    City _____ State _____


* This form may be used by tenant as a 30 day notice to landlord to terminate month-to-month tenancy, or to give
  landlord 30 day notice prior to end of term created by rental agreement. It is also suggested that you retain a fully
  executed, and conformed copy of this notice, and on your copy, make a note of the name on whom same was served,
  and date and time of service.
```

ARIZONA RENTAL RESIDENTS ASSOC.

5-5 In some cases, if you do not give written notice that you will be moving when your lease expires, the landlord will automatically renew the lease. Once it is renewed, you are bound to the lease for another time period.

Assigning and subletting a lease

If you have signed a lease, but you wish to move out early, you have three options:

1. Continue paying the rent until the lease expires.
2. Assign the lease.
3. Sublet the lease.

To *assign* the lease, you transfer the entire unexpired portion of the lease to someone else. After the assignment is transacted, you can no longer be held responsible for the lease.

To *sublet* the lease, you transfer part interest in the property. For instance, you could turn over your apartment to another person for a period of time. Both you and the other person would be held responsible to the landlord for all terms of the lease.

Breach of contract

Landlords and tenants are sometimes unable to fulfill promises. If you cannot keep your agreement, you should try to work it out with your landlord. You should be aware that a lawsuit can be started against you for *breach of contract*. This is a legal term for not living up to an agreement. Lawsuits are costly and time-consuming.

The most common breach of contract on the part of the renter is failure to pay rent. In case of the loss of your job, you may not be able to pay the rent on schedule. You will want to make arrangements with your landlord if possible.

A landlord may also be guilty of breach of contract. If there is failure to provide water or a means of heating your dwelling, there is guilt. Major repairs are usually the responsibility of the owner. If such repairs are needed, you should give written notice to your landlord. If the repairs are not made, you will have grounds for breach of contract.

Eviction

Eviction means forcing a renter to leave the property before the rental agreement expires. Landlords may begin a court action leading to eviction only if a tenant fails to live up to his or her responsibilities.

The eviction process varies from state to state. Nearly all states require a warning before a tenant can be evicted. The warning is a written legal notice.

A PLACE TO BUY

Home ownership has always been the American dream. The fact that it has been on the rise since 1930 attests to this. Home ownership has advantages. It gives a real and emotional sense of freedom. There are also financial advantages.

Home ownership is a hedge against inflation. That means homes tend to increase in value at a higher rate than the rate of inflation. (People who pay rent must make higher payments for the same housing as inflation rises.) Houses have increased in values on an average of five to 25 percent each year for 25 years. See 5-6.

As the value of your home increases and you make payments on the principle of the mortgage, you build up *equity*. Equity is the money value of your house to you beyond what is owed on the house. Renters are not able to build equity in their dwellings. But home owners can gain from equity if they sell or refinance their houses.

Home ownership also gives a tax advantage. The federal government permits deductions for the taxes you pay on your house and the interest paid on the mortgage. Some states allow these deductions, too.

Buying the right home is not a simple task. You will want a home in which you are comfortable and happy. How can you judge what

If your home was built in:	and the original cost was:			
	$40,000	$60,000	$80,000	$100,000
	the approximate cost to rebuild in 1984 is:			
1960	$158,700	$238,100	$317,500	$396,800
1965	148,500	222,800	297,100	371,300
1970	114,100	171,000	228,000	285,000
1975	72,500	108,800	145,000	181,300
1978	57,300	86,000	114,600	143,300
1980	45,200	67,800	90,400	113,100
1983	41,200	61,800	82,400	103,000

REPRINTED WITH PERMISSION OF STATE FARM FIRE AND CASUALTY COMPANY. HOME OFFICE: BLOOMINGTON, IL.

5-6 The dollar value of a house tends to increase over time.

is the right home for you? First of all, it must be one that you can afford.

The price is right

You can estimate your ability to pay housing costs in several ways. Three of them will be discussed here. When you compare housing costs computed by each of these three methods, you will be able to judge which one is best for you. To make figuring easy, suppose that your living unit has a $30,000 annual income.

Method one. Probably the oldest method is to allow 2 1/2 times your annual income for the purchase price of a home. Using this method, you should be able to afford a $75,000 home.

Method two. Divide your annual income by 60 and limit monthly housing costs to that amount. This method, as well as the first one, is based on your gross income. *Gross income* is income before deductions are made. Using this method, you could spend up to $500 monthly for housing. (Both methods two and three can be applied to renters as well as to buyers.)

Method three. Keep monthly housing costs to approximately one-third of your monthly net income. *Net income* or take-home pay is the amount of money you receive after social security, income tax, and other deductions have been taken from your paycheck. Because deductions vary from state to state and from job to job, this method can be used only when you know exactly what your take-home pay is. As a rule, method three allows you to spend more for monthly housing costs than method two.

Methods two and three mention "housing costs." These are more than just the mortgage loan payments which are the regular long-term installment payments. Housing costs include property taxes and home insurance payments. They also include the cost of utilities—water, gas, and electricity. Repairs and maintenance should also have a place in the monthly housing budget.

None of the methods described above is absolute. The amount you can afford depends on many other factors. If you have other debts, you will not be able to afford as much for housing. Other limitations would include having many members in your living unit (which means higher food, clothing, and education bills) or having members who are in poor health. Also, if your new home will require many repairs before you can live in it, you will have to save some of your money for this work.

On the other hand, if you have a large savings account, or if you have a good job and expect your salary to grow, you may be able to spend more for housing.

To build or to buy?

Once you have decided what you can afford to spend for a house, you will want to decide whether to build one or buy one.

Building a house. Buying a lot and building a house involves four projects. They are done in the following order.

1. Choose a region, community, neighborhood, and site. Finding the right location may take weeks or months. (Review Chapter 4.)
2. Find a house plan you like and one that "fits" the site. The plan may be custom-designed by an architect or chosen from stock plans.
3. Select the contractor. The process of choosing the right one starts with a check on the reputation and character of each contractor you are considering. Each one will need to look at your plans and specifications. (Specifications are a list of the type and quality of materials being used for the house.)

When you have narrowed your choices down to a few contractors, you should ask each one for a *bid*. In other words, you should ask what each one would charge to construct the house. The bid should include the cost for both materials and labor.

You also need to know when work can be started and how long the job will take. Ask about the method and time of payments. Builders or contractors generally get paid by installments. These payments begin once the work is in progress.

4. Find enough money to pay for the house. If you don't have enough cash, you will have to borrow it. When you apply for a loan, you must furnish the appraised value of the dwelling. This can be estimated using the information given in your plans. The first loan will be for construction of the house. After the house is finished, you can receive a long-term mortgage loan.

Buying a new house. A popular way to acquire a new house is to buy one that has already been built. This process requires much less time than buying the lot and having a house built on it.

If the house was built by a reputable builder, the workmanship will be guaranteed for a period of time, usually one to two years after completion. Some top builders guarantee their work for up to five years. You should have the guarantee in writing for your protection.

Buying a completed new house has some unique advantages. The most important one may be that you can move in as soon as the deal is *closed,* or when all the legal and financial matters have been settled.

Another advantage of buying a home that has already been built is that you can see the finished product before you buy. If you are not a person who can visualize (imagine) how a house will look by studying the plans, this will be important to you.

Buying a "used" house. Many home buyers choose houses that have been previously occupied. These houses do have some advantages. The same number of rooms and the same amount of space will usually cost less in used houses than in new ones. Sometimes, you can see how the people living there have made use of the space. When you look at rooms that are furnished, you can get a better idea of their sizes. This can help you visualize how your furniture will fit into the same space.

Some of the things that usually do not come with a new house may be included in the sale price of a used one. Draperies and the hardware to hang them are sometimes left by the previous owner. The carpeting may also be left in the dwelling. The lot may have mature trees and shrubs. Fences, walls, and screens may have been added. These are costly in time, money, and effort. See 5-7 and 5-8.

Another bonus is that taxes in established communities are not likely to increase as rapidly as those in new areas.

While you may find that some used houses are bargains, others will not be. Before you sign a contract agreeing to buy, you should check carefully for serious defects such as:

- The lack of a concrete foundation. This would indicate that the house will probably sag or shift. This will weaken the structure.
- Rotten or sagging roofs, walls, or supports. These are signs of poor care. They are major construction defects and are costly to repair.
- Insect damage. The damage may need major repairs. And it may mean defects that are not visible to the inexperienced observer.
- A bad neighborhood. It is not likely to improve.

These conditions can be repaired if you want to spend some time, money, and effort:

- The structure is good, but it needs paint.
- The plumbing is old and may need to be replaced soon.
- The walls, ceilings, or floors show slight damage.
- Windows are broken.
- The roof needs repair.
- There is trash lying around the house.
- The yard looks shabby.

WESTERN WOOD PRODUCTS ASSOC.

WESTERN WOOD PRODUCTS ASSOC.

5-7 A fence adds beauty to a yard. It can enclose the entire property. It may also serve to contain pets and protect children.

5-8 A patio wall screens activities from public view and helps block cold winds.

There is no perfect house. You will want to know the shortcomings before you buy. If you do not find out about them until after you have moved in, it can be a shock. The shock becomes greater when you realize how much it will cost to fix them.

You may want to have the house inspected. An *inspector* will judge the construction and present condition of the house.

You should have the house appraised before you buy it. The *appraiser* will give you an expert estimate of the quality and value of the property.

Shopping for a place to buy

When you know what you can afford and what you want, it is time to go shopping. How do you shop for a house? One way is to contact a reliable real estate firm. Real estate firms

5-9 Advertisements in local newspapers can help you find real estate firms.

are in the business of selling land and buildings. They advertise in the real estate section of newspapers, 5-9. Not all of the properties they have contracted to sell are advertised in the paper. They have additional listings in the real estate agent's catalog. See 5-10.

Real estate agents can give you information about the community and neighborhood you are considering. They can screen out places that would not appeal to you. Sometimes they can help you get financing.

Someone will pay a *real estate agent's commission* (fee) for these services. The commission will range from 5 to 10 percent of the selling price. It is usually paid by the seller. However, the price of the home may be raised to include it.

Sometimes you can buy directly from the owner and save the fees paid to real estate firms. See 5-11. However, you need a great deal of time and knowledge to shop on your own. If you do not have a general knowledge about real estate deals, the mistakes you might make could be much more costly than realtor fees.

When shopping for a house, do not rely totally on real estate agents. Tell people you know that you are looking for a place to buy. They may know about certain houses that you would like. They may even know of other people's plans to sell their houses in the near future.

Drive or walk through neighborhoods you like. You may find a model house on display. Or you may find places with "for sale" signs in the front yards, 5-12.

As you look at places and talk with people, keep a written record about each house. Note the price and the location. Get the name and address of the owner. Write down the features of each house—the number of rooms, the size of the rooms, the size of the lot, the condition of the structure, and any reactions you had when you saw it.

Steps in buying a home

After you have found a home you want and have agreed to pay the price that is asked for it, you must settle many legal and financial matters.

ADDR. 41184 Maple, Urbandale				RMS. 5	BDRM 3	BATH 1	GAR/CRPT 1½ ATT. NO	PRICE $ 51,900
STYLE Bungalow		CONSTR Brick		BSMT Full	SLAB —	CRAWL —	SQ.FT — AGE 25	MLS# 82833
LOT SIZE 30x125			STRM.WD Alum	DRS. Alum	FRPL No	A/C Central	HEAT Gas F.A.	TAXES $ 520.00

ROOM	SIZE	LEV	CPT	DP	FLR	Range Yes Ref Yes
LIV	19.4x12	1	Y	Y	HW	Dhwh No Disp. No
DIN						Elem. Jefferson
FR						Jr. Hi Prairie
KIT	12x12.4	1	Y	Y	HW	High Prairie
BKFT						Paroc Queen of Apost.
BDRM	9.6x12.6	1	Y			Poss 30 DAC
BDRM	10.6x10.9	1				R. Sell Relocating
BDRM	9x10	1				Mtg. Bal N/A
BDRM						Assume N/A
BDRM						Type N/A
BATH	6.9x5	1				Int. N/A
BATH						Held by N/A

REMARKS: 1½ Car garage with patio — Alum awnings — Gas central air — Roof 2 yrs. old — Fenced yard — Plaster walls — Walk to Bus — Basement finished — Humidifier

Owner Tom and Sally Jones	Phone 555-7334
Salesman Ned Talon	Phone 555-1417

| Realtor 3524 | Phone 555-4040 | LIST DATE | TO | PROP TYPE # 1. |

5-10 Real estate agents have many listings besides those you read about in ads. This sample is from a real estate agent's catalog.

Agreement of sale. When a buyer agrees to buy and a seller agrees to sell, both of them sign a contract called an agreement of sale. Sometimes this goes by another name, such as a contract of purchase, a purchase agreement, or a sales agreement.

The agreement of sale should include a detailed description of the real estate and its legal location. The total purchase price, the amount of the down payment, and the delivery date of property should also be included. It should state that the sale will be complete only if the seller has clear title to the property.

Any specific terms and conditions of the sale should be spelled out in writing. For instance, an owner may agree to leave the draperies, carpeting, range, and refrigerator in the house. Each of these items should be listed in the agreement of sale. This way, the buyer knows exactly what he or she is buying. Other specific terms that should be explained are how the cost of property taxes will be divided at the end of the year and who bears the risk of loss to the property as a result of fire, wind, etc., while the deal is being completed.

Earnest money. Earnest money is deposit money the potential buyer gives to the seller to show that he or she is serious about buying the home. If the deal goes through, the earnest money will go toward the payment of the total price. If the deal does not go through, the buyer may forfeit the money. If the buyer wants the earnest money to be refundable, he or she should insert a clause in the agreement of sale.

5-11 Houses can be sold by owners themselves. This saves the expense of the real estate commission.

The clause should list the conditions under which it will be refunded.

Abstract of title. Before a buyer buys a home, he or she must be sure the seller is the legal owner. An *abstract of title* (a copy of all public records concerning the property) is reviewed by a lawyer or title insurance company. The abstract reveals the true legal owner and any debts that are held on the property. This is important since the buyer becomes responsible for any such debts when he or she becomes the owner of the property. Often, the buyer purchases *title insurance* for protection against financial loss caused by errors in the abstract of title.

Survey. A survey is often done to assure the lender of the mortgate that a building is actually sited on the land according to the legal description.

Securing a mortgage. A mortgage is a claim against property that a borrower gives to a lender as security for borrowed money. The lender is usually a bank, savings and loan association, or insurance company. However, the seller may also be the lender.

Interest is a major factor in the cost of a mortgage. A difference of only 1/2 percent in interest rates can have a dramatic effect on the cost of a mortgage.

For years, the "standard" home mortgage was a long-term, fixed-rate loan. This means that the mortgage was written for a long period of time, usually 20 to 30 years. During that time, the interest rate and monthly payments remained the same. The conventional, FHA-insured and the VA-guaranteed are the three common fixed-rate mortgages.

A *conventional mortgage* is a two-party contract between a borrower and a lending firm. This type of mortgage is not insured by the government. Therefore, the lending firm has a greater risk in conventional loans. This type of mortgage usually requires a larger down payment and a shorter repayment period than other mortgages.

FHA-insured loans are three-party contracts. They involve the borrower, the lending firm and the FHA. FHA stands for the Federal Housing Administration. It is part of the U.S.

5-12 A real estate firm's sign advertises that a used house is for sale.

Department of Housing and Urban Development (HUD). FHA does not make loans, but it insures the lender against the borrower's possible default.

Anyone can apply for an FHA-insured loan by going to an approved lending institution. The lending institution submits the application to the local FHA office.

When you compare FHA-insured loans to conventional ones, you will find that FHA-insured loans can often be secured with a smaller down payment. They have interest rates that are set by the government. And they usually allow a longer period of time for repayment.

VA-guaranteed loans generally cost less than the other types. They are three-party loans involving the borrower, the lender, and the Veterans Administration.

106

Veterans of the U.S. Armed Forces may apply for a VA-guaranteed loan at a lending institution. Their applications will be submitted to a VA office. Eligibility requirements are set by Congress.

The VA does not require a down payment, but the lender may. The size of the down payment and the length of the repayment period are decided by the veteran and the lender.

Although conventional, FHA-insured, and VA-guaranteed mortgages are still popular, several alternative mortgages have come into being. These alternatives keep lenders and borrowers from having to finance long-term mortgages at fixed interest rates. Lenders want greater flexibility so they can keep up with changes in interest rates. Borrowers want affordable mortgages. Three alternative mortgage plans are discussed below—the adjustable rate mortgage, the renegotiable rate mortgage, and the graduated payment mortgage. Other creative home financing plans are presented in 5-13.

With an *adjustable rate mortgage,* the interest rate is adjusted up or down periodically according to a national interest rate index. Depending on interest rate changes, monthly payments may increase or decrease. However, some of these mortgages have rate caps. This means the interest rate will never exceed a certain rate regardless of the national interest rate index.

In a *renegotiable rate mortgage,* sometimes called a rollover mortgage, the interest rate and monthly payments are fixed for a stated length of time. Every three to five years, interest rates are reviewed and may be changed according to the current rate of interest. If the new interest rate is below the original one, monthly payments will decrease. If the new interest rate is above the original one, monthly payments will increase.

The *graduated payment mortgage* allows the buyer to pay low monthly payments at first and higher payments in the future. This mortgage is designed to help young home buyers. The concept behind this mortgage is that the buyer's income will increase as the monthly payments increase. The interest rate and the monthly payments (including increases) are all fixed when the mortgage is signed.

Home financing alternatives will vary from state to state and lender to lender. Research all the options to find the method of financing that is best for you.

Foreclosure. Suppose that you have secured a mortgage and have bought a home. It is the largest purchase you have ever made. You have agreed to make monthly payments for many years. What would happen if you lost your job or became ill and could not make your mortgage payments.

Legally, the lending institution could foreclose your mortgage. To recover the money you borrowed, persons from the lending institution could take your mortgaged property away from you and sell it.

You may be able to avoid mortgage payments until your financial situation returns to

CREATIVE HOME FINANCING	
TYPE	**DESCRIPTION**
Balloon Mortgage	Monthly payments based on a fixed interest rate; usually short-term. Payments may cover interest only, with principal due in full at term end.
Shared Appreciation Mortgage	Below-market interest rate and lower monthly payments in exchange for a share of profits on a specified date or when property is sold.
Assumable Mortgage	Buyer takes over seller's original, below-market interest rate mortgage.
Wraparound	Seller keeps original low-rate mortgage. Buyer makes payments to seller who forwards a portion to the lender holding original mortgage. Offers lower interest rate on total transaction.
Land Contract	Seller retains original mortgage. No transfer of title until loan is fully paid. Equal monthly payments based on below-market interest rate with unpaid principal due at loan end.
Rent with Option	Renter pays "option fee" for right to purchase property at specified time and agreed-upon price. Rent may or may not be applied to sales price.

5-13 Many creative home financing plans are now available to meet the varying needs of home buyers or sellers.

normal. To find out if this is possible, make a personal visit to the lending institution. Let people there know you are concerned because you cannot make payments. Ask them for an extension of time. Know your financial situation and be prepared to answer these questions:

- Why did you miss your payments?
- From where are you currently getting income?
- When will you begin payments again?
- When can you pay the payments you missed?

Closing costs. Before the sale of real estate is final, many legal and financial matters must be settled. The fees and charges for settling these matters are called closing costs. They are paid by cash or check and are in addition to the price of the property. Closing costs can amount to several hundred dollars. The buyers should ask for an estimate and should be sure to have enough money to pay for them.

Closing costs may include these items:

- Documentary stamps. (These are a state tax, in the form of stamps, required on mortgages and deeds when a title passes from one owner to another.)
- Recording the deed and mortgage.
- Escrow fees. (These are funds paid to an escrow agent to hold until a specified event occurs. After the event has occured, the funds are released to designated persons. In practice, this often means that when the home owner makes mortgage payments, he or she pays an additional sum which is placed in a trust fund. Other expenses, such as insurance premiums, taxes, and special assessments, are paid with the money in this fund.)
- Attorney's fee.
- Abstract of title and title insurance.
- Appraisal.
- Survey charge.
- Points. (These are a type of interest paid to offset interest lost by the lender. One point equals one percent.)

The seller also has some closing costs. These may include the real estate commission and his or her share of the year's insurance costs, taxes, and other assessments. The seller's closing costs may actually be higher than those of the buyer,

but the price of the house may be raised to cover them.

The title and deed. When the sale is closed, the *title* is passed to the new owner. The title is the rights of ownership and possession of particular property. The legal document by which the title is transferred is called a *deed*. The deed describes the property being sold. It is signed and witnessed according to the laws of the state where the property is located.

Several types of deeds are used to transfer property. A *general warranty deed,* 5-14, transfers the title of the property to the buyer. It guarantees that the title is clear of any claims against it. If any mortgage, tax, or title claims are made against the property, the buyer may hold the seller liable for them. This type of deed offers the greatest legal protection to the buyer.

A *special warranty deed* also transfers the title to the buyer. But it guarantees that during the time the seller held title to the property, the seller has done nothing to the property which has, or which might in the future, impair the buyer's title.

A *quitclaim deed* transfers whatever interest the seller has in the property. By accepting such a deed, the buyer assumes all legal and financial risks for the property.

Insurance. A home is a big financial burden. Home owners insurance or property insurance can help protect the investment of a home owner. Most mortgage holders require the home buyer to protect the home from loss through fire and other hazards. Several types of coverage are available, 5-15.

Refinancing. At some point after you have purchased your home, you may decide to refinance your mortgage. The main reasons people refinance are to lower monthly payments or to save money because interest rates have dropped.

You may need to lower monthly payments because you are having trouble meeting present payments. Using the equity in your house may allow you to get a loan with smaller payments that are spread over a longer period of time. Even though your payments are lower, refinancing for this reason probably won't save you money. Many times, it costs you more in

WARRANTY DEED

Statutory (ILLINOIS)

(Individual to Individual)

(The Above Space For Recorder's Use Only)

THE GRANTOR _____

of the _____ of _____ County of _____ State of _____
for and in consideration of _____ DOLLARS,
in hand paid,

CONVEY ___ and WARRANT ___ to _____

of the _____ of _____ County of _____ State of _____
the following described Real Estate situated in the County of _____ in the
State of Illinois, to wit:

hereby releasing and waiving all rights under and by virtue of the Homestead Exemption Laws of the State
of Illinois.

DATED this _____ day of _____ 19 ___

_____ (Seal)   _____ (Seal)

PLEASE
PRINT OR
TYPE NAME(S)
BELOW   _____ (Seal)   _____ (Seal)
SIGNATURE(S)

State of Illinois, County of _____ ss.   I, the undersigned, a Notary Public in
and for said County, in the State aforesaid, DO HEREBY CERTIFY that _____

personally known to me to be the same person___ whose name___
IMPRESS   subscribed to the foregoing instrument, appeared before me this day in person,
SEAL   and acknowledged that ___ h ___ signed, sealed and delivered the said instrument
HERE   as _____ free and voluntary act, for the uses and purposes therein set
forth, including the release and waiver of the right of homestead.

Given under my hand and official seal, this _____ day of _____ 19 ___

Commission expires _____ 19 ___   _____
NOTARY PUBLIC

AFFIX "RIDERS" OR REVENUE STAMPS HERE

ADDRESS OF PROPERTY:
_____

MAIL TO: { (Name) _____
(Address) _____
(City, State and Zip) _____ }

THE ABOVE ADDRESS IS FOR STATISTICAL PURPOSES
ONLY AND IS NOT A PART OF THIS DEED.

SEND SUBSEQUENT TAX BILLS TO:

(Name) _____

OR   RECORDER'S OFFICE BOX NO. _____

(Address) _____

5-14 A general warranty deed transfers the title of the property to the new owners and guarantees that the title is clear of any claims.

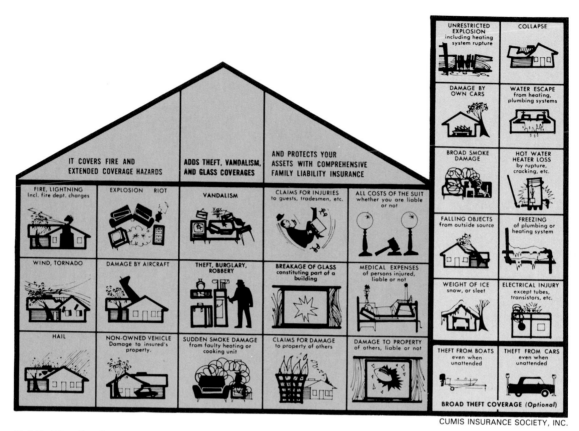

The following text appears within the illustration:

UNRESTRICTED EXPLOSION including heating system rupture

COLLAPSE

DAMAGE BY OWN CARS

WATER ESCAPE from heating, plumbing systems

BROAD SMOKE DAMAGE

HOT WATER HEATER LOSS by rupture, cracking, etc.

FALLING OBJECTS from outside source

FREEZING of plumbing or heating system

WEIGHT OF ICE snow, or sleet

ELECTRICAL INJURY except tubes, transistors, etc.

THEFT FROM BOATS even when unattended

THEFT FROM CARS even when unattended

BROAD THEFT COVERAGE (Optional)

IT COVERS FIRE AND EXTENDED COVERAGE HAZARDS

ADDS THEFT, VANDALISM, AND GLASS COVERAGES

AND PROTECTS YOUR ASSETS WITH COMPREHENSIVE FAMILY LIABILITY INSURANCE

FIRE, LIGHTNING Incl. fire dept. charges

EXPLOSION RIOT

VANDALISM

CLAIMS FOR INJURIES to guests, tradesmen, etc.

ALL COSTS OF THE SUIT whether you are liable or not

WIND, TORNADO

DAMAGE BY AIRCRAFT

THEFT, BURGLARY, ROBBERY

BREAKAGE OF GLASS constituting part of a building

MEDICAL EXPENSES of persons injured, liable or not

HAIL

NON-OWNED VEHICLE Damage to insured's property.

SUDDEN SMOKE DAMAGE from faulty heating or cooking unit

CLAIMS FOR DAMAGE to property of others

DAMAGE TO PROPERTY of others, liable or not

CUMIS INSURANCE SOCIETY, INC.

5-15 The basic coverage offered in this home owners insurance policy is shown in the main part of the house. Additional types of coverage are shown in the "chimney."

the long run. But in an emergency, refinancing can be an alternative to foreclosure.

You can refinance to save money if the going interest rate drops two or more percent below your rate. If you decide to refinance for this reason, shop for the best deal. Start with the institution carrying your present mortgage. By staying with them you may eliminate some costs, such as closing costs. Another institution would need to charge them.

Before making a decision about refinancing, find the answers to these questions:
• Is there a prepayment penalty—will paying the old mortgage early cost more?
• Is a title search, appraisal, survey or inspection required? (These will cost extra money.)
• Are there other costs?
• Who pays the recording and escrow fees?

• How much will your monthly payment change?
• How many months will it take for you to recover the cost of refinancing?
• Do you plan to live in the house long enough to make refinancing worthwhile?

Condominium ownership

In the past few years, *condominium* units have become very popular. The word condominium means common ownership. A condominium is not a type of building. The types of units range from duplexes to high-rise buildings, 5-16.

When you buy a condominium unit, you own your individual unit. In addition, you share ownership of the grounds, stairways, and other common areas. In a way, you are both owner and renter. Although you own your unit, you must answer to the desires of the entire group of owners for certain things. For instance, the appearance of the outside of your unit and your yard may be under the control of the group's management.

The advantage of condominium ownership is that many facilities and services are usually provided. Swimming pools, tennis courts, yard care, and snow removal are a few of the common ones. Condominium owners have the same financial advantages conventional homeowners have. They are investing in real estate and can take advantage of certain income tax deductions. They also build equity in their property.

Condominium units are usually less expensive to build than free-standing, single-family houses. However, because of the "extras" you buy, the purchase price may be high. You will want to approach the purchase of a condominium unit carefully.

Buying a condominium unit is much like buying a house. You will need to choose a condominium you can afford and a location you like. You will have to decide between a new and a used unit. You will probably deal with either a real estate agent or the developer. You will sign an agreement of sale, make a down payment, secure a mortgage, pay closing costs, and sign a deed.

You should take some extra precautions if you plan to buy a condominium unit. Be sure to read the *declaration of ownership* carefully. It contains the conditions and restrictions of the sale, ownership, and use of the property within a particular group of condominium units. Check to see that you can sell your unit at any time and that you are liable for only the mortgage and taxes for *your* unit. Find out who has control of the management of the units. Get a detailed breakdown of your monthly payments. Besides mortgage payments and taxes, you will have to pay utilities, insurance, and a *maintenance fee*. Maintenance fees vary widely and are usually subject to change. They are used for the repair and maintenance of the common areas. Check to see that the fee seems reasonable.

5-16 Some high-rise multifamily dwellings are condominium units.

Cooperative ownership

The word cooperative, like the word condominium, refers to a type of ownership, not a type of dwelling. Cooperative units are dwellings that are owned by a corporation. The members of the corporation are all residents of the dwellings.

In a cooperative, the corporation owns title to the real estate. A resident buys stock in the corporation which entitles him or her to occupy a unit. For larger units, more stock is purchased. Instead of owning a particular unit, the resident owns an undivided interest in the entire building. However, he or she has an absolute right to occupy the unit for as long as the stock is owned.

As in any other corporation, the stockholders (in this case, the residents) elect a board of directors who operate the corporation for the benefit of all stockholders.

Buying a cooperative unit is different than buying a house. The first step—finding a unit—may be the most difficult one. Although the concept is growing in popularity, relatively few cooperative dwellings exist today.

The legal and financial aspects of cooperative housing are unique. When a corporation buys an entire building and a lot to begin a cooperative housing project, it secures a mortgage on the property. When you move into a cooperative building, you cannot get a mortgage since you are buying stock, not real estate. In many cases, you will need to pay the full price of the stock in cash. You will not pay closing costs since you will deal directly with the corporation.

The tax advantages are different than those for other types of home ownership. Most home owners can deduct the amount of money they pay for real estate taxes and for interest on their mortgages from their income tax. In a cooperative situation, the corporation owns the building; the corporation pays real estate taxes; and the corporation makes the mortgage payments. You, as a stockholder, can deduct a certain portion of what the corporation pays in real estate taxes and mortgage interest from your income tax.

Once you are in a cooperative dwelling, you will pay a monthly fee. This money is used for maintenance and taxes. It is also used to make the corporation's mortgage payments on the property. If some residents failed to pay this for any length of time, the corporation might be unable to make mortgage payments and would face the possibility of foreclosure. Because of this risk, check the financial stability of the corporation before you buy any stock.

Cooperative ownership has some advantages. Residents are likely to become a closeknit group. It is a "friendly" type of housing, and residents have no maintenance worries.

to Know

asbtract of title . . . adjustable rate mortgage . . . agreement of sale . . . appraiser . . . assign . . . bid . . . breach of contract . . . carrying charges . . . closing costs . . . condominium . . . conventional mortgage . . . cooperative . . . declaration of ownership . . . deed . . . down payment . . . eviction . . . equity . . . FHA-insured loan . . . finance charge . . . foreclosure . . . general warranty deed . . . graduated payment mortgage . . . gross income . . . inspector . . . installment buying . . . interest . . . lease . . . lessee . . . lessor . . . maintenance fees . . . mortgage . . . net income . . . quitclaim deed . . . refinancing . . . renegotiable rate mortgage . . . security deposit . . . special warranty deed . . . sublet . . . survey . . . title . . . VA-guaranteed loan

to Review

Write your answers on a separate sheet of paper.

1. Acquisition involves _____ and _____.

2. Give examples of the following as related to housing:
   a. Cost in effort.
   b. Cost of financing.
   c. Initial acquisition.
   d. Maintenance cost.
   e. Replacement cost.

3. List four advantages of renting a home.

4. Define the term written lease and name eight things it should include.

5. True or False. When you sublet your apartment, you are no longer responsible for it.

6. If a tenant fails to pay rent, he or she could be sued for _____.

7. What are the three ways of figuring what you can afford to spend on housing?

8. As the new owner of a house on which you have a mortgage, you want to figure your monthly housing costs. Which of the following items would you include?
   a. Income tax.
   b. Mortgage loan payments.
   c. Home insurance payments.
   d. The heating bill.
   e. Car payments.
   f. Real estate taxes.
   g. Maintenance allowance.

9. An appraiser will tell you:
   a. What houses are available for sale.
   b. If your mortgage is accepted or rejected.
   c. What a particular house is worth.

10. Define an agreement of sale and name five things it should include.

11. Why should the buyer of a home purchase title insurance?

12. Name three types of housing loans. Give one characteristic of each type.

13. List two reasons for refinancing.

14. How are the terms title and deed related?

15. When you buy a condominium unit, you buy:

    a. Stock in a corporation.

    b. Your individual unit.

    c. Your individual unit and an undivided interest in all common areas.

to Do

1. Study the cost of buying a color television with cash, by check, with a credit card, or on an installment buying plan from the store. Which process costs the most in terms of money?

2. Visit an apartment building and ask the landlord for a copy of the lease used for those apartments. Does it include all that it should? Does it include any additional restrictions?

3. Have a class debate: Renting vs. Buying.

4. Working in small groups, consider various incomes of living units. Figure out how much each one can afford to spend on housing.

5. Look through the classified ads in your local newspaper. Working with the figures obtained in the previous exercise (4), choose a home for each of those living units. Assume that some living units will rent and some will buy.

6. Discuss the advantages and disadvantages of buying each of the following:

    a. A used house.

    b. A new house that is already built.

    c. A new house that will be custom-built.

7. Find a classified ad offering a house for sale. Investigate the monthly cost of buying it with three different types of loans.

8. Ask the manager of some condominium units for a copy of the declaration of ownership for the units. Examine it closely. Discuss the advantages and disadvantages of condominium ownership.

part 3

The inside story

Holly and Ken Sukel use their home often for entertaining. Since Ken is an account executive for an ad firm, he and his wife often host small dinner parties and larger gatherings.

Decorating this living room was a challenge for the Sukels. They needed a large space to accommodate many guests. But they needed smaller areas within the room for a few people to sit and talk. And they wanted the room to have an elegant appearance without needing too much care.

The Sukels arranged the room with one large conversation area and a smaller one to the side. Plenty of space is left for people to walk by the seating without interrupting conversations. Large window areas make the room bright and cheery in the day, and lamps are used to give softer light in the evening.

The Sukels chose a simple color scheme based on shades of blue. Holly uses seasonal fresh flowers to add an accent. White was chosen for backgrounds to make the room seem spacious. The Sukels chose a no-wax floor for the room to make cleaning easier. The furniture has durable upholstery that is treated for stain resistance.

How can you fill the space within your home so that it is pleasing and functional for you? What kinds of knowledge will you need as you plan parts of the home other than the living room, such as the kitchen or bedrooms?

By using space to its best advantage, you can make your home seem larger.

The question of space

After studying this chapter, you will be able to:
- Evaluate the use of space in a home.
- Interpret a floor plan.
- Organize space by grouping rooms according to function.
- Plan safe and convenient traffic patterns.
- Make the most of storage space.
- Extend the space within a home.

Frank Lloyd Wright once said, "The reality of the building is the space within."

Designers of homes know this. They are as concerned about the *interior* (inside) as they are about the *exterior* (outside) of their buildings.

In all parts of the home, the way space is divided is of great importance. It is one of the most basic concerns in housing.

Interior space is divided into areas according to its intended use. To give satisfaction to the people living there, the space divisions must satisfy their needs and taste. The life-style of the people in the living unit will determine how the space is used. Only the members of the living unit will know exactly what suits them. When planning how to use the space in their home, they should consider their activities, habits, and life situations.

6-1 Real estate ads have more appeal when they give information about kinds of living space. Ads like these appear in newspapers every day.

The most common method of arranging space is to divide it into rooms. Buyers or renters almost always want to know the number of rooms in a home. This is usually their first concern. Realtors know the importance of describing the different rooms. They often indicate the number and uses of the rooms in their advertisements. See 6-1.

WHAT A FLOOR PLAN SHOWS

The easiest way to see what a home looks like is to walk through it. But if that is not possible, the next best thing is to look at a drawing of it.

A *floor plan,* 6-2, is a drawing of all the rooms on one floor of a building. Most floor plans that are shown to prospective home buyers are simple drawings. Their main purpose is to show the location of rooms, doors, windows, storage areas, and hallways. In 6-3, you can see the symbols used in floor plans. By studying 6-4, you will learn how to interpret a floor plan.

The builder of a home uses a *blueprint* as a guide, 6-5. This is a photographic reproduction

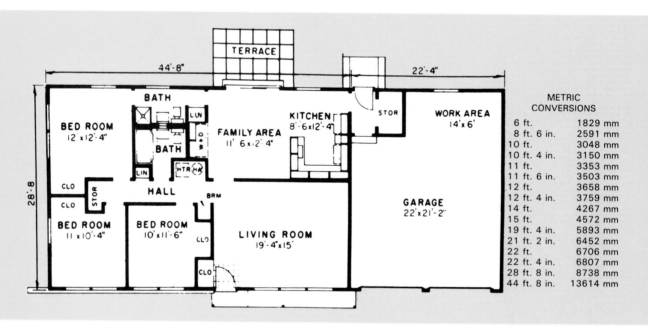

METRIC CONVERSIONS	
6 ft.	1829 mm
8 ft. 6 in.	2591 mm
10 ft.	3048 mm
10 ft. 4 in.	3150 mm
11 ft.	3353 mm
11 ft. 6 in.	3503 mm
12 ft.	3658 mm
12 ft. 4 in.	3759 mm
14 ft.	4267 mm
15 ft.	4572 mm
19 ft. 4 in.	5893 mm
21 ft. 2 in.	6452 mm
22 ft.	6706 mm
22 ft. 4 in.	6807 mm
28 ft. 8 in.	8738 mm
44 ft. 8 in.	13614 mm

6-2 This simple floor plan shows the location of each room. Few details are included.

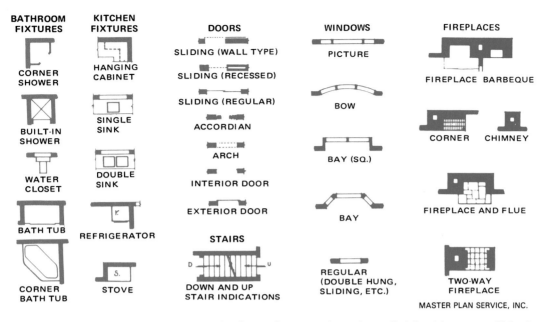

BATHROOM FIXTURES
CORNER SHOWER
BUILT-IN SHOWER
WATER CLOSET
BATH TUB
CORNER BATH TUB

KITCHEN FIXTURES
HANGING CABINET
SINGLE SINK
DOUBLE SINK
REFRIGERATOR
STOVE

DOORS
SLIDING (WALL TYPE)
SLIDING (RECESSED)
SLIDING (REGULAR)
ACCORDIAN
ARCH
INTERIOR DOOR
EXTERIOR DOOR

STAIRS
DOWN AND UP
STAIR INDICATIONS

WINDOWS
PICTURE
BOW
BAY (SQ.)
BAY
REGULAR
(DOUBLE HUNG,
SLIDING, ETC.)

FIREPLACES
FIREPLACE   BARBEQUE
CORNER   CHIMNEY
FIREPLACE AND FLUE
TWO-WAY FIREPLACE

MASTER PLAN SERVICE, INC.

6-3 These are some symbols used in floor plans to show how finished homes will look.

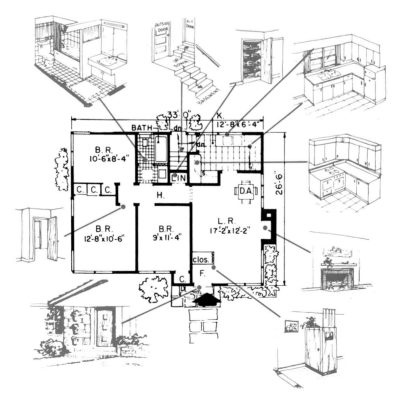

6-4 "Reading" a floor plan is a matter of picturing what the symbols mean.

of the original floor plan. A blueprint is an accurately *scaled drawing*. That means that it is less than full size, but everything in it is reduced proportionately. For instance, every 1/4 in. may represent 1 ft. (20 mm may represent 1 m).

Blueprints are more detailed than most floor plans. They include the following:
- Size and location of rooms.
- Form and location of doors and windows.
- Thicknesses of walls and partitions.
- Stairways.
- Kitchen cabinets, major appliances, and fixtures.
- Bath fixtures.
- Built-in storage such as closets, counters, and shelves.
- Electrical outlets and switches.
- Any additional features such as a terrace, patio, garage, or carport.

If neither a blueprint nor a floor plan is available, you can draw a simple floor plan. You will need to take many measurements and convert them to scaled dimensions. Using graph paper will make your task easier. See 6-6 and 6-7. The most common scale is 1/4 in. equals 1 ft. (For metric measurements, use the scale 20 mm equals 1 m.)

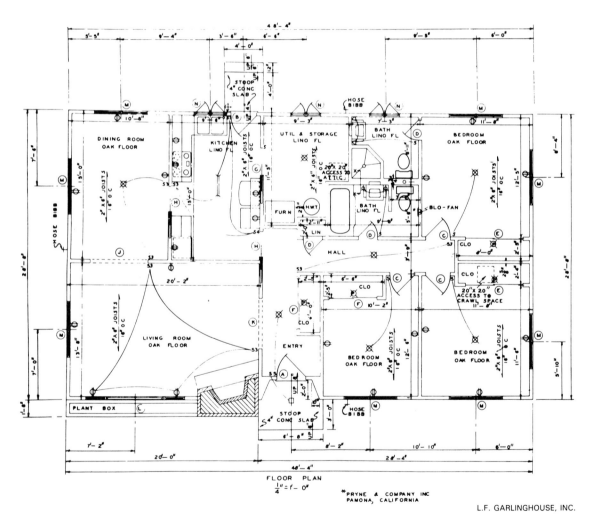

FLOOR PLAN
$\frac{1}{4}'' = 1'-0''$

*PRYNE & COMPANY INC
PAMONA, CALIFORNIA

L.F. GARLINGHOUSE, INC.

6-5 Blueprints have details and dimensions not found in simplified floor plans. From them, builders can get the exact information they need.

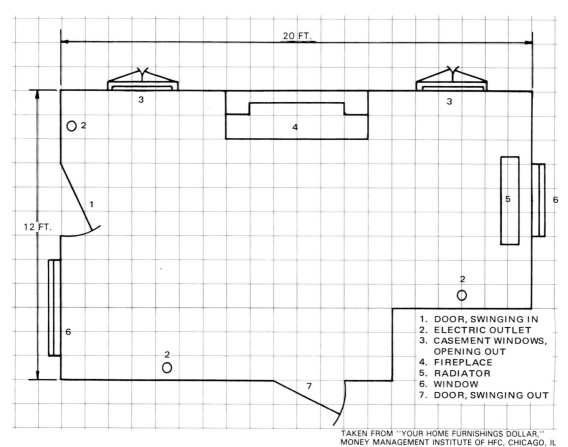

20 FT.

12 FT.

1. DOOR, SWINGING IN
2. ELECTRIC OUTLET
3. CASEMENT WINDOWS,
   OPENING OUT
4. FIREPLACE
5. RADIATOR
6. WINDOW
7. DOOR, SWINGING OUT

6-6 Graph paper simplifies the use of a scale. Here, 1/4 in. represents 1 ft. Note the use of symbols.

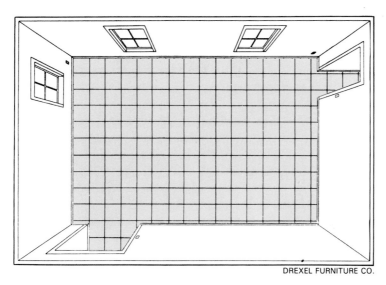

DREXEL FURNITURE CO.

6-7 Miniature rooms can be made by adding walls to a floor of graph paper. Doors and windows are sketched on the walls which are then folded up and fastened at the corners.

GROUPING BY FUNCTION

As you look at floor plans, you will notice that certain rooms of a home are usually located next to each other. This is because those rooms are used for similar purposes or functions. Grouping rooms together by function is an efficient way to organize space.

Most of the space within a home will fall into one of these three groups:

1. The *quiet area,* including bedrooms and bathrooms.
2. The *work area,* including the kitchen, laundry area, utility room, and garage.
3. The *social area,* including the dining room, living room, family room, and entrances.

The quiet area

The quiet area in most homes consists of bedrooms and bathrooms, 6-8. These rooms provide space for sleeping, resting, grooming, and dressing.

Sleep and rest are primary needs. They are among the first needs to be considered when planning the use of space. The quiet area of a home offers the best setting for rest and relaxation, 6-9. It is usually a comfortable and private place.

SUN LAKES DEVELOPMENT CO.

6-9 Bedrooms in the quiet area of a home offer space for relaxation.

In many homes, each person has a separate room. In other homes, this is not possible or even desirable. The important goal is to insure comfort for each person. In the quiet area, the spatial needs of individuals should be placed ahead of those of the group.

Space for dressing and grooming is another part of the quiet area. These activities require

6-8 The shaded portion represents the quiet area.

ARMSTRONG WORLD INDUSTRIES, INC.

6-10 Space for storage and use of grooming items, as well as space for exercise, is plentiful in this bathroom.

privacy and storage space for clothes and grooming supplies. Both bedrooms and bathrooms help fulfill these spatial needs. See 6-10 and 6-11.

Many rooms with sleeping or dressing space also provide space for other activities. These rooms are called *multipurpose rooms.* They are used during waking hours as well as during sleeping time. Rooms may provide space for resting, sleeping, dressing, reading, and studying. Other "living-bedrooms" may include space for watching television, listening to music, and working on hobbies.

The work area

Some rooms in a home are set aside as places to do work. This group of rooms is called the work area, 6-12. It includes all parts of the home that are needed to maintain and service the other areas. Sometimes it overlaps with the service zone that is outside the home. (See Chapter 4.)

The space devoted to a work area varies from home to home. The kitchen, laundry area, utility room, and garage are generally part of the work area. A workshop, sewing center, or place for hobbies may also be included.

ARMSTRONG WORLD INDUSTRIES, INC.

6-11 Storage near the bathroom provides well-organized space for dressing.

The question of space   123

6-12 The shaded portion represents the work area.

For most living units, the kitchen is used more often than any other room in the work area, 6-13. Centers of activity in a kitchen are the places where food is stored (refrigerator), where food is prepared (range), and where cleaning is done (sink). The imaginary lines that connect these three places form a *work triangle*. Anyone preparing a meal in a kitchen will walk along the lines of that triangle several times before the meal is ready. In a well-designed kitchen, the total length of all sides of the work triangle will not exceed 22 ft. (6700 mm). Six basic kitchen designs are shown in 6-14. Notice that the distance around the work triangle in each design is less than 22 ft. (6700 mm).

The social area

Members of a living unit spend much of their time in the social area of their home. The social area, 6-15, provides space for daily living, entertaining, and recreation. It includes living rooms, family rooms, dining rooms, and entrances.

Living rooms, as shown in 6-16, provide space for family activities as well as for entertaining guests. If a dwelling has both a living room and a family room, the family room often has a more casual atmosphere. It is used for recreation and relaxation, 6-17.

Every home needs a place where people can eat. Some have a separate room, as in 6-18, that is used only for dining. It can be used for family meals and for entertaining guests. If it is not used regularly, the cost of having a separate dining room may be too great. In that case, the living unit may prefer to eat in a multipurpose room. Dining space can be shared with space for other activities. The only limitation is that

ARMSTRONG WORLD INDUSTRIES, INC.

6-13 The kitchen is usually the busiest room of the work area.

6-14 Work triangles are shown in six different kitchen layouts. Shorter work triangles save more time and energy.

6-15 The shaded portion represents the social area.

ARMSTRONG WORLD INDUSTRIES, INC.

6-16 A living room is part of the social area of the home.

the eating area should be located near the place the food is prepared. See 6-19.

Dining space can double as a center for sewing or hobbies. It can be part of a family room or living room, as shown in 6-20. It can also be part of the kitchen. A lowered kitchen counter provides enough space for quick meals and snacks. Large kitchens sometimes have room for a separate table.

If you enjoy being outdoors, you may want to use outside space for eating and relaxation. See 6-21.

An *entry* or *entrance* is a place where guests are identified and greeted. It is here that outer wear is often removed and placed in nearby storage. If a dwelling has more than one entrance, each may have a slightly different purpose. Yet each entrance is probably part of the social area.

All entries help direct the movement of people throughout a home. The front entrance in 6-22 is typical. It leads into either the family room or living room.

ARMSTRONG WORLD INDUSTRIES, INC.

6-17 Family rooms are places for relaxing activities such as working on jigsaw puzzles.

Ways of separating areas and rooms

You have just read about the three main areas within a dwelling: quiet, work, and social. These areas can be separated in several ways. A certain area can be located in one end of the home or on a different level. For instance, the quiet area may be upstairs while the social and work areas are on the ground floor.

Hallways are another way of separating areas in a dwelling. They range from 36 in. (914 mm) to 42 in. (1066 mm) wide. A 36 in. (914 mm) width is for very short halls. A 40 in. (1016 mm) width is the most common one. A 42 in. (1066 mm) width is for very long halls or for halls where wheelchairs are used regularly.

Besides physically separating rooms and areas, hall space also acts as a buffer zone for noises. A hallway between the quiet area and social area makes it possible for some people to rest or sleep while others are entertaining guests, dining, or watching television. Hallways near work areas help reduce the amount of noise from appliances and tools that reaches the quiet and social areas.

Individual rooms are usually separated by walls. However, some dwellings have large

JOHN RUNNING

6-19 In this home, both the snack bar and the separate dining room are near the food preparation area.

open areas. Within these open areas, some divisions of space can be seen. Alcoves (small recessed sections of a room) and balconies are sometimes used. Screens, free-standing storage units, and careful arrangements of furniture are also used to separate space according to function. Look again at 6-20. There is no wall between the dining and living areas of the room, but you can see that the room is designed for two different activities.

THOMASVILLE FURNITURE INDUSTRIES

6-18 A separate dining room is often found in large homes.

SUN LAKES DEVELOPMENT CO.

6-20 This multipurpose room serves as a dining-living area.

6-21 Outside eating areas appeal to those who enjoy the outdoors.

6-22 The main entrance provides space for greeting visitors. It also begins the movement of traffic through a home.

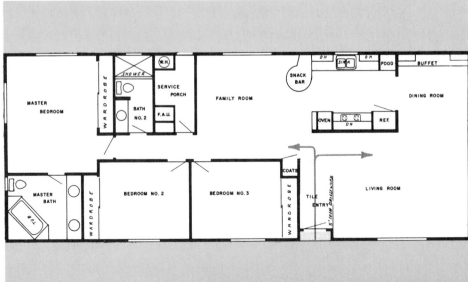

An advantage of open areas is that people in the home can be involved with more than one activity. For instance, the kitchen may be open to the family room or living room. This allows the persons preparing meals or washing dishes to take part in other activities.

GROUPING FOR CONSERVATION

When you look at a floor plan, you can see how rooms are located in relation to quiet,

work, and social areas. You can also see that structural considerations are made when floor plans are designed.

In a well-planned house, all of the plumbing lines are located near each other. This helps to conserve money, water, and fuel. Fewer plumbing materials are needed, and hot water is not wasted to heat long pipes. Look at 6-23. Notice that the kitchen, bathrooms, and laundry room are all located close to one another.

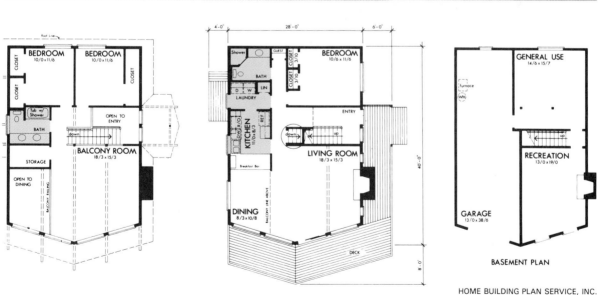

HOME BUILDING PLAN SERVICE, INC.

6-23 This house has well-planned plumbing. The upstairs bath is directly above the kitchen. The kitchen is close to the laundry room and the downstairs bath.

You do not always have the chance to make decisions about the structure of a dwelling. Decisions about plumbing lines and other structural details have been made by someone else when you rent a dwelling or when you buy a house that is already built. In that case, you must decide if you would be satisfied living there or if you should look for another place to live.

TRAFFIC PATTERNS

Have you ever been in a traffic jam as you were leaving a football game or some other school event? Often the local police make a plan to relieve the congestion.

Planning will also help prevent or reduce congestion in the traffic throughout a dwelling. When space is organized well, people can move easily within a room, from room to room, or to the outside. The paths they follow are called *traffic patterns.*

Traffic patterns need enough space for persons to move about freely. Yet using more space than is needed is wasteful. As a rule, traffic patterns that are about 40 in. (1016 mm) wide are adequate.

People should be able to move throughout a home without disturbing other activities.

Major traffic patterns should avoid the quiet area of a home so it can remain quiet. Work areas are unsafe if people frequently walk through them. To avoid accidents, traffic patterns should lead to work areas, but should not go through them. Conversation, study, and television viewing are interrupted when traffic patterns are located through social areas.

The easiest way to evaluate traffic patterns is to study floor plans. Look at 6-24, and 6-25. Do they follow these guidelines for safe and convenient traffic patterns?

- Traffic patterns should be convenient and direct.
- Have adequate space, but do not waste it.
- Provide easy access from the entrances to other parts of the dwelling.
- Separate traffic patterns to the work area from traffic patterns to the quiet and social areas.
- Avoid cutting through the middle of rooms.
- Should not interfere with a good furniture arrangement, nor interrupt activities within a room.
- Should not interfere with privacy in areas of the home where privacy is expected.
- Do not cut through kitchen work area or any other hazardous work area.

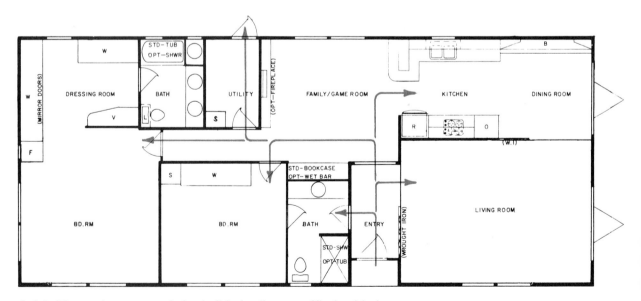

6-24 The main entry and the hall help direct traffic in this house.

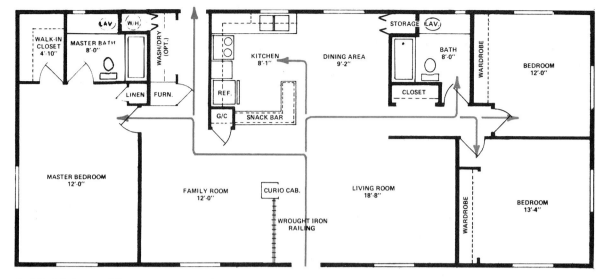

6-25 Major traffic patterns go through the social area. Entertaining might be difficult in such a house.

- The kitchen should have easy access to all areas of the home.
- If a home has a service entrance, direct access to a clean-up area is desirable.
- Have access from service entrance to quiet area without going through social area.
- Provide direct access from utility area to outside service zone.

Space for doors

Outside doors and those between rooms help determine the flow of traffic. Other doors within a room may conceal storage. It is important that the space around them remain free. Blocked doors will stop traffic and cut off access to items that are stored.

Not only should the space immediately in front of doors be free, but there must be space for them to swing and stand open. In addition, people need room to go through the doors or to get what they need from storage areas. In 6-26 and 6-27, you can gather an idea of the amount of space that is needed.

SURVEY THE STORAGE SPACE

Well-planned homes have plenty of storage space that is scattered throughout all areas of the home: quiet, work, and social.

You may be renting a place to live, or you may be buying a home that is already built. In either case, you will need to survey the available storage space. Is there enough space to store all your things? Is the storage located in convenient places? If you plan to use some of the

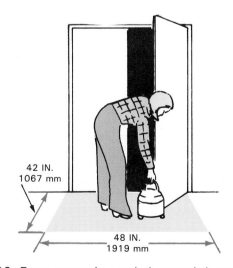

42 IN.
1067 mm

48 IN.
1919 mm

6-26 Extra space is needed around doors to storage areas for swinging the door and removing the stored items.

rooms for more than one activity, do they have the kind of storage space you need? For instance, suppose you plan to use the dining room as both a study area and a place to eat. You would need space to store paper, pens, and reference books as well as dishes and table linens.

If you spend a lot of time on hobbies, you may want extra space to use as a hobby center. A gardener would enjoy having a work area like the one shown in 6-28. How much space would you need to store your hobby supplies?

A floor plan, 6-29, helps you evaluate the storage space of a home. They show the location of *built-in storage* units. (However, they do not show the number of shelves and drawers.) Floor plans also show how much floor space is available for additional storage such as shelves and bookcases.

Planning for storage

If you are making plans to build a house or to have one built for you, you will want to plan for storage. First, you must determine the storage needs of each member of your living unit. You will also want to plan *common-use storage*. This is storage used by all who live in a home. Common-use storage includes the

6-28 An attractive and well-organized hobby center makes working with plants even more fun.

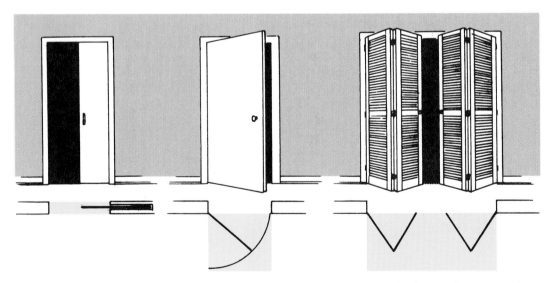

6-27 The colored areas show the amount of space that must be kept clear around each type of door.

6-29 This floor plan shows the location of a pantry, kitchen cabinets, and closets. These are types of built-in storage.

storage near the entrance where outdoor clothing is kept. It also includes storage for food, tools, and other items that are shared.

Storage furniture can add a great deal to the available storage space in a dwelling. Desks, chests, and dressers are popular pieces. Another type of storage furniture is shown in 6-30. If you have such furniture, you can get by with less built-in storage.

If you had a choice of putting built-in storage in a home or using storage furniture, which would you choose? Both types of storage have

ARMSTRONG WORLD INDUSTRIES, INC.

6-30 This bed unit is a type of storage furniture. It offers a place to sleep as well as storage.

some advantages. If you are typical, you will move at least 14 times during your lifetime. You can not take built-in storage, 6-31, with you, so you would not have the cost of moving it. Also, your home would increase in value if you included built-in storage. On the other hand, storage furniture can be handy and attractive. If you like pieces of storage furniture, you can take them with you to any home.

EXTENDING SPACE

Many people want larger homes than they have. Even if they cannot add rooms to their homes, they can make their homes look and feel more spacious. This may be due to an extension to the outside such as a patio. In other cases, it may be because of the illusion of a larger size. (An illusion is something that is misleading.)

NORTHERN HOMES, INC.

6-32 Large amounts of glass help combine indoor and outdoor living space.

Carpeted outdoor areas and screened porches are extensions of living space. Terraces, patios, decks, and balconies are also used to extend inside space to the outdoors. They are commonly used as extensions of the social area, but they are sometimes added to the quiet area or work area. In fact, some homes completely surround a terrace or court.

Patios, decks, and other extensions are often connected to the inside space by the use of glass, 6-32. Large windows and glass doors seem to bring the outdoors inside. Indoor gardens give the same effect although the technique is the reverse of extending rooms to the outside.

Illusion of size

The illusion of size can be created by extension and repetition. Look at the two houses in 6-33. In each, certain features give the illusion that the houses are larger than they really are.

In the upper house, an attached garage and an enclosed patio make the house appear longer. The wide overhang of the roof at the sides of the house also adds to the visual length.

The other house has an attached garage too. In addition, it has a porch which is an extension of the main section of the house. The

ARMSTRONG WORLD INDUSTRIES, INC.

6-31 Built-in storage is a permanent part of a home. It can not be sold, replaced, or moved like pieces of furniture.

6-33 Roof extensions and repetition of lines are included in the designs of these houses to give them the illusion of greater size.

brickwork along the front of the house carries your eyes from one end of the house to the other, giving an illusion of length. The repetition of vertical lines in the siding, chimney, windows, and porch pillars also creates eye movement and a feeling of vastness.

Inside space. Illusions of size and space are used inside homes as well as outside. For instance, mirrors can make a room look larger, 6-34. This is because the space is "repeated" in the reflection. Mirrored tiles or strips can be used on all or part of a wall. If an entire wall

ARMSTRONG WORLD INDUSTRIES, INC.

6-34 A mirror helps make this room seem larger.

is covered with mirrors, the room will look twice its actual size.

Repeating color or texture inside a room also helps make the space seem larger. Using the same floor covering helps the room appear more unified and larger. Using floor coverings that are close in color to the walls makes the room appear even more spacious.

The types of colors in a room also affects the feeling of spaciousness. Light, neutral colors make a room appear larger. Dark colors "move" objects closer together, making a room seem smaller. To make a space look larger, choose light colors for walls and floors. Light colored furnishings also help to make rooms appear larger.

Placement of walls affects how spacious a dwelling seems. The same amount of space seems larger if no walls divide it. Many smaller houses and apartments have open floor plans. In these dwellings, different rooms such as the dining room and living room are not divided by walls. This arrangement helps make rooms seem spacious even if they are small.

6-36 Mirrors, adequate lighting, and light colors are used together to make this room seem more spacious.

Space through lighting

Another method of making a dwelling seem more spacious is to use lighting. Light makes rooms seem larger. Both sunlight and artificial light can be used. Good artificial light is especially important in rooms without windows such as some dens, kitchens, bathrooms, and basements.

If a dwelling has an extension to the outdoors, 6-35, artificial lighting can be used to extend the inside space in hours of darkness.

Light and color are closely related. Without light, you cannot see any colors. With dim lights, even a large, light-colored room may seem small. With a great deal of light, a small and dark room may seem larger. To make a small area look as large as possible, combine good lighting with light colors and mirrors, 6-36.

to Know

blueprint . . . built-in storage . . . common-use storage . . . entry . . . extending space . . . floor plan . . . illusions of size and space . . . multipurpose room . . . open areas . . . quiet area . . . scaled drawing . . . social area . . . storage furniture . . . traffic patterns . . . work area . . . work triangle

6-35 By using outdoor lights, living space can be extended to the outdoors even at night.

to Review

Write your answers on a separate sheet of paper.

1. A _____ _____ shows the location of all the rooms in a home.

2. Which of the following would NOT be found in a blueprint?
    a. Dimensions for the garage.
    b. Location of built-in storage.
    c. Location of furniture in a room.
    d. Room sizes and locations.

3. The space in a home can be divided into three areas according to function. Name the three areas.

4. What is the maximum distance around a work triangle in a well-designed kitchen?

5. Explain two functions of hallways.

6. List five guidelines for good traffic patterns.

7. Name one advantage of built-in storage and one advantage of storage furniture.

8. Give two examples of how living space can be extended.

9. Describe three methods of creating the illusion of spaciousness inside a dwelling.

to Do

1. Look at the floor plan shown on page 129. Evaluate it as a home for your living unit by answering the following questions:
    a. Would all members of your living unit have enough space to satisfy their needs?
    b. Are the rooms grouped according to function?
    c. Are quiet areas away from public view and traffic?
    d. Which rooms could be used for more than one purpose?
    e. Are eating areas close to the kitchen?
    f. Is space provided for entertaining as well as for daily living?
    g. Are the entrances located in convenient places?
    h. Are the rooms grouped well for plumbing?
    i. Are the traffic patterns safe and convenient?
    j. Is storage adequate and convenient?
    k. How is living space extended to the outside?

2. Draw a room to scale, using graph paper.

3. Using a number of floor plans, do each of the following:
    a. Shade the quiet area, social area, and work area with different colors. Tell whether or not the division is as it should be. Justify your answer.
    b. Show the traffic patterns. Check them with the guidelines listed in this chapter. Tell if they are safe and convenient.
    c. Tell which storage is for individual use and which is for common use.
    d. If living space has been extended, indicate how it has been done.

4. Find or draw pictures to show one or more of the following:
    a. Multipurpose rooms.
    b. Ways to extend inside living space.
    c. Ways to create the illusion of spaciousness.
    d. Ideas for increasing storage space.

Color and design are used within a home to make living spaces more attractive and comfortable.

Color and design

After studying this chapter, you will be able to:

- Plan pleasing color harmonies.
- Describe the elements of design.
- Give an example of the use of each design principle.
- Explain the goals of design.
- Describe several treatments for the backgrounds of a home.

Design is the result of artistic effort, and color is probably its most important element. Design is the arrangement of color, line, form, and texture in a pleasing manner. The guidelines that determine how these elements are arranged are called design principles. These are proportion, balance, emphasis, and rhythm. The final goals of the arrangement are beauty, appropriateness, and unity with variation.

You can plan or change a design by using color, line, form, and texture in different ways. Color is probably the most important factor in design. A decision about color is usually the first one made when decorating a room. Color sets the mood for a room and leaves a lasting impression with most visitors.

COLOR

Color is the first thing others notice about your housing. If you understand color, you can use it to make your microenvironment exciting, attractive, and satisfying.

Each color has certain psychological effects on people. For instance, *red* is associated with danger and power. It is bold, aggressive, exciting, and warm. See 7-1. The color red demands attention. It can make you feel energetic, but too much red in a room can be overpowering.

Orange is less aggressive than red. It is lively, cheerful, and warm.

Yellow is friendly, happy, and warm. Yellow rooms are light and airy.

Green is nature's color. It mixes well with other colors and looks especially good next to white. Green is cool, peaceful, and friendly.

Blue is cool, quiet, and reserved. It brings thoughts of oceans, sky, and ice to mind. It can be soothing and peaceful, but too much blue in a room can be depressing.

Violet is a royal color. It works well with most other colors. It is dignified and can be very dramatic.

Black is sophisticated. It is severe and dramatic. Small amounts of black help to give a room a crisp, clear appearance, 7-2.

ARMSTRONG WORLD INDUSTRIES, INC.

7-1 The color red helps create a mood of excitement.

White is fresh and youthful. It can add sparkle to a room. Like black, small amounts of white make rooms look cleaner and livelier. *Off-white* is popular for backgrounds. It makes the other colors and the furniture in a room look good.

People feel most comfortable when they are surrounded by colors that reflect their personality. For instance, outgoing people might choose bright red or orange for the main color in a room. Shy people might feel awkward in a red room. They would probably feel better in a room that was decorated with blue or green.

When making color decisions for a home, the preferences of each member of the living unit should be considered. No single color will satisfy everyone, but the social area of the dwelling should be decorated to make all members feel as comfortable as possible. Individual preferences can be satisfied in the more private rooms of the quiet and work areas.

THE COLOR WHEEL

The *color wheel,* 7-3, is the basis of all color relationships. Three of the colors on the color wheel—red, yellow, and blue—are called *primary colors.* By mixing, lightening, and darkening the primary colors, all other colors can be made.

Mixing equal amounts of any two primary colors produces a *secondary color.* Orange, green, and violet are secondary colors. Orange is a mixture of red and yellow. Green is a mix-

7-2 Small amounts of black help give this area a livelier appearance.

ture of yellow and blue. Violet is a mixture of red and blue. Look again at the color wheel in 7-3. Notice that the location of each secondary color is between the two primary colors used to make it.

The other colors on the color wheel are called *intermediate* or *tertiary colors*. They are named after the two colors used to make them, with the primary color listed first. Red-orange, yellow-orange, yellow-green, blue-green, blue-violet, and red-violet are the intermediate colors.

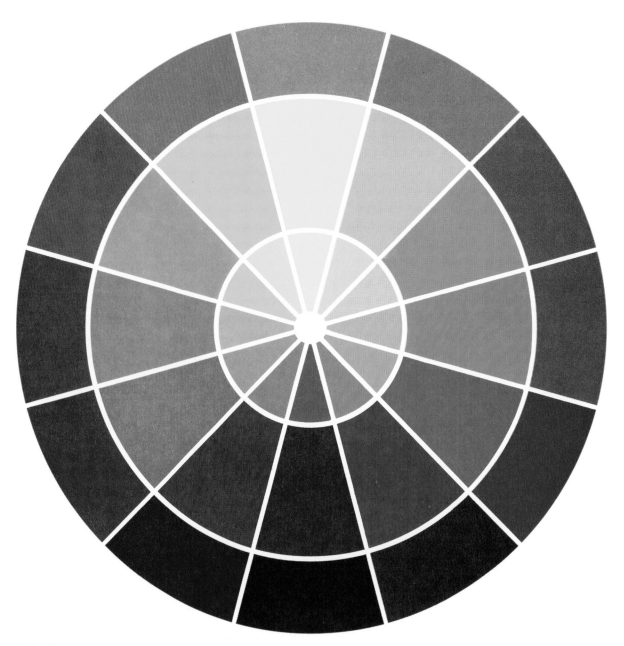

7-3 The arrangement of colors in a color wheel provides a basis for all color relationships.

Hue

A *hue,* or color name, is the one characteristic that makes a color unique. It is hue that makes blue different from red, yellow, green, blue-green, blue-violet, etc. If you begin with blue, making that blue lighter, darker, brighter, or duller will not change the hue. It will still be blue.

Value

The *value* of a hue refers to its lightness or darkness. The *normal value* of a hue is the value shown on the center ring of the color wheel. The normal values of some hues are lighter than the normal values of others. Yellow has the lightest normal value. As you move away from yellow on the color wheel, normal values of hues become darker. Violet has the darkest normal value.

To lighten the value of a hue, white is added. The result is called a *tint.* For instance, pink is a tint of red. It is made by adding white to red. For lighter tints, more white is added. Tints are shown on the inner ring off the color wheel in 7-3.

The value of a hue can also be made darker. This is done by adding varying amounts of black to the hue. The result is called a *shade.* Navy is a shade of blue. Burgundy is a shade of red. Shades are shown on the outer ring of the color wheel in 7-3.

A *value scale* is pictured in 7-4. It shows the full range of values for a hue, from tints to shades.

Intensity

Intensity refers to the brightness or dullness of a hue. The hues on the color wheel are of normal intensity.

Most colors used in a home are of lower intensity. One way to lower the intensity of a color is to add some of its *complement.* The complement of a hue is the hue directly across from it on a color wheel. For instance, blue is the complement of orange. To lower the intensity of orange, varying amounts of blue are added, 7-5.

Another way to lower the intensity of a color is to add some black or white to it. However,

7-4 Values ranging from tints to shades are shown on a value scale.

7-5 By adding blue to orange, the intensity of orange is reduced to make a more dull color.

this method changes the value as well as the intensity.

Neutrals

Black, white, and gray are *neutrals*. They look good next to colors. By adding a neutral to a hue, the value of the hue is changed to either a tint or a shade. Adding a neutral to a hue also makes the hue less intense. When any of these changes are made, the hue is *neutralized*. Neutralized hues blend more easily with other colors.

Warm and cool colors

Some colors seem warm, and others seem cool. See 7-6. The *warm colors* are the "sun colors." Red is the warmest. The colors that are close to red on the color wheel are also considered warm.

Does your home have some rooms in which you always feel warm? If so, look at the colors used in those rooms. Do they appear on the left-hand side of the color wheel?

Warm colors are called *advancing colors*. Objects that are warm-colored appear nearer to you. Walls that are warm-colored appear closer together. Thus, a room that is painted red or orange appears smaller than it really is.

Warm colors attract your attention. They can make you feel happy, energetic, and full of excitement. Many advertisements use warm colors to make you notice them. Restaurants use warm colors to increase your appetite. Locker rooms use them to generate excitement. Homes use them to make members of the living units feel lively and cheerful. However, large amounts of warm colors may make you feel nervous, especially if the colors are of full intensity.

On the opposite side of the color wheel are the *cool colors*. These include blue, green, and the colors near them.

Cool colors are called *receding colors*. They make objects seem smaller and walls seem farther away than they are. A room painted light green seems larger than it is.

Cool colors are quiet and restful. They are often used in hospitals to help keep patients calm and relaxed. They are also popular for bedrooms. If cool colors are overused, they can make people feel depressed.

Warm and cool colors are not different in temperature. They just create different atmospheres that make people feel different ways. To illustrate this point, a story is often told about a lunchroom in an office building.

7-6 Yellows give a room a warmer feeling than blues.

The workers in the office complained that the lunchroom was always cold. It was painted light blue. The employer had the room painted orange. The workers quit complaining even though the temperature did not change.

COLOR HARMONIES

When certain colors are used together in a pleasing manner, they create a *color harmony* or *color scheme*. There are no absolute "rights" or "wrongs" in using colors, but there are some guidelines that can help you. See 7-7. Following one of the standard color harmonies is the surest and easiest way to achieve success with color.

Monochromatic color harmony

The simplest color harmony is the *monochromatic* one, 7-8. In it, a single hue is used. Variation is added by changing the value and intensity of the hue. For example, if you like green, you may use a dark green carpet, medium green upholstery, and light green walls. Accents of very intense green, white, and black can also add variety. A room with this type of color harmony is shown in 7-9.

Analogous color harmony

An *analogous color harmony,* 7-10, is made by combining related hues. These are hues that are next to each other on the color wheel. Usually, between three and five hues are used. Because they are related, they blend together easily. One color seems to float into another. An example of an analogous color scheme is shown in 7-11.

The result will look best if you choose one color as the main one. Use smaller amounts of the others to add interest and variety. See 7-18. In addition, you may want to use a tiny amount of an unrelated color for an accent.

Complementary color harmony

Complementary color harmonies, 7-12, are made by combining complementary colors (colors directly across from each other on the

1. Use colors that the members of your living unit enjoy.
2. Colors based on blue give coolness to a room.
3. Colors based on red give warmth to a room.
4. Light values, dull intensities and cool hues have receding qualities that make rooms appear larger.
5. Dark values, bright intensities and warm hues have advancing qualities that make rooms appear smaller.
6. Contrasting values draw attention.
   a. A white sofa against a dark-colored wall will draw more attention than a white sofa against a white wall.
   b. Too many strong value contrasts in a room may produce a tiring and confusing appearance.
7. Similar values create a restful mood.
8. Light colors soil easily and may require extra cleaning. Dark colors show dust.
9. Intensity of color varies according to the amount that is used. The larger the area of color, the more intense it appears.
10. Large areas look best when covered with colors of low intensity. Bright colors should be used in small amounts.
11. When colors are used side-by-side, the differences between them will be emphasized.
    a. When light and dark colors are used together, the light ones appear lighter, and the dark ones appear darker.
    b. When bright and dull colors are used together, the bright ones appear brighter, and the dull ones appear duller.
    c. When warm and cool colors are used together, the warm ones appear warmer, and the cool ones appear cooler.
12. When complementary colors are used together, they make each other appear brighter.
13. Color harmonies look best when one color dominates.
14. Neutral colors are an important part of any color scheme.
15. Colors change as light changes. Artificial light "softens" colors. Colors that appear attractive under artificial light may not be pleasing in the daylight.
16. Surfaces with rough textures make colors appear darker than surfaces with smooth textures.

7-7 These guidelines can help you achieve success with color.

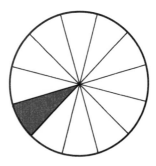

7-8 A monochromatic color harmony uses a single hue.

Color and design 145

color wheel). In 7-13, red and green are used in a complementary color harmony.

Complementary colors make each other look brighter and more intense. When blue is next to orange, the blue looks "more blue," and the orange looks "more orange." A complementary color harmony can make a room look bright and dramatic. Although such sharp contrast is fine for some rooms, most rooms look better if the contrast is lessened. To do this, the values and intensities of the colors can be varied. Also, the colors can be used in varied amounts. The more one color is allowed to dominate the other, the less the contrast is noticed. This idea follows the guideline that one color should dominate in any color harmony.

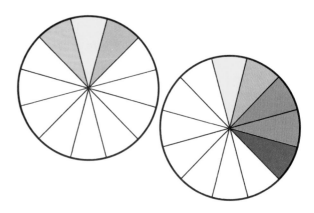

7-10 An analogous color harmony uses three to five hues that are next to each other on the color wheel.

7-9 Yellow is the basis for this monochromatic color harmony.

MARILYN BRANDOM, PHOTO BY PHILIP BARTHOLEMEW

7-11 An analogous color harmony using yellow, yellow-green, and green gives this room a refreshing appearance.

Variations of the complementary color harmony

The complementary color harmony can be altered to create other color schemes. They are all somewhat alike because they all use contrasting colors.

A *split complementary color harmony* is pictured in 7-14. The first step is to choose one color. Then the two colors on each side of its complement are used with it.

A *double complementary color harmony,* 7-15, is one step further than the split-complementary one. In this case, neither of the two basic complementary colors are used. Instead, the two colors on each side of both of them are used.

A *triad color harmony,* 7-16, uses three colors that are spaced evenly around the color wheel. The three primary colors form a triad color scheme, 7-17. The three secondary colors can also be used for this type of color scheme.

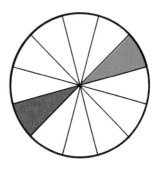

7-12 A complementary color scheme uses two opposite colors on the color wheel.

THOMASVILLE FURNITURE INDUSTRIES, INC.

7-13 A complementary color harmony can look formal and dramatic.

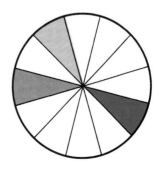

7-14 Split complementary color harmony.

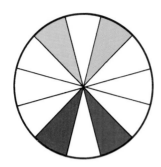

7-15 Double complementary color harmony.

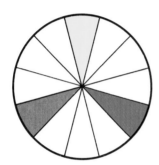

7-16 Triad color harmony.

KIRSCH CO.

7-17 A triad color harmony using the three primary colors is used in this child's room.

KIRSCH CO.

7-18 A dramatic look is created by the large contrast in value between white and dark brown in this neutral scheme.

The two other possible color combinations are yellow-orange, red-violet, and blue-green; or red-orange, blue-violet, and yellow-green.

Neutral harmonies

Although black and white are not hues of the color wheel, they are the basis for some color schemes. Combinations of black, gray, and white create *neutral harmonies*.

Brown is not a neutral color. But because brown, tan, and beige blend well with almost all other colors, they are sometimes treated as neutral. In 7-18, brown and white are used to create a neutral scheme. If black had been used instead of dark brown, the room would have had even more contrast and a harsher mood. The orange flowers and green plants are accents. They add a needed spark of variety to the scheme.

OTHER ELEMENTS OF DESIGN

Color is used with the other design elements — line, form, and texture — to create a design. Together, they can be used to give a room or space a pleasing appearance. By using the elements of design, you can make a space seem open or cozy, formal or informal, active or restful. Understanding how to use these elements can help you achieve your goals for a comfortable, pleasing living space, 7-19.

USE DESIGN ELEMENTS	ACCORDING TO DESIGN PRINCIPLES	TO ACHIEVE DESIGN GOALS
Color	Proportion	Beauty
Line	Balance	Appropriateness
Form	Emphasis	Unity with
Texture	Rhythm	variation

7-19 This chart explains the relationship among the elements, principles, and goals of design.

Line

Lines give direction to a design. They cause your eyes to move left and right or up and down. The direction of lines creates certain effects in a design. *Vertical lines,* 7-20, add height, strength, and dignity. They can be seen in columns or pillars, in tall pieces of furniture and in long, straight folds of draperies.

Horizontal lines add stability and restfulness. See 7-21. Long, low roofs, shelves, and long pieces of furniture such as sofas and chests are sources of these lines.

Diagonal lines, 7-22, suggest activity. Too many of them in a room can be tiring. Diagonal lines are seen in gable roofs, slanted ceilings, and staircases.

Curved lines are pictured in 7-23. They add a graceful, softening effect. They are found in doorway arches, ruffled curtains, and furniture with curved edges.

You have learned that one color should dominate a design. Others can be added for variety and interest. The same guideline applies to other design elements. One type of line

SUN LAKES DEVELOPMENT CO.

7-20 Vertical lines add height and dignity to this wall.

VENTARAMA SKYLIGHT CORP.

7-21 Horizontal lines help give this kitchen a restful look.

Color and design 149

should dominate a design. Others can be added for interest. In 7-24 you can see how lines are used in the exterior of a dwelling.

Form. Any object that has height, width, and depth has form. The form of an object should fit its function. Consider some different forms of chairs. Dining room chairs have a form that allows people to sit close to a table. Chairs for a family room have a form that allows people to sit comfortably and relax while talking, reading, or watching television. The form of lounge chairs allows people to stretch their legs while remaining in a sitting position.

Imagine a chair with a seat that slanted to one side. Imagine one with very short legs or very tall legs. Imagine one so frail that it could not support an average person. These forms would not be suited to the function of chairs.

Forms within a room should be related. Some pieces of furniture have the form of cubes or rectangular prisms. Look at the room in 7-25. It is dominated by "boxy" forms which look good together. A chair with a different form would look out of place in this room.

Texture. Texture refers to the way the surface of something feels — or the way you expect it to feel. Texture appeals as much to the sense of sight as it does to the sense of touch. What do you see in your mind when you hear descriptions such as lustrous, shiny, or dull?

Rigid, crisp, harsh, flexible, and limp describe the hardness and softness of texture. Terms that describe the roughness or smoothness of texture are nubby, crinkled, fuzzy, quilted, ribbed, uneven, and even.

Texture affects color. Rough textures cast tiny shadows on the surface of an object that make the color look darker. Smooth, shiny textures make colors look lighter than rough ones.

Texture adds interest to a room. Rooms look best if one texture dominates and others are added for interest. Interest can be added by using visual texture as well as real texture. Objects with visual texture feel different than they look like they would feel. For instance, a wallpaper may feel smooth. But the pattern printed on it may make it look rough. The room in 7-26 has a good combination of textures including visual texture.

7-23 The curved lines of the walkway and the roof tile help soften the appearance of this house.

ARMSTRONG WORLD INDUSTRIES, INC.

7-22 The diagonal lines of the fabric on the furniture in this room add interest.

7-24 Horizontal, vertical, diagonal, and curved lines are balanced on the exterior of this house.

7-25 The forms of the furniture in this room are similar. Each piece looks like it belongs in the room.

7-26 Smooth textures dominate in this room, but the grooves of the furniture add interest. The design of the wallpaper adds a rough visual texture.

Color and design 151

Principles of design

When you understand the principles of design, you can use the elements of design successfully. Then you can achieve the goals of beauty, appropriateness, and unity with variation. The principles of design are proportion, balance, emphasis, and rhythm.

Proportion. Proportion is the ratio of one part to another part or to the whole. It involves the shape, size, and visual weight of an object.

Unequal amounts are more pleasing to the eye than equal amounts. Thus, a rectangle has more pleasing proportions than a square. Ratios such as 2:3, 3:5, and 5:8 are better than 2:2 or 2:4. This guideline applies to rooms, furniture, and accessories. See 7-27.

Visual weight is another factor in proportion. Look at the two chairs in 7-28. Both have the same dimensions. Yet one *looks* larger and heavier than the other. Thick lines, bold colors, coarse textures, and large patterns all add to visual weight.

If you were decorating a small room, you would choose furniture that was light in visual weight. This would prevent the furniture from making the room look crowded. Likewise, you would choose accessories that were in proportion to the furniture. In a small room, it is wise to think small in everything from sofas to ashtrays.

Balance. Balance gives a design a feeling of equilibrium. Balance can be either formal or informal.

Formal balance is pictured in 7-29. If you draw an imaginary vertical line through the front door, one side of the house is the mirror image of the other. The same thing can be seen in a room, 7-30.

Informal balance is pictured in 7-31. The two ends of the house are not alike, but neither side overpowers the other. The room in 7-32 also illustrates informal balance. The sofa and end table on one side are balanced by the chair, small table, and wooden chair on the other side. The boldness of the red fabric makes the chair "heavy" enough for the arrangement to work.

Emphasis. Emphasis creates a center of interest in a design. It is the feature that is seen first and that repeatedly draws attention. Common points of emphasis in rooms are fireplaces, pleasant outdoor views, colorful rugs, and striking works of art, 7-33.

The point of emphasis gives order and direction to a room. Everything else in the room should relate to it through color, type of line, texture, or proportion.

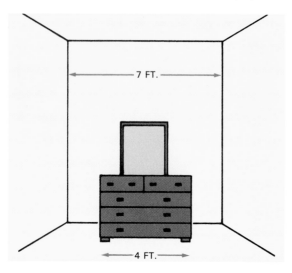

7-27 Good proportion is important in furnishing a room.

7-28 Although these two chairs are the same size, one looks larger because of visual weight.

7-29 Formal balance gives this house a stately appearance.

Rhythm. Rhythm leads the eye from one area to another with smooth movement. This can be achieved by radiation, repetition, opposition, gradation, or transition. See 7-34.

In rhythm by *radiation,* lines flow out from a central point. This is usually found in accessories.

Rhythm by *repetition* is created when a

design element is repeated. Color, line, form, or texture may be repeated.

In rhythm by *opposition,* lines meet to form right angles. Opposition may be found in the corners of the windowpanes, picture frames, and fireplaces.

Gradation is the type of rhythm created by a gradual change in color value from dark to light. It can also be created by a regular change from smaller to larger parts that all have the same shape.

Curved lines are sources of rhythm by *transition* when they carry the eye over an architectural feature or piece of furniture.

Several types of rhythm can be seen in 7-35.

Goals of design

The goals of design are beauty, appropriateness, and unity with variation.

Beauty cannot be defined. Each person has a unique concept of beauty. However, the elements and principles of design have been developed as a result of studying what most people see as being beautiful. If design elements are arranged according to design principles, the result will appear beautiful to most people.

7-30 Formal balance creates a mood of stability and peace within a room.

7-31 Although the two sides of this house do not match, they are balanced. For instance, the tall, thin trees are balanced with short, wide bushes. It takes practice to achieve good informal balance.

ETHAN ALLEN, INC.

7-32 The furniture in this room is arranged with informal balance.

7-33 The large fan on the wall is the point of emphasis in this room.

7-35 Rhythm by radiation can be seen in the lines radiating from the center of the sections of glass above the curtains in this dining room. Rhythm by repetition is seen in the pattern of the furniture wood carvings. Rhythm by opposition is shown in the china closet. Rhythm by transition is seen in the arches of the windows.

Appropriateness or suitability has many meanings. Furnishings should be appropriate for the dwelling as a whole. (A vacation cabin does not need formal dining furniture.) Furnishings should be appropriate for each room. (A refrigerator is not appropriate in a living room.) The form of any furnishing should be appropriate for its function. Above all, your home should be appropriate for your personality, life-style, needs, and wants.

Unity with variation has been mentioned several times. In any design with unity, one color dominates. One type of line dominates. One type of form dominates. One texture dominates. The proportion is mostly large or mostly small. Balance is mostly formal or mostly informal. One point of emphasis is needed. One type of rhythm dominates. All of these guidelines are stated to assure unity or harmony in the design. With unity, the overall appearance of a room is pleasing. Without unity, a room can be a confusing combination of parts.

On the other hand, too many limitations on design elements and principles can result in a boring, lifeless room. Some variety is needed. Therefore, the goal is "mostly unity with some variation."

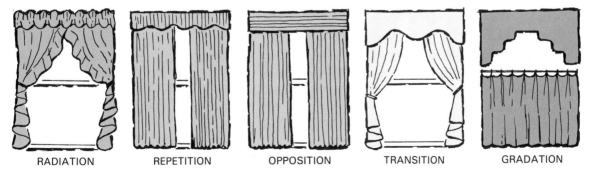

RADIATION   REPETITION   OPPOSITION   TRANSITION   GRADATION

7-34 Rhythm can be achieved in several different ways.

Color and design 155

7-36 This vinyl floor covering is beautiful and easy to keep clean.

BACKGROUNDS

Floors, walls, and ceilings are important parts of a room. They hide construction details and provide insulation. They also serve as backgrounds for everything else. The way they are used helps to determine the total look of the room. They can help show off the furnishings in the best way. They can also help create the desired mood.

Floors

A floor is usually the first background to be planned. It underscores the entire room and helps tie the many parts of a room together.

In many homes, floor treatments are chosen separately for each area. In others, a single treatment such as carpeting is used throughout.

The main types of floor treatments are resilient, nonresilient, wood, and carpet. Before choosing one, you should consider its beauty, comfort, durability, maintenance, and cost.

Resilient floor treatments. Resilient surfaces are those which have some "give" but retain their original shape. They are nonasborbent, durable, easy to maintain, and fairly inexpensive. They provide some walking comfort and noise control.

Asphalt tile, vinyl, and cork tile are types of resilient floor treatments. They are available in a wide range of colors and patterns and can be used in any decorating scheme.

Asphalt tile is the least costly type of tile. It is not affected by moisture, so it can be used in places where moisture is a problem such as basement floors. It is durable, but dents and stains can be problems.

Vinyl floor coverings, 7-36, can offer any color, pattern, or texture desired. They are very resistant to wear and to stains, but abrasion can damage the surface. They are available in either tile or sheet form. Vinyl tile is the most costly kind of tile, but it is the easiest to maintain. Little or no waxing is needed. Some sheet vinyl is made with a layer of vinyl foam behind it. The result is a floor with good walking comfort and good sound absorption.

Cork tile has a beautiful, rich appearance. It is great for foot comfort and sound control. But it wears rapidly and dents easily. It is difficult to maintain and is damaged by grease stains. When covered with a coating of vinyl, it is water resistant, more durable, and easier to maintain.

Nonresilient floor treatments. Nonresilient floor treatments are extremely durable and attractive. However, they offer little foot comfort, noise control, or warmth. They are difficult to install and costly.

Ceramic tile, clay tile, concrete tile, terrazzo, stone, and brick are types of nonresilient floor treatments.

Ceramic tile, 7-37, is a hard, durable covering for both floors and walls. Its glaze is water and stain resistant, so it is easy to maintain. Ceramic tile is used most often for entries and bathrooms, but the wide range of sizes, colors, and patterns makes it appropriate for any room.

Clay or *quarry tile,* like ceramic tile, is very strong and durable. It resists grease, chemicals, and changes in temperature. Colors are limited to its natural range of golds, reds, browns, grays, and blacks. The shapes and textures vary. It can be glazed or unglazed. When needed, glazed clay tile should be washed with warm water and soap. Unglazed tile may need to be waxed.

Concrete with a smooth surface can be used as a finished floor. Color may be added to it as a powder before it dries or by using a special floor paint. This type of floor is extremely sturdy and durable. It is used for some entries, basements, patios, and garages. Indoor floors need a heavy coat of wax for maintenance.

Terrazzo is made of a mixture of cement, mortar, and marble chips. It is ground and polished to a smooth finish. It comes in a limited range of colors. Terrazzo floors are easy to maintain because they are hard, durable, and very resistant to moisture. They are usually used in areas with heavy traffic such as entries and halls.

KOHLER CO.

7-37 Ceramic tile gives this bathroom a fresh, clean appearance.

Stone floors are beautiful and durable, but costly. Stones vary in size and quality. They may be laid in natural shapes or cut into regular ones. Colors are limited to natural grays and browns. Stone floors are fairly easy to maintain. A vinyl coating protects them from grease stains. They are used in areas of heavy traffic, some dining rooms, and patios. They can look either formal or informal.

Brick floors, like stone ones, are beautiful, durable, and costly. Bricks come in many sizes, colors, and textures. See 7-38. The care of brick floors is similar to that of stone floors. A vinyl coating protects them from stains. The floors should be dusted regularly and washed occasionally. They look best in informal settings.

Wood floor treatments. Wood has always been a popular floor treatment. It looks good with any style of furniture. It offers beauty and warmth to a room. It has some resilience, yet it is durable and resists dents. The cost is moderate to high, depending on the type of wood chosen.

Oak, maple, beech, birch, hickory, mahogany, cherry, and teak are used for *hardwood* floors. Oak is the most common because of its beauty, warmth, and durability. Maple floors are also common. They are smooth, strong, and hard.

Southern yellow pine, Douglas fir, western hemlock, and larch are the common *softwoods* used for floors. Redwood, cedar, cypress, and eastern white pine are used where they are readily available.

KIRSCH CO.

7-38 Brick floors are beautiful and durable. Their rough texture adds interest to any informal setting.

ETHAN ALLEN, INC.

7-39 Various widths and lengths of wood are used for random plank floors. They look great in informal settings.

Wood floors are laid in several ways. The most common method is to nail down thin strips of wood which are tongue and grooved to keep them close together. Decorative patterns such as random plank, 7-39, and parquetry, 7-40, add interest to a wood floor.

Today, wood finishes of plastic, such as vinyl, make the task of maintaining wood floors easy. They protect the wood from moisture, stains, and wear.

Carpets and rugs. Carpets and rugs are among the most popular floor treatments of today. They have many advantages. They make a room warmer. They provide sound control and walking comfort. They add color and texture to a room. They serve as an attractive

7-40 Parquet floors are often assembled in factories for easier installation.

foundation for other furnishings. With a good vacuum cleaner, maintenance of carpets and rugs is usually easy.

Wall-to-wall carpeting, 7-41, covers an entire floor. It makes a room appear larger and more luxurious. It can hide a poor floor. A disadvantage is that it cannot be moved, so some parts show wear before other parts.

A *room-size rug* exposes a small border of floor. It can show off a beautiful wood floor while keeping the warmth and comfort of the rug. See 7-42. Room-size rugs can be turned for more even wear. However, maintenance is a disadvantage. Separate cleaning processes are needed for the rug and exposed floor.

Area rugs vary in size, but they do not cover the entire floor. They are used to define areas of a room. See 7-43. Area rugs are versatile. They can add interest to a room and can even serve as the point of emphasis. They can be moved from one furniture grouping to another

PPG INDUSTRIES

7-42 A room-size rug combines the beauty of the original floor with the comfort of a rug.

MARILYN BRANDOM, PHOTO BY PHILIP BARTHOLEMEW

7-41 A wall-to-wall carpet makes a room seem larger because the floor space is not divided into sections.

for a new look. They can be used in almost any room in any dwelling.

Two factors that affect the quality of rugs and carpets are *density* and *fiber content*. Density refers to the number of tufts or yarns per square inch or square centimeter. Carpets with a high density look better and are more durable.

Wool, nylon, acrylic, rayon, olefin, and cotton are the major fibers used for carpets and rugs. Wool is an ideal fiber for carpet. It is very resilient. (It regains its shape after you step on it.) It is beautiful and durable, and it resists soil and stains. However, wool is expensive.

Nylon is the most-used fiber for carpets today. It is very durable. It has very good resilience and resistance to soil. (But oily stains are difficult to remove.) It is less costly than wool.

Acrylic looks much like wool. It has good resilience, durability, and resistance to soil. (But oily stains are difficult to remove.) It costs less than wool, but more than nylon.

Rayon rugs are attractive, but not very practical. They are low in resilience, durability, and resistance to soil. However, they are low in price. Therefore, they are used where quality is not a major factor. Scatter rugs and inexpensive room-size rugs are often made of rayon.

Cotton rugs are attractive and durable, but low in resilience and resistance to soil. Prices vary according to the type of cotton, but they are usually fairly low. Cotton is used mostly for washable scatter rugs.

Many kitchen, bathroom, and outdoor carpets are made of olefin. It is very durable and very resistant to soil and stains. It is fairly resilient. The price range of olefin is from medium to low.

Walls

Walls make up the largest surface area of a room. They have many functions. They give protection from the outdoors. They hide pipes, wires, and insulation. They divide space within a dwelling and provide privacy. They help reduce noise, and they serve as backgrounds for the furnishings of a room.

ETHAN ALLEN, INC.

7-43 The eating area in this room is set apart from the sleeping and dressing areas by an area rug.

Before choosing a wall treatment, the size and shape of the room should be considered. If the room is small, smooth walls of light, dull colors will help it look larger. If the room is large, it will look more cozy when dark, bright colors, large patterns, or rough textures are used on the walls.

If the room is long and narrow, the room's proportions will look better when one of the short walls is covered with a dark color.

Other considerations should also be made before choosing a wall treatment. It should harmonize with the ceiling and floor treatments. It should add to the general mood of the room. And most of all, it should reflect the personalities of the persons who use the room.

Walls and wall treatments vary a great deal. Each one has advantages and disadvantages. Choose the one that meets your needs and priorities and that fits the room's mood.

Gypsum board or dry wall is the most common material used for interior walls. It comes in 4 ft. by 8 ft. (1219 mm by 2438 mm) panels. Joints are taped, hidden by a fast-drying compound, then sanded. The smooth surface is covered by paint, wallpaper, or fabric.

Paneling is another common type of wall. It is usually made of plywood in 4 ft. by 8 ft. (1219 mm by 2438 mm) panels. Paneling can be applied directly to framing materials, but it is much more substantial if applied over gypsum board. Paneling comes in many different colors and textures. It is appropriate in any room. See 7-44 and 7-45.

Brick or *stone* is used mostly for decorative walls and fireplace walls, as in 7-46. It is beautiful and durable and requires little or no upkeep. However, it is costly to install. It belongs in informal settings, where it can add to the warm, cozy atmosphere.

Cement blocks can make attractive walls when painted. They are large, so they belong in large rooms with large pieces of furniture, rough textures, and bold colors.

Plaster is seldom used except in older homes and commercial buildings. Applying it requires special skills and facilities. Therefore, it costs more than most other types of walls. Walls of plaster can be either smooth or rough. They are usually covered with paint.

Ceramic tile comes in many sizes, shapes, and patterns. A wall of decorative tiles can be the point of emphasis in a room. Walls of ceramic tile are durable and easy to maintain.

Plastic wallboard comes in both enamel and plastic (such as Formica) finishes. It is used mostly in bathrooms and kitchens, and it is easy to maintain.

Carpet is sometimes used on walls as well as on floors. Its texture adds interest to the room. Carpet is very effective in absorbing noise.

Cork, like carpet, is a good wall treatment for rooms where sound insulation is needed. It adds warmth and textural interest to a room.

Fabric can be used to cover walls. it can be attached to the wall with glue, tape, or staples. Sometimes it is stretched between two curtain rods—one at the ceiling and one at the floor. Fabric can add color, warmth, texture, and interest to a room. Closely woven fabrics of

CALIFORNIA REDWOOD ASSOC.

7-44 Paneling with a satin finish looks good in this kitchen.

ETHAN ALLEN, INC.

7-45 Paneling is a beautiful background for this elegant room.

medium weight are the best choices for wall coverings.

Wallpaper can copy almost any imaginable surface. It can look like brick, stone, wood, or leather. It can look like a painted mural of an outdoor scene. Because of the variety of patterns, wallpaper can be used to enhance any room. See 7-47.

Wallpaper is practical as well as beautiful. Some wallpapers are coated with thick layers of vinyl. These resist stains and water, so they can be used in kitchens and bathrooms. They are durable and can be scrubbed clean. Some can even be peeled off a wall and used again in another room.

Paint is the fastest and least costly way to cover wall surfaces and to change the look of a room. See 7-48.

When you choose paint, choose a color that is slightly lighter than the color you want. When color is applied to walls, it looks stronger and darker because you see so much of it.

SUN LAKES DEVELOPMENT CO.

7-47 Wallpaper is used to make this bathroom seem bright and cheery.

PPG INDUSTRIES

7-46 A stone wall is an attractive background for an informal room.

7-48 Paint has been used to give this room a bright, youthful look.

(A good tip to remember when you have finished painting a room is to paint one side of a recipe card. Take the card with you when you shop for curtains, carpet, or furniture so you can choose harmonious colors. On the back of the card, write the brand name and color name of the paint. Then if you ever want to match it, you'll have the information you need.)

Paints vary in the amount of gloss or sheen they have. Enamel paints have the most gloss. They give a protective and decorative finish to kitchen and bathroom walls, wood trim, windowsills, radiators, masonry, and heating pipes.

Semi-gloss paints have less sheen and are slightly less durable than enamel paints. They can be used in most of the places enamel paints are used as well as for ceilings and walls of dry wall.

Flat wall paints have no gloss. They give a soft finish to walls and ceilings. They should not be used for the walls or woodwork in kitchens and bathrooms, nor for windowsills.

Textured paints give walls a rough surface. They can be used to cover ceilings and walls that have cracks or irregularities.

7-49 This ceiling treatment helps create a formal mood.

Ceilings

The ceiling of a room is the least-noticed background, but it performs many tasks. It holds and conceals insulating materials which help control the temperature in a building. It hides electrical wiring. Some ceilings also hide water and gas lines.

Ceilings affect the appearance of rooms by helping to create certain moods. See 7-49. Average ceilings are 8 ft. (2438 mm) from the floor. Higher ceilings give a feeling of spaciousness and usually create a formal atmosphere. Lower ceilings make rooms seem smaller and usually create an informal mood.

You can create the illusion of height by using vertical lines on the walls or by running the wall treatment up onto the ceiling a short distance. A ceiling will appear lower if you use horizontal lines on the walls or extend the ceiling treatment down a short distance onto the walls.

Another way to make it look lower is to use dark or patterned materials.

The three most common materials used for ceilings are plaster, acoustical plaster, and acoustical tile.

Plaster (or wallboard finished to look like plaster) is appropriate for any room. Its surface can be either smooth or rough. It is usually covered with a flat paint.

Acoustical plaster has a rough texture. It helps absorb sound and thus reduces the noise in a room. It is applied by spraying it onto the ceiling's surface.

Acoustical tile, 7-50, is decorative and functional. It comes in many patterns and colors. It absorbs sound and is easy to clean.

When planning backgrounds for your home, keep the goals of design in mind. This will help you achieve pleasing results in any room throughout the dwelling.

7-50 Vinyl-coated acoustical tile absorbs sound and is easy to clean.

to Know

analogous . . . appropriateness . . .
backgrounds . . . balance . . . beauty . . .
ceilings . . . color . . . color harmony . . .
complementary . . . cool colors . . . design . . .
double complementary . . . elements of design . . .
emphasis . . . floors . . . form . . . hue . . .
intensity . . . intermediate colors . . . line . . .
monochromatic . . . neutrals . . .
primary colors . . .proportion . . . rhythm . . .
secondary colors . . . shade . . .
split complementary . . . texture . . . tint . . .
triad . . . unity with variation . . . value . . .
visual weight . . . walls . . . warm colors

to Review

Write your answers on a separate sheet of paper.

1. List the three secondary colors and explain how each one can be made from primary colors.

2. Explain the difference between value and intensity of color.

3. Describe how to neutralize a hue.

4. Colors related to red are _____; colors related to blue are _____.

5. Give an example of each of the following:
   a. Monochromatic color harmony.
   b. Analogous color harmony.
   c. Complementary color harmony.

6. _____ is the design element that gives direction to a design.

7. The form of an object should fit its _____.

8. The way a surface looks and feels is known as _____.

9. When you are concerned with the shape, size, and visual weight of objects, you are using the design principle of _____.

10. What is the difference between formal and informal balance?

11. Explain the importance of emphasis in a design.

12. Define rhythm in design.

13. List three kinds of rhythm and give an example of each.

14. Explain the design goal of unity with variation.

15. Describe three floor treatments.

16. Describe three wall treatments.

17. Describe two ceiling treatments.

to Do

1. Using only red, blue, and yellow paints, mix colors to make a color wheel.

2. Make a value scale by adding black and white to a hue.

3. With paints, practice making a color less intense by adding varying amounts of its complement.

4. Place a piece of green paper next to a red paper. Then place another piece of green paper next to a gray paper. Which green looks brighter?

5. Place a piece of very light blue paper next to very dark blue paper. Place another piece of very light blue paper next to medium blue paper. Which light blue is lighter?

6. Make two small "rooms" of cardboard. Cover the walls of one with light, dull, cool colors. Cover the walls of the other with dark, bright, warm colors. Which one looks larger?

7. Find pictures in magazines to illustrate the following:
   a. Warm or cool colors.
   b. Each type of color harmony.
   c. Each design element.
   d. Each design principle.
   e. Various background treatments.

8. Make a collage showing a variety of textures that are used in housing design. You may want to choose one topic for your collage, such as floor coverings or upholstery fabric.

8

Decisions about lighting

After studying this chapter, you will be able to:

◼ Explain variations in natural light and describe several types of window treatments.

◼ Differentiate between incandescent and fluorescent light.

◼ Plan good lighting for a home in terms of visual comfort, safety, and beauty.

Light is an important part of your housing, inside and out. It can help you make the most of all the available space in your home. It can make your home a safe place to work and play. And it can add beauty to any living area.

Wherever you live, you will need to make many decisions about light. These decisions will be easier for you if you understand light and know how to make it work for you.

NATURAL LIGHT

The availability of natural light varies in many ways. It depends on the weather, the time of day, and the season of the year. More light is available on sunny days than on cloudy ones. More light is available at noon than at any other time of the day. Summer months offer more sunlight than those of spring, autumn, or winter.

Natural light varies in yet another way. Light coming from the north gives a feeling of coolness. Light from the south or west gives a warm feeling. Eastern light is in between the others. It is warmer than northern light, but it is cooler than light from the south or west.

The warmth or coolness of light should be considered when planning a color scheme. As you read in Chapter 7, reds and oranges are warm colors. You may not want to use them as the main colors in a room that faces west or south. They would multiply the effect of the warm sun. However, rooms on the north side of a dwelling may feel more comfortable if decorated with warm colors since the light they receive is cool.

Windows and window treatments

Windows have many uses in a room. They provide natural light, air circulation, and a view. They also add to the design of a dwelling. Both the interior and exterior appearances of a building are affected by the size, shape, and location of windows. Look at the house in 8-1. Its appeal depends on the use of windows. Inside, windows can serve as the point of emphasis in a room or as part of the background.

Windows have many different styles as shown in 8-2. Each style gives a different look to a room. A closer view of a double-hung window is shown in 8-3 so you can learn the parts of a window.

The style of window, its size, and its location are factors that affect the choice of a

PPG INDUSTRIES

8-1 Windows make both the exterior and interior designs of this house interesting.

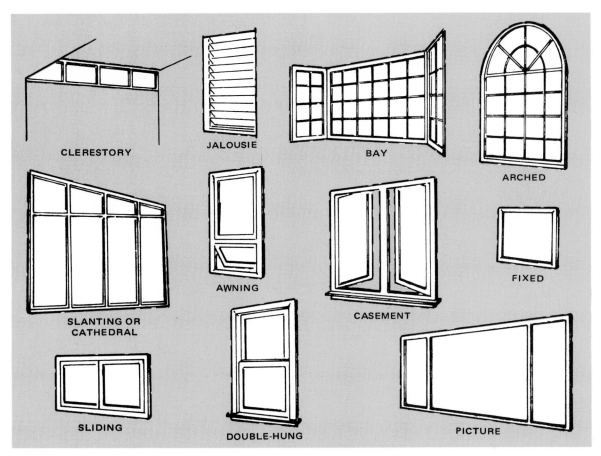

CLERESTORY

JALOUSIE

BAY

ARCHED

SLANTING OR
CATHEDRAL

AWNING

CASEMENT

FIXED

SLIDING

DOUBLE-HUNG

PICTURE

8-2 These different types of windows require different window treatments.

window treatment. Another important factor is the window's major function.

One of the functions of a window is to provide natural light. Window treatments can help you control the amount of light that enters a room. Some window treatments will allow you to block out all or part of the natural light. Others will help you get as much light as possible in a room. Look at 8-4 to see ways of controlling light.

Perhaps you have windows that usually let in pleasant amounts of light, but for an hour or two each day, the sunlight is too bright for comfort. *Shades,* as shown in 8-5, 8-6, and 8-7, can block out the sun's glare. Shades vary in appearance to go with almost any decor.

Windows used for air circulation cannot be covered with draperies that block air move-

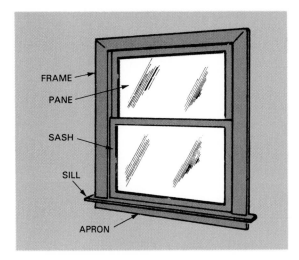

FRAME

PANE

SASH

SILL

APRON

8-3 The five main parts of a window are the frame, sash, pane, sill, and apron.

8-4 Sheer pleated shades provide privacy while allowing some light to enter. The draperies could be closed to darken the room.

8-5 Shades can be raised and lowered as needed to allow varying amounts of natural light and privacy.

8-6 As you raise Roman shades from the bottom, they form soft, accordian folds.

ment. *Shutters* are more appropriate for windows with that function.

Blinds are also good window treatments where light and air need to be controlled. See 8-8 and 8-9. Blinds can be tilted to any degree to control the amounts of air and light that enter a room. Horizontal blinds can be raised completely, and vertical blinds can be moved to one side to leave a window uncovered. Blinds can be made of wood, metal, plastic, or shade cloth.

Suppose you had a large picture window that overlooked a beautiful view. You would want to treat the window so the view could be enjoyed. One way to do this is shown in 8-10.

Where privacy is not a concern, windows can be left untreated. Look at the room in 8-11. The unusual shape of the window would make it difficult to treat. By leaving it uncovered, it adds a dramatic look to the room. Light can enter the room freely, and the view can always be enjoyed.

DEL MAR

8-8 These metalcrafted blinds are colorful, convenient, and easy to clean.

KIRSCH CO.

8-7 Colorful pleated shades can dress up any window.

Decisions about lighting 171

8-9 Vertical blinds of shade cloth permit light to enter.

8-11 This striking window needs no treatment.

8-10 This window treatment does not interfere with the pleasant outdoor view.

Curtains and draperies. Curtains and draperies are the most common window treatments. They are extremely versatile. They can fit into any decor. They can emphasize an attractive window or hide the faults of an awkward one. They can frame a beautiful view or provide privacy. They can allow sunlight to pour into a room or block it out completely. The treatment you choose depends on the room's decor and the functions of the window.

Although the variations of curtains and draperies seem endless, most will fit into one of three groups: draw draperies, curtains, and cafes.

Draw draperies are pinch-pleated panels which can cover windows completely or be pulled to the sides. They can be lined or unlined. They can be translucent (allowing some light to enter) or opaque (blocking out all light). Draw draperies can be used alone or with other window treatments such as curtains, shades, or blinds. In 8-12, pleated shades are used with draw draperies. The inside ones are sheer. They filter the light that enters the room

8-12 Draw draperies with coordinating pleated shades are an attractive part of this dining room.

and provide some privacy. The outer draperies are made of heavier fabric. When they are closed, they block out almost all of the sunlight, provide complete privacy, and help insulate the room.

Curtains are flat fabric panels with a pocket hem at the top. They slip onto a curtain rod and are gathered or shirred to the desired fullness. Curtains are somewhat limited because they cannot be opened and closed. The amount of light or privacy they provide depends on the fabric that is used. Curtains of sheer fabric, as shown in 8-13, give the room a light, airy feeling. If more privacy is needed, a simple roll-up shade can be hung behind the curtains. Heavier fabric also provides privacy, but it makes the room darker.

Cafes cover part of a window. When more than one tier is used, the window can be completely covered. The top of each panel is joined to rings which slip over a rod. They cannot be opened by pulling a cord as draw draperies are, but you can open them by pushing them to the sides. This allows you to control air, light, and

8-13 Curtains of sheer fabric give a window a soft, graceful appearance.

privacy. By changing the width or the number of tiers, almost any look can be achieved with cafes.

The length of almost all curtains and draperies fits into one of three groups: *sill length, apron length,* or *floor length.* If the bottom edge of a window treatment falls at any other place, it will look either too short or too long. To measure the length of draw draperies, curtains, and cafes, use the methods in 8-14.

Fabrics. When choosing fabric for curtains and draperies, the major concerns are color, texture, opaqueness, and durability. The color and texture of the fabric should harmonize with the room's furnishings, 8-15. The opaqueness of the fabric should allow the window to do its job—to provide either light or privacy.

The durability of a fabric depends largely on its fiber content. The chart in 8-16 describes *fiber characteristics* related to curtains and draperies. Fibers that are sunlight resistant are not weakened by the sun. Draperies made of abrasion resistant fibers are not damaged by rubbing against the floor or windowsill when they are opened and closed. Since burning draperies can cause serious home fires, fire resistant fibers are good choices. Cleaning curtains and draperies can be easy if the fibers do not need special care.

Fibers often receive special finishes to improve one or more of their characteristics. Some finishes make the dyes sunfast so they will not fade. Other finishes can make the fibers more fire resistant or easier to clean.

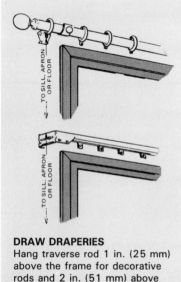

DRAW DRAPERIES
Hang traverse rod 1 in. (25 mm) above the frame for decorative rods and 2 in. (51 mm) above the frame for conventional rods. In either case, the rod should be at least 4 in. (102 mm) above the glass.

Measure from either the bottom of the decorative rings or the top of the conventional rods. Measure to the sill, apron, or floor. If measuring to the floor, subtract 1 in. (25 mm) for clearance.

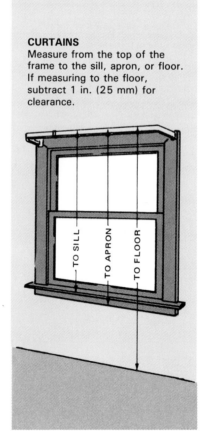

CURTAINS
Measure from the top of the frame to the sill, apron, or floor. If measuring to the floor, subtract 1 in. (25 mm) for clearance.

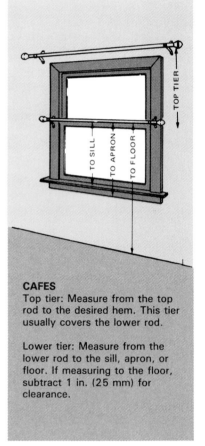

CAFES
Top tier: Measure from the top rod to the desired hem. This tier usually covers the lower rod.

Lower tier: Measure from the lower rod to the sill, apron, or floor. If measuring to the floor, subtract 1 in. (25 mm) for clearance.

8-14 Different methods are used to measure for draw draperies, curtains, and cafes.

8-15 These plaid curtains fit well with the casual appearance of this room.

FIBER	SUNLIGHT RESISTANCE	ABRASION RESISTANCE	FIRE RESISTANCE	CLEANING PROCESS	COMMENTS
Fiberglass	High	Low	High	Washable No ironing	Often feels stiff
Polyester	Medium	High	Melts	Washable No ironing	Most popular fiber for sheers
Nylon	Low	High	Melts	Washable Little ironing	Overall durability affected by finishes
Acrylic	High	Medium	Low	Washable Little ironing	Good appearance Very durable
Modacrylic	Medium	Medium	High	Washable Press with low heat	Used in blends with other fibers
Cotton	Medium	Medium	Burns	Washable Ironing depends on finish	Low cost Soils easily
Rayon	Low	Low	Burns	Shrinks unless given a special finish	Low cost Used in blends Improved by finishes
Acetate	Low	Low	Burns	Dry-clean	Good appearance Low cost Poor durability

8-16 Fiber characteristics play a big part in the performance of curtains and draperies.

Decisions about lighting   175

Draperies are sometimes lined to protect them from the sun. Other reasons for using linings are that they add body to draperies and make them hang batter; they make draperies look better from the outside of the home; and they provide better insulation.

Cost. The cost of curtains and draperies varies widely. It depends on the quality of fabric and the amount of fabric needed. Floor-length curtains usually cost more than short ones. Lined draperies cost more than unlined draperies.

Another factor in the cost of curtains and draperies is the process you use to acquire them. The least costly process is to make them yourself. Curtains and cafes are easy if you know how to sew. Draperies are a little more difficult. The next least costly method is to buy ready-mades in a store. If your windows are a standard size, this is usually an easy process. If your windows have odd shapes or unusual sizes, or if you want a special effect, you will need custom-made curtains and draperies. Someone will come to your home, measure your windows, and perhaps offer suggestions to you. Then he or she will make just the right window treatments for your home.

Windows and energy

Plain glass windows provide little insulation for a home. In warm weather, heat can enter a home through windows. In cold weather, coolness can enter, and heat can escape. This transfer of heat wastes energy. One solution to this problem would be to eliminate windows, but few people are willing to do that.

Some insulation is provided by window treatments. Foam-backed or lined draperies are the best. The problem with draperies is that they must be closed to block the transfer of heat.

By using special insulating glass for windows, you can enjoy the beauty of windows and conserve energy. Insulating glass reduces the transfer of heat between the inside of a home and the outdoors. It helps lower heating and air-conditioning bills.

In summer, heat enters a home through sunlight as well as through warm air. A special type of glass is available that reflects sunlight and helps keep the inside of a home cool. It works like a one-way mirror. Inside, it increases privacy and reduces the glare of the sun. Outside, it reflects its surroundings. In warm climates, this type of glass can be installed permanently, 8-17. In areas with hot summers and cold winters, storm windows with this glass can be installed for the summer and replaced with conventional storm windows for the winter. When windows are treated to control temperature, they become part of a passive solar system.

PPG INDUSTRIES

8-17 Glass that reflects sunlight helps keep the inside of a home cool and conserves energy.

ARTIFICIAL LIGHT

Since natural light is not always available, artificial light is also needed. The two main kinds of artificial light for homes are incandescent and fluorescent.

Incandescent light

Incandescent light is produced when an electric current passes through a fine tungsten filament inside a bulb. The filament is heated by the electricity until it glows and gives off light. See 8-18. The bulbs may vary in shape and size, but they all work the same way. See 8-19.

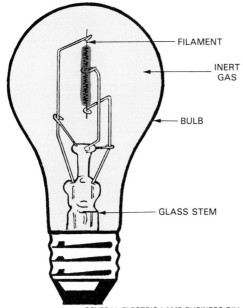

FILAMENT

INERT GAS

BULB

GLASS STEM

GENERAL ELECTRIC LAMP BUSINESS DIV.

8-18 Inside an incandescent light bulb, inert gas surrounds a filament. Electric current heats the filament and makes it glow.

Incandescent light bulbs for household use range from 15 to 300 watts. *Watts* indicate the amount of electrical power used by the bulb. When comparing two incandescent bulbs, the one with the higher wattage will give off more light. The chart in 8-20 lists the recommended wattages for some household activities.

Many kinds of special incandescent bulbs are available. One is the three-way bulb. Sets of filaments can operate separately or together to give off different amounts of light. Some sizes and uses for three-way bulbs are listed in 8-21.

Most incandescent bulbs used in homes have a *frost finish* which covers the entire inside surface of the bulb. The main purpose of the finish is to cut down glare so the light appears smoother and shadows are softened. The frost finish also makes the bulb last longer and keeps the surface of the bulb fairly cool. A lamp shade that accidently touches a bulb with this finish is not likely to be damaged by it.

A clear bulb without a finish produces a great deal of glare. It should be used only in fixtures which hide it completely from view.

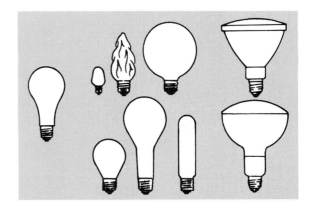

8-19 Incandescent bulbs have many different shapes and sizes. The most common shape is shown at left.

SELECTION GUIDE FOR INCANDESCENT BULBS

ACTIVITY	MINIMUM RECOMMENDED WATTAGE*
Reading, writing, sewing Occasional periods Prolonged periods	150 200 or 300
Grooming Bathroom mirror 1 fixture each side of mirror 1 cup-type fixture over mirror 1 fixture over mirror Bathroom ceiling fixture Vanity table lamps, in pairs (person seated) Dresser lamps, in pairs (person standing)	1—50 or 2—40s 100 150 150 100 each 150 each
Kitchen work Ceiling fixture (2 or more in a large area) Fixture over sink Fixture for eating area (separately from workspace)	150 or 200 150 150
Shopwork Fixture for workbench (2 or more for long bench)	150

*white bulbs preferred

U.S. DEPT. OF AGRICULTURE

8-20 Your activities determine the quantity of light you need.

SIZES AND USES FOR THREE-WAY INCANDESCENT BULBS

	WATTAGE	FINISH	USES
Bulbs with Standard (medium) Three-way Bases	30-70-100	Soft white	Dressing table or dresser lamps. TV or decorative lamps, small pin-ups.
	50-100-150	Soft white	End table or junior floor and swing-arm lamps, study lamps with diffusing bowls.
	50-200-250	Soft white	End table or junior floor and swing-arm lamps, study lamps with diffusing bowls.
Bulb with Large (mogul) Three-way Bases	100-200-300	Soft white	Senior table and floor lamps with mogul sockets.

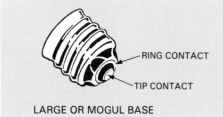

RING CONTACT

TIP CONTACT

LARGE OR MOGUL BASE

STANDARD OR MEDIUM BASE

Lower wattage filaments connect with ring contact. Higher wattage filaments connect with tip contact. The filaments can be used separately or together, depending on the amount of light desired.

GENERAL ELECTRIC LAMP BUSINESS DIV.

8-21 The standard or medium base of three-way bulbs is suited to most household uses.

Some bulbs have silver or aluminum coatings. Two such bulbs are shown in 8-19. They focus the light in a certain direction. Other bulbs are coated with silicone rubber. This coating prevents the glass from shattering if the bulb breaks.

Another variation in incandescent bulbs is color. Colored bulbs can be used to set the mood of a room. Blue lights are sometimes used to make a room seem restful or romantic. On the other hand, a red bulb gives off the kind of light that creates a feeling of excitement. Bulbs with yellow coatings are used to keep insects away. They do not repel insects, but the yellow coating blocks the light rays that attract them.

Fluorescent light

Fluorescent light was introduced around 1950. Mercury vapor is sealed in a long tube. When the vapor is activated by electricity, it produces invisible ultraviolet rays. These rays are converted into visible light rays by a coating of fluorescent material on the inside of the glass tube.

Changing the coating of fluorescent material changes the color of the light. Red, pink, gold, green, and blue can be used for decorative purposes. Several different "whites" are also available. *Cool white* is the most widely used fluorescent light in schools and offices. It is very efficient, blends well with sunlight, and makes colors look good. *Warm white* is the most cost efficient white fluorescent light. But it is not flattering to some colors. *Deluxe cool white* most closely imitates natural daylight. *Home-lite* is the most common fluorescent light for homes and restaurants. It imitates incandescent light closely and has a warm, friendly glow.

Fluorescent tubes may be either straight or curved to form a circle. They are available in various sizes. The lengths of the straight tubes

POPULAR SIZES OF FLUORESCENT TUBES

	WATTAGE	LENGTH	
Straight Tubes	14	15 in.	(38 cm)
	15	18 in.	(46 cm)
	20	24 in.	(61 cm)
	30	36 in.	(91 cm)
	40	48 in.	(122 cm)
	WATTAGE	**OUTSIDE DIAMETER OF CIRCLE**	
Circline	22	8 1/4 in.	(21 cm)
	32	12 in.	(30 cm)
	40	16 in.	(41 cm)

8-22 The wattages for fluorescent tubes depend on the lengths of the straight tubes or the diameters of circuline tubes.

or the diameters of circline ones determine their wattages. See 8-22.

Wattage refers to the amount of current used, not the amount of light produced. Fluorescent light is more efficient than incandescent light. A fluorescent tube produces about four times as much light at an incandescent bulb with the same wattage.

Incandescent and fluorescent lighting differ in other ways. Incandescent bulbs are less expensive to install and replace, but fluorescent tubes last longer and are less expensive to use. Incandescent bulbs light up as soon as current is supplied. With fluorescent tubes, there is a delay between current and light. Incandescent bulbs give off more light for their size than fluorescent bulbs. However, fluorescent tubes produce less heat.

LET LIGHT WORK FOR YOU

If used to its best advantage, light can work for you in many ways. It can be either reflected or absorbed. It can shine directly on a certain spot or lighten a room in general. It can help make your home visually comfortable, safe, and beautiful.

Reflection of light

Light, color, and texture are closely related. Without light, there is no color. In turn, colors reflect and absorb various amounts of light.

Surfaces with rough textures look darker because tiny shadows fall in the places light cannot reach. Together, light, color, and texture greatly affect the appearance of a room.

Light is *reflected* by light colors and smooth, shiny surfaces. Reflected light is the light that bounces off surfaces. Light seems to come from these surfaces as well as from the real source.

Have you ever been blinded by light reflected from a smooth, shiny object? The chrome on a car in front of you sometimes reflects sunlight into your eyes. The more directly the light rays strike the car, the more directly they are reflected into your eyes.

Light reflects off smooth surfaces in your home too. One of the functions of backgrounds in a home is to reflect light. Study 8-23 to learn how much light can be reflected by background areas.

Absorption of light

Rough textures and dark colors *absorb* most of the available light rays. If light is absorbed, it cannot be reflected.

Have you noticed how well you see the light-colored lines in the middle of the highway? The next time you travel, notice the appearance of the road. The light-colored stripes reflect light while the dark-colored road absorbs light.

You can use this same concept in your home. Use light colors in large areas such as backgrounds to make a home appear lighter and brighter. You will have a more comfortable home while using less electricity for light.

BACKGROUND	MINIMUM	MAXIMUM
Ceilings Pale Color Tints	60%	90%
Walls Medium Shades	35%	60%
Floors Carpeting, Tiles, Woods	15%	35%

8-23 This chart suggests minimum and maximum amounts of light that are reflected by background areas.

Measuring light

Amounts of light can be measured with the use of a light meter. The unit of measure is the footcandle. A *footcandle* is the amount of light a standard candle gives at a distance of one foot. (In metric terms, 1 footcandle equals about 10 lux or .1 hectolux.)

Through research, amounts of light needed for various activities under normal conditions have been determined. These are listed in 8-24.

Diffused light

The word diffused means widely spread or scattered. *Diffused light* is light that is scattered over a large area.

Glare is the most troublesome aspect of lighting. Diffused light has no glare. It has a "soft" appearance. The devices used to scatter light are called diffusers. Diffusers are usually made of frosted or translucent glass.

Direct and indirect lighting

Direct lighting is so called because it shines directly toward where it is used, 8-25. Very little is reflected from other surfaces. Direct lighting provides the most light possible to a specific area. If used alone, direct lighting can create a sharp contrast between light and dark. This can cause eye fatigue. To prevent this, do not use direct lighting by itself. If direct lighting is needed for a task, use it in addition to other room lighting.

Indirect lighting is usually directed toward ceilings and walls. The majority of the light is reflected from these surfaces. See 8-26. Indirect lighting provides "soft" light for a large area. It does not provide enough light for detailed work.

Lighting for visual comfort

To have visual comfort in your home, you need two basic types of lighting: general and specific. The type and the amount you need vary for each room.

General lighting provides a low level of light. This type is needed throughout your home. Without it, you cannot see things clearly nor move about safely.

SEEING TASK	AMOUNT OF LIGHT (in footcandles*)
Dining	15
Grooming	
Shaving	50
Applying make-up	50
Handcrafts	
Ordinary seeing tasks	70
Difficult seeing tasks	100
Very difficult seeing tasks	150
Critical seeing tasks	200
Ironing	50
Kitchen Duties	
Food preparation and cleaning that involves difficult seeing tasks	150
Serving and other non-critical tasks	50
Laundry Tasks	
Preparation, sorting, hand wash	50
Washer and dryer areas	30
Reading and Writing	
Handwriting, reproductions, poor copies	70
Books, magazines, and newspapers	30
Reading Piano or Organ Scores	
Advanced (substandard size)	150
Advanced	70
Simple	30
Sewing	
Dark fabrics	200
Medium fabrics	100
Light fabrics	50
Occasional, high contrast	30
Study	70
Table Games	30

*Divide by 10 to determine approximate number of hectolux.

U.S. DEPT. OF AGRICULTURE

8-24 Use this chart to determine the approximate amount of light you need for a certain activity. For instance, when you dine, the amount of light falling onto the table should be about 15 footcandles.

GENERAL ELECTRIC LAMP BUSINESS DIV.

8-25 Direct lighting shines straight ahead. It is not reflected until it has lighted the surface to be used.

The amount of general lighting you need depends on the size, shape, and use of the lighted area. The chart in 8-27 can serve as a guide as you plan the amount of general lighting needed throughout your home.

General lighting does not always supply enough light for visual comfort. In these cases, it can be supplemented by *specific lighting.*

Specific lighting can be called "task" lighting when it is used to help you see well enough to do a certain task. Writing letters, carving wood, and sewing are just a few of the tasks that require specific or "task" lighting. The amount

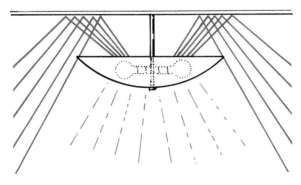

8-26 Indirect lighting is reflected by background surfaces.

of specific lighting you need depends on your activity. Having the right amount will prevent eyestrain. The finer the detail or the faster the action taking place, the more light you need. For instance, playing ping pong requires more light than playing pool.

Reading also requires specific lighting. If you plan to read for quite a while, you need about 70 footcandles (7.0 hectolux) of light over the reading area. A lamp in the correct position with a 200 watt bulb can give this amount of light. See 8-28.

Specific lighting in one part of a room can serve as general lighting for another part. For instance, if you are reading in one corner of a family room, the lamp that you use for specific lighting would add to the general lighting of the entire room.

To get the right amount of good quality light, combine general and specific lighting. Together, they give adequate light without sharp contrast.

Lighting for safety

Darkness can be unsafe. To guard against accidents, plan lighting where it will work best for you. If you can answer "yes" to the following questions, you will know your lighting is planned for safety. Can you:

- Light your way as you go from room to room?
- Switch lights on or off from each doorway?
- Turn on stairway lighting as you go up or down?
- Light entrances as you enter?
- Control garage or carport lighting from the house?
- Control outside lighting from inside the house?

Another aspect of lighting for safety concerns safe wiring. To assure safety, the wiring used for lighting should meet certain standards which are set by various groups. The National Electrical Code is a standard with which all wiring should comply. There are often local requirements as well. When you purchase anything with an electrical part, look for the Underwriters Laboratories seal of approval,

MINIMUM GENERAL LIGHTING NEEDED FOR VARIOUS ROOM TYPES AND SIZES

ROOM TYPE	FIXTURES	STRUCTURAL	RECESSED	
	Ceiling-Mounted or Suspended	Valance/Cornice Wall Bracket*	Directional Flood Type**	Nondirectional—Square or Rectangular Boxes
LIVING				
Areas	(light widely distributed)			(Recreation or Family Rooms)
Living Room, Family, Bedroom				
Small (under 150 sq. ft.)	3 to 5-socket fixture, total 150-200 watts	8-12 ft.	Four 50 watt units	Four 75 watt incandescent Two 40 watt fluorescent
Average (185-250 sq. ft.)	4 to 6-socket fixture, total 200-300 watts	16-20 ft.	Five to Eight 75 watt or 150 watt units	††Four 100 watt incandescent Three 40 watt or four 30 watt fluorescent
Large (over 250 sq. ft.)	1 watt per sq. ft. and 1 fixture per 125 sq. ft.	1 foot/15 sq. ft.	One 75 watt unit for each 30 to 40 sq. ft.	Incandescent: ††One 100 watt or 150 watt per 40-50 sq. ft. Fluorescent: Two 40 watt or three 30 watt or six 20 watt per 100 sq. ft.
SERVICE				
Kitchen, Laundry, Workshop				
Small (under 75 sq. ft.)	150 watt incandescent or total 60 watt fluorescent	Use single row of fluorescents on top of open-to-ceiling cabinets—or in soffit extended 8-12 in. beyond cabinets	Not suitable for general lighting in these areas	††Two 150 watt incandescent or two 40 watt fluorescent
Average (75-120 sq. ft.)	Incandescent: 150-200 watt or Fluorescent total 60-80 watt	or		††Four 100 watt incandescent or two 40 watt fluorescent
Large (over 120 sq. ft.)	Incandescent: 2 watts per sq. ft. or Fluorescent: 3/4 to 1 watt per sq. ft.	5 to 6 watts/sq. ft. in fluorescent for luminous ceiling		Incandescent: ††One 100 watt per 30 sq. ft. or ††one 150 watt per 40 sq. ft. Fluorescent: Two 40 watt or three 30 watt or six 20 watt per 60 sq. ft.

*Or use equal length of wall lighting with recessed wall washers or floodlights.
**Should not be located above heads of seated persons; may be 18 in. or more in any direction from this point.

††Minimum Size: 10 in., 12 in. or 14 in. preferable.

GENERAL ELECTRIC LAMP BUSINESS DIV.

8-27 You need different amounts of light for rooms with different functions and sizes.

8-29. It tells you that the appliance was manufactured according to safety standards. However, it does not assure you that the parts will continue to be safe. You have the responsibility of using the appliance safely and watching for any possible dangers. If instructions for the use and care of an appliance are available, read them and follow them. Know what to expect of appliances and how to use them.

Electrical circuits should not be overloaded. Do not plug too many appliances into one socket. The excess load could blow a fuse and you would be without electric power in all or part of your home. Even worse, a fire could start.

Lighting for beauty

While all light can be decorative, some lighting is used for beauty alone. Soft light can create a quiet, restful mood, 8-30. Sharper light can be used to focus on the point of emphasis in a room such as an art object. When lighting is used in this way, it is called *accent lighting*.

AGRICULTURAL RESEARCH SERVICE

8-28 Lamp shades above eye level should be farther behind you, but closer to your side, then lamp shades at eye level.

8-29 The Underwriters Laboratories seal of approval assures you that an appliance was made according to safety guidelines.

ARMSTRONG WORLD INDUSTRIES, INC.

8-30 Soft lighting, such as candlelight, can be used to give a room a quiet, elegant mood.

Decorative lighting can be used outside as well as inside a home, 8-31. Huge yard lights are often used in rural settings, while smaller ones are used in urban areas. Lights near entrances are also common. Patios can be lighted for night use. In such areas, you will want the light to be attractive. Harsh and glaring light should be avoided. With the right choices, you can have pleasant, glowing light.

STRUCTURAL AND NONSTRUCTURAL LIGHTING

When lighting is a part of the built-in design of a home, it is called *structural lighting*. It is either included in the original blueprint or added during a remodeling project. If you buy a house that is already built or if you rent a home, the decisions about structural lighting will have been made for you.

Types of structural lighting are pictured in 8-32. *Valance lighting* is used over windows. Fluorescent light is directed upward and downward, giving both direct and indirect lighting. Valance lighting restores the daytime lighting balance to a room.

Wall bracket lighting is just like valance lighting except that is used on plain walls instead of over windows. Light is directed both upward and downward. It can be used for general or accent lighting.

Cornice lighting begins at the ceiling. All the light shines downward, giving direct light only. It can be used on almost any wall for a variety of effects.

Cove lighting begins near the ceiling. All the light is directed upward, giving indirect lighting only. It is good general lighting, but it must be supplemented with specific lighting. Cove lighting gives a room a feeling of height.

Recessed downlights are installed in ceilings. When several are used together, they supply

8-31 Lighting gives this home a dramatic appearance.

COVE LIGHTING

RECESSED DOWNLIGHT/TRACK LIGHT

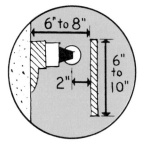

VALANCE LIGHTING

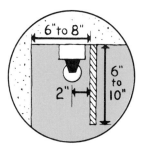

CORNICE LIGHTING

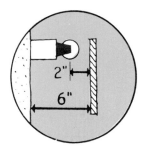

WALL BRACKET LIGHTING

SOFFIT LIGHTING

LUMINOUS CEILING

8-32 Structural lighting can create special effects in a room. It must be planned while the dwelling is being built or remodeled.

good general lighting. A few of them can be used for accent lighting. The typical "scalloped" pattern of light and shadow gives a dramatic look.

Surface-mounted downlights are just like recessed downlights except that the housing (can or cylinder) is in plain view below the ceiling.

Wall washers are also installed in the ceiling. They have a contoured inner reflector that directs nearly uniform light on a wall from ceiling to floor. It gives a smooth look to walls.

Soffit lighting may be built into a ceiling or attached to it. Soffit lighting is used where a large amount of light is needed.

Luminous ceilings are made of panels that cover recessed lights. They make a room feel spacious.

Track lighting consists of several fixtures mounted on a track. The fixtures can be arranged in varying positions to create different effects.

Light fixtures

The wiring for light fixtures is a part of the dwelling's structure, but the fixtures are not. You may have a chance to choose fixtures for a home even if it is not custom built. You can select a style in harmony with other aspects of the room's design. Some styles from which you can choose are pictured in 8-33.

When choosing fixtures, consider these points:
- Diffused light gives more visual comfort than exposed bulbs which can produce glare.
- Fixtures whose positions can be changed can be used in more than one way. Some fixtures may be raised or lowered. Others swing or swivel for a variety of effects.
- Fixtures that provide for changing the quantity of light (as three-way bulbs) have more uses.

Lamps

Movable lamps are the oldest type of lighting for homes. Since they can be moved, changed, and replaced more easily than any other form of lighting, you can make many choices about them.

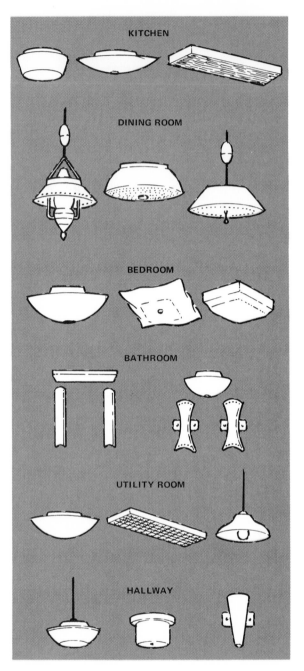

8-33 Fixtures for different rooms have many different forms.

When you choose a lamp, you may want it for decorative purposes only. Or you may need good light for safety or visual comfort. You can find a lamp to fill any of these needs.

8-34 Wall bracket lighting and lamps provide artificial light for this room. A large window area provides natural light during the daytime.

In choosing lamps, the following points can be useful:
- A sturdy or heavy base prevents tipping.
- A diffusing bowl prevents glare.
- A harp makes it possible to change the height of the lamp shade. (A harp is a metal hoop or arch that supports a shade.)
- The colors and textures of lamps and their shades should harmonize.
- Light-colored translucent shades give off the most light.
- Lamps that can be adjusted are the most practical. Some can be raised and lowered, such as swag lamps. Some have swinging arms, and some can use three-way bulbs.

Lamps, light fixtures, structural lighting, and natural light can be combined in many different ways, 8-34. The goal is always to achieve good lighting throughout the dwelling. Study 8-35 to gain a better understanding of the choices you can make about lighting.

STRUCTURAL AND NONSTRUCTURAL LIGHTING

DECISIONS	RANGE OF AVAILABLE CHOICES		
Location	Ceiling fixtures Wall fixtures Movable lamps		
Form	Surface mounted Suspended Recessed Bracket Valance Cornice Cove		
	Incandescent	or	Fluorescent
	General	or	Specific
	Direct	or	Indirect
Acquisition Process and cost	Initial Operating Maintenance Replacing		

8-35 You have many decisions to make when choosing lighting for a home.

to Know

absorbed light . . . accent lighting . . .
artificial light . . . blinds . . . cafes . . .
curtains . . . diffused light . . . direct lighting . . .
draw draperies . . . fluorescent light . . .
footcandle . . . general lighting . . . hectolux . . .
incandescent light . . . indirect lighting . . .
light fixtures . . . natural light . . .
nonstructural lighting . . . opaque . . .
reflected light . . . shades . . . shutters . . .
specific lighting . . . structural lighting . . .
task lighting . . . translucent . . . watts

to Review

Write your answers on a separate sheet of paper.
1. Name three factors that affect the availability of natural light.
2. Which light gives the coolest feeling?
   a. Northern light.
   b. Eastern light.
   c. Southern light.
   d. Western light.
3. List three functions of a window.
4. The bottom edge of curtains, cafes, and draw draperies should fall at one of three places; the sill, the floor, or the _____.
5. Describe two ways to reduce the amount of heat transfer through windows.
6. Compare incandescent and fluorescent light in terms of installation cost and operating cost.
7. List three ways light can work for you in your home. Give an example of each.
8. Match the following:
___ a. Unit of measure for amounts of light.
___ b. Unit of measure for current used.
___ c. Part of incandescent bulb.
___ d. Gives off ultraviolet rays when activated by electricity.
   1. Bulb.
   2. Rough, dull surface.
   3. Diffuser.
   4. Tungsten filament.
   5. Footcandle or lux.
   6. Mercury vapor.
   7. Watt.

to Do

1. Given a floor plan, list activities which would take place in each room. Then indicate the location, form, and amount of light needed in each room.
2. To study glare, do the following projects under a bright light. Cut a 3 in. (7.6 cm) circle from a piece of dark, mat-finished cardboard. Place it on a larger piece of white, reflective cardboard. Look at the dark circle for a while and notice how tired your eyes become. Then write several words on the white cardboard. Notice how difficult it is to read the words. Finally, place circles of light and dark cardboard on a piece of kitchen aluminum wrap. Observe that it is almost impossible to see their outlines.
3. Compare light from several different sources: a frosted bulb, colored bulbs, a cool white fluorescent tube and a warm white fluorescent tube. Place lights near each other. Compare each light with sunlight. Turn on all lights and observe the different colors of light. Shine all lights on a white surface and note the differences. Then shine them all on a colored surface and note the differences.
4. Working in small groups, examine the illustrations throughout this book that show lighting. Make a list of the different types you find and give reasons you think they were used.
5. Find out the code for electrical wiring in your locality. Who is responsible for inspection?
6. Look for the Underwriters' Laboratories seal of approval on lamps and electrical appliances in your classroom and home.
7. Find and mount pictures of various window treatments on a bulletin board.
8. Make a bulletin board entitled, "Types of structural lighting." For each type of lighting, include the following:
   a. Picture or drawing of the light fixture.
   b. Picture or drawing of the fixture as it is used within a room.
   c. Description of the type of lighting provided by the fixture.
   d. Suggestions for locations where the fixture would be most suitable.

9

Choosing home furnishings

After studying this chapter, you will be able to:
- List points to check in determining the quality of furniture.
- Describe various furniture styles.

The type of housing you have will affect the number of decisions you must make about how it is furnished. For instance, if you choose furnished housing, you will have fewer decisions to make. Most furnished units are rented apartments or multifamily dwellings. Choosing unfurnished housing, on the other hand, will require you to make more decisions. Most single-family houses are rented or sold unfurnished.

Whatever type of housing you have, you will probably furnish at least part of it yourself. You will have some decisions to make about furnishings.

CHOOSING FURNITURE

If you are like most people, you cannot afford to buy all of the furniture you would like at one time. You must decide what to get first.

Getting started

You begin by listing your needs and knowing how much you can afford to spend. You will consider location, form, and acquisition, the three major areas of housing decisions. (Refer to Chapter 3 if you want to review decision-making.)

This list of ideas will help you get started.

1. Buy the things you need most. Select basic pieces for sleeping, eating, seating, and storage.
2. Select furniture that can be used for more than one purpose. A sofa bed can be used for sitting and for sleeping. A bench can serve as either a seat or a coffee table. Some dining chairs look good in living rooms too.
3. Plan for the future. Choose pieces that you can recycle. For instance, you might choose a durable table and chair set. It can be used inside until you have more money to spend. Then you can use it on a patio or porch and replace it with nicer furniture.
4. Use makeshift furniture from garage sales, secondhand stores, and relatives until you decide which styles you really like and until you can afford furniture of good quality. When you are ready, buy well-made furniture. It is worth the higher price because it lasts longer.
5. Check pieces of furniture carefully before you buy. Do all movable parts operate? Are the joints tight and well-made? Is the finish smooth and durable? Is it well-braced at points of stress?
6. Plan around the larger pieces of furniture. Small items like lamps should be chosen to go with sofas and other large pieces.
7. Choose pieces of furniture that fit your life-style. Even beautiful pieces of furniture are of little value if you do not use them.
8. If your budget is tight, see Chapter 11 for bargain ideas.

Consider the consequences

Suppose you made a spur-of-the-moment decision and bought a king-size water bed. What would the consequences be? If you have never slept on one, you might find it uncomfortable. Because it is so large, it might take up most of the floor space in the room. You may not have enough space for other activities such as dressing, studying, and working on hobbies. You may not have enough space to add other furnishings such as a dresser, a desk, or a comfortable chair. Can you see that one choice influences other choices as you furnish a room or house?

Your decisions should be made to satisfy you and the members of your living unit. They should not be made for the satisfaction of friends or neighbors since they only visit you. Those living in the dwelling need satisfaction from its furnishings more than anyone else.

FURNITURE CONSTRUCTION

Wood, metal, plastic, glass, and fabric are all used in the construction of furniture. Sometimes a combination of materials is used. The materials you choose depend on the desires of your living unit, the mood of the room, and the amount of money you can afford to spend.

Wood

Each kind of wood has its own characteristics. However, the part of the tree from which the piece of wood comes adds certain characteristics. See 9-1.

A *grain* or pattern is formed as a tree grows. The stump or base of the tree has a beautiful, irregular grain caused by the twisted and irregular growth of the tree's roots. Crotchwood has a special grain caused by branches growing out from the trunk of a tree. Lumber is cut to show off this grain. Trees that have been damaged and healed have a unique and highly prized grain called burl.

The way the trunk of the tree is cut into pieces can affect the appearance of wood grain. Quartered, rotary, and flat cut methods each give a different look to the same kind of wood.

Hardwood and softwood. Wood for furniture can be either hardwood or softwood. Hardwood comes from deciduous trees (trees that lose their leaves). The most popular hardwoods used for quality furniture include

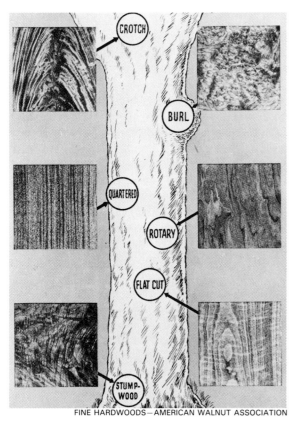

FINE HARDWOODS—AMERICAN WALNUT ASSOCIATION

9-1 Wood grain varies according to the part of the tree from which the lumber comes and the way that it is cut.

THOMASVILLE FURNITURE INDUSTRIES, INC.

9-2 Cherry wood was used to make this furniture because of its beauty and strength.

walnut, mahogany, pecan, cherry, maple, and oak. See 9-2. Hardwood does not dent easily. It is stronger than softwood, but it costs more.

Softwood comes from evergreen trees. It does not have the beautiful grain of hardwood, and it dents easily. Cedar, redwood, pine, fir, and spruce are the most common softwoods used for furniture.

Furniture can be made of all hardwood, all softwood, or a combination of the two.

Solid wood and bonded wood. Solid wood furniture construction means that all of the exposed parts are made of whole pieces of wood. Such furniture is usually expensive, especially if it is made of hardwood. The disadvantage of solid wood is that it has a tendency to warp, swell, and crack.

Veneered wood or plywood furniture is more

common than solid wood furniture today. The wood is a "sandwich" of three, five, or seven thin layers of wood. Layers are bonded to each other, to a solid wood core, or to a pressed wood core, 9-3. The outside layers are veneers of fine wood. Rare woods and beautiful grains can be used. Veneering makes fine woods available at a moderate cost. It also permits the use of fragile woods since the inside layers add strength. Most of the furniture made since 1900 is at least partly veneered.

Other bonded woods are *pressed woods*. They are made of shavings, veneer scraps, chips, and other small pieces of wood. These types of wood are less expensive than solid or veneered wood. Called particle board, waferboard, or composition plywood, they are often used on parts of furniture that do not show.

Choosing home furnishings 191

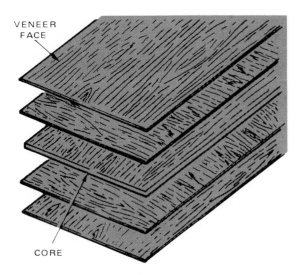

VENEER
FACE

CORE

9-3 In plywood, the grains of alternate veneers run at right angles. This adds strength to the plywood.

Or they may be covered with a more expensive wood or with a plastic laminate.

Wood joints. Wood pieces can be fastened together in many different ways. The most common wood joints are pictured in 9-4.

Gluing is used on all joints for added strength. Today, some glues are stronger than wood!

A *mortise and tenon* joint is one of the strongest joints used for furniture. The glued tenon fits tightly into the "hole" or mortise. No nails or screws are used. Common uses are for chairs and headboards where stretchers are joined to leg posts or where top rails are joined to back posts.

Double dowel joints are very common and very strong. Glued wooden dowels fit into drilled holes in both pieces of wood.

Corner blocks support and reinforce the furniture frame. They are used in the construction of chairs and tables. They keep one side from pulling away from the other.

Dovetail joints are used in fastening two pieces of wood that meet at right angles. They are always found in drawers of good quality furniture.

Tongue and groove joints are invisible if they are made skillfully. They are used where several boards are to be joined lengthwise as for table tops.

Butt joints are the weakest of the joints. One board is simply glued or nailed flush to another board.

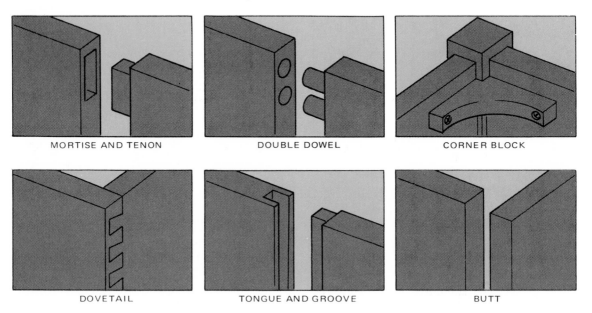

MORTISE AND TENON   DOUBLE DOWEL   CORNER BLOCK

DOVETAIL   TONGUE AND GROOVE   BUTT

9-4 Joints are an important factor in determining the quality of pieces of furniture.

Finishing wood furniture. Wood furniture may be left unfinished or given a finish for added protection or beauty.

In unfinished furniture, the wood is left as it was when the furniture was constructed. There is no sealer, wax, nor varnish on the surface. You are expected to finish it. Much of the unfinished furniture comes unassembled (not put together). The initial cost of unfinished furniture is low. But before you buy, be sure to consider the cost of finishing it yourself. It will cost you money, time, and effort.

Finished furniture has been treated in some way to protect and/or improve the wood surfaces. Some finishes are plastics which resist moisture, stains, and burning. Some are decorative and bring out the natural beauty of the wood. Others, such as paint, are sometimes used to hide a surface that is not attractive.

When you buy wood furniture, read the labels carefully. They will tell you what finishes have been applied, the purpose of the finishes, and the care they should receive. Be sure you understand all the terms on the labels; the meanings can be confusing. For instance, the term "genuine walnut" on a label means that actual walnut wood was used as the face veneer. However, the term "walnut finish" means only that the wood has been finished to look like walnut.

Other points to check before buying wood furniture are listed in 9-5.

Plastic, metal, and glass furniture

Plastic furniture is usually less expensive than wood. It is lightweight, sturdy, easy to clean, and often brightly colored. Generally, it looks best in contemporary settings as the one in 9-6.

When you choose plastic furniture, pay attention to the following:
• Is the piece strong and durable?
• Are the edges smooth and the surfaces without flaws?
• Are color and gloss uniform?
• Are the parts that reinforce the piece hidden unless they are part of the design?

If plastic is used, it should not be made to imitate other materials. The design should take advantage of the special properties of plastic.

CHECKLIST WHEN SHOPPING FOR WOOD FURNITURE

____ Do doors shut tightly without sticking?

____ Have corner blocks been used for reinforcement?

____ Are dust panels provided between drawers?

____ Do drawers slide easily?

____ Are legs attached with mortise and tenon or dowel joints?

____ Do legs stand squarely upon the floor?

____ Have insides of drawers, backs of chests, and undersides of tables and chairs been sanded and finished?

____ Are surfaces smooth?

____ Are surfaces solid, veneered, or laminated?

____ Has a protective plastic coating been used on surfaces that will receive hard wear?

____ Will the furniture piece fulfill your use, style, color and size requirements?

____ Is the furniture within your budget?

SEARS CONSUMER INFORMATION SERVICES

9-5 You may find this checklist useful when choosing wood furniture.

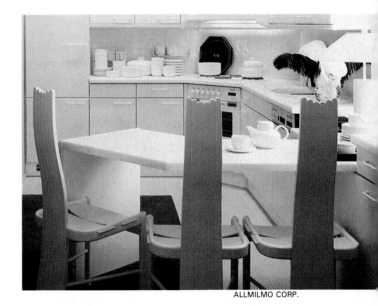

ALLMILMO CORP.

9-6 Molded plastic gives this dining set a clean, contemporary look.

Metal is popular for both indoor and outdoor furniture. Wrought iron, steel, aluminum, and chrome are all used for different furnishings. Metal is often combined with other materials such as wood, fabric, or glass. See 9-7.

These guidelines will help you choose furniture of metal:
- Is the metal or metallic finish rustproof?
- Is the surface smooth?
- Are sharp edges coated or covered?

Glass is usually combined with metal or wood, 9-8. It is popular for tabletops and doors of china cabinets or other display cabinets.

When glass is a part of furniture that you are choosing, check for the following:
- Is the glass tempered for safety and durability?
- Is the furniture designed to hold the glass firmly in place?
- Are glass surfaces free of bubbles, scratches, and other defects?

Upholstered furniture

Chairs, sofas, and other pieces of padded furniture are called upholstered furniture. See

9-7 Brass is popular for furniture pieces such as this coffee table and matching end table.

9-8 Tinted glass is combined with wood in this coffee table.

9-9. The greater part, and sometimes all, of the exposed surface is covered with fabric. This outer covering hides the inner construction details. Because these details are hidden, choosing good-quality upholstered furniture can be difficult. Shop in stores you can trust, and buy brand names you recognize. Read all labels attached to the piece. If you have questions, talk with a knowledgeable salesperson. The following information will give you some background knowledge so you will know what to look for yourself and what questions you should ask.

Upholstery fabrics. Fabric is an important part of upholstered furniture. It is also a clue to the overall quality of a piece. Furniture of good quality will have durable and well-tailored upholstery fabric.

The three classes of fabrics are:
1. Woven.
2. Nonwoven.
3. Knitted.

Woven fabrics. Most upholstery fabrics are woven. Woven fabrics are made by crossing two sets of yarns (warp yarns in the lengthwise direction and filling yarns in the crosswise direction).

Woven fabrics are made of only three basic weaves. All other weaves are variations of these three. The basic weaves are:

1. Plain weave, 9-10.
2. Twill weave, 9-11.
3. Satin weave, 9-12.

They vary according to the way the yarns are crossed or interlaced. Two common variations of the basic weaves are shown in 9-13 and 9-14.

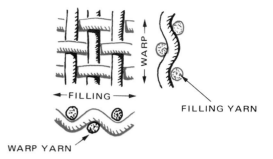

9-10 In the plain weave, each filling yarn passes over, then under, each warp yarn.

9-9 Upholstered furniture may be completely covered with fabric as in this couch. Or some wood may be exposed as in the chair.

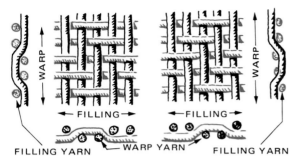

9-11 Each warp or filling yarn passes over two or more yarns to form the twill weave. The interlacings progress by one to either the right or left to create a pattern of diagonal lines.

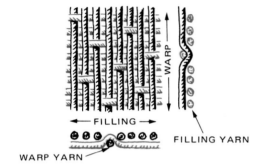

9-12 One yarn crosses over several yarns and then under one yarn to form the satin weave. The interlacings progress by two to either the right or left. A smooth surface results.

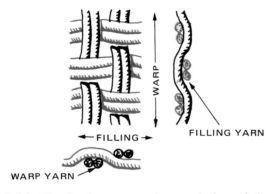

9-13 The basket weave is a variation of the plain weave. Two or more filling yarns are interlaced with two or more warp yarns.

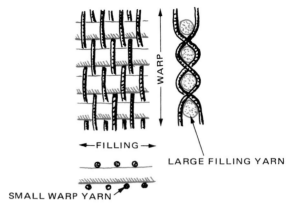

9-14 The rib weave is a variation of the plain weave. The warp and filling yarns are of different sizes.

Pile weaves are variations of the basic weaves. They have yarn loops or cut yarns standing away from the base of the fabric. In 9-15, you can compare a plain weave, loop-pile weave, and a cut-pile weave.

Frieze is a heavy, coarse, pile fabric used mainly for upholstery. Velvet, velveteen, corduroy, and terry cloth are other pile-weave fabrics.

Another special weave that is sometimes used for upholstery fabrics is the Jacquard weave. Designs are woven into the fabric with different colors of yarn. Each warp yarn is individually controlled. This allows beautiful, detailed designs to be made. Parts of the design are often emphasized by raised areas.

Upholstery fabrics of good quality are durable and easy to clean as well as beautiful. When choosing upholstery fabrics, consider the following points:
• Tight, close weaves are of better quality than loose weaves.
• Heavyweight fabrics are more durable than medium-weight fabrics.
• Long floats (as in the satin weave) tend to snag.
• Fabrics in which the warp and filling yarns are equal in number and in size are durable.
• Stain-resistant finishes make woven fabrics easier to clean.
Nonwoven fabrics. Leather and vinyl are the

two most common nonwoven fabrics used for upholstery.

Natural leather is strong and durable. With special finishes, it resists stains, fading, and cracking. The disadvantage of leather is its high cost.

Vinyl is durable, easy to clean, and low in cost. Vinyl fabric for upholstery should be medium-weight or heavyweight. It is usually backed with a knit fabric to give it more stability and strength.

Knitted fabrics. Knitted fabrics are made of interlooping yarns. The closeness and size of the loops may vary as well as the way the loops are joined. See 9-16.

Though knitted fabrics are increasing in use as upholstery material, they are not as popular as woven fabrics. They lack the stability and body needed for durable upholstery. Their major use is for backing other fabrics.

Fabric design. Designs or patterns in fabrics may be structural or applied. *Structural* designs are made by varying the yarns as the fabric is

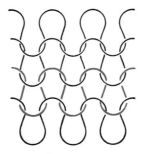
WEFT STITCH

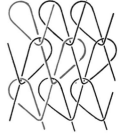
WARP STITCH

9-16 Knitted fabrics vary according to yarn size, yarn texture, and loop construction. The weft stitch allows more stretch than the warp switch.

either woven or knitted. The size, texture, and placement of the yarns all affect the final pattern.

Applied designs offer even more variety to fabrics. Any pattern can be printed onto a fabric, and dyes can be used to achieve any color.

Whether it is structural or applied, the fabric design you choose should fit into the overall design plan for the room. Consider the size and the style of the piece of furniture, the other colors and patterns used in the room, and the general mood of the room.

Fiber facts. Many kinds of fibers are used to make fabrics. A few—cotton, flax (or linen), wool, and silk—are *natural* fibers. They come from plants and animals. Other fibers are *manufactured* from chemicals.

Each fiber has its own characteristics. The characteristics have a great influence on the quality and performance of the fabric. Before you buy upholstered furniture, find out what fibers are used in the fabric. Some are more durable than others, so they will look nicer for a longer time. Here are some guidelines to follow:

- Nylon is very strong and very resistant to abrasion (rubbing action).
- Polyester and olefin are strong and resistant to abrasion.
- Wool, acrylic, flax, and cotton are fairly strong and fairly resistant to abrasion.

PLAIN WEAVE

LOOP-PILE WEAVE

CUT-PILE WEAVE

9-15 A pile-weave fabric has additional yarn covering its surface.

- Rayon and acetate are weak and have poor resistance to abrasion.

By altering manufacturing processes, manufactured fibers can be made stronger. The performance of fabrics can be improved by using a combination of types of fibers or by adding special finishes. Changes like these are mentioned on labels of upholstered furniture. Always read the labels before you buy.

Frames, springs, and cushions. Frames of upholstered furniture are made of wood or metal. Many of the points you would check when buying wood or metal furniture also apply to the frames of upholstered furniture.

Springs are a part of the inner construction. The type and number of springs help determine the quality. There are two types of springs: *coil* and *flat*. See 9-17. Coil springs are used in heavier furniture. You can "sink into" furniture with coil springs. Lightweight pieces of furniture with sleek lines usually have flat or zigzag springs. They offer firm comfort at lower cost.

Cushions are often made of urethane foam or foam rubber. These materials are durable, lightweight, and resilient. They can be molded into any shape, and they come in many sizes and degrees of firmness.

Covered or pocketed coils, as shown in 9-18, are sometimes used in cushions. They are usually covered with a thin layer of foam rubber and a layer of fabric. Other cushions are filled with down and feathers. These are very comfortable, but not as durable as foam.

The cutaway illustration in 9-19 shows the inner construction of a sofa. You can see how different materials are combined to provide seating comfort.

Comfort is one of the most important factors to consider when choosing upholstered furniture. Regardless of the quality, a sofa that does not feel comfortable is a poor buy. Sit in it. Check the height and depth of the seat. Check the height of the back and arms. Be sure it fits your body's proportions.

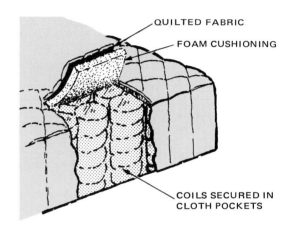

9-18 Covered or pocketed coils provide great seating comfort.

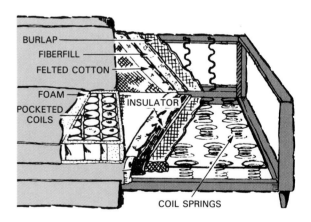

9-19 Double-cone coil springs are used in the seat of this sofa, and flat springs are used for back support. Pocketed coils, foam, and layers of fibers provide maximum seating comfort.

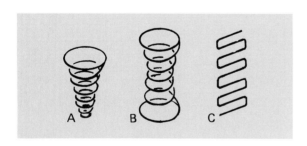

9-17 Single-cone springs (A) are used in medium-priced furniture. Double-cone springs (B) are more comfortable. Flat, zigzag springs (C) are used when a minimum of bulk is desired.

198

9-20 Check these points before you buy pieces of upholstered furniture.

SPIEGEL, INC.

9-21 Quality is more important in sleep furniture than in most other types of furniture. Buy sleep furniture in a store that you can trust.

Some points to consider when shopping for upholstered furniture are listed in 9-20.

Sleep furniture

Comfort is most important when choosing sleep furniture. Before you buy a bed, be sure to lie on it. That is the only way to see if it is comfortable for you.

About one-third of your life is spent sleeping, so you should choose the best sleeping furniture you can afford. Since you cannot see the inside construction of a bed, you need to choose a reliable dealer, 9-21.

Most beds have a mattress, springs, and a frame as shown in 9-22. Headboards and footboards may or may not be added.

Mattresses. The most popular type of mattress is the *innerspring* mattress. It is filled with a series of coil springs. The springs vary in number, size, placement, gauge (thickness of wire), and whether or not they are individually pocketed. This type of mattress also varies in

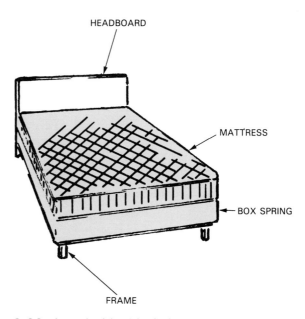

9-22 A typical bed includes a mattress, springs, and a frame. Headboards and footboards are optional.

the amount of padding that covers the springs. These factors determine the firmness and comfort of the mattress. Manufacturers say that a good quality innerspring mattress should have these features:

1. At least 300 heavy coils firmly anchored.
2. Good padding and insulation placed over and between coils.
3. A tightly woven cover with a nonsag border.

Foam mattresses are also popular. They are made of latex or polyurethane foam. The foam is cut or molded to shape and is usually covered with a ticking (a tightly woven cotton cloth) like other types of mattresses. Foam mattresses are lighter in weight and lower in cost than innerspring mattresses.

Foam mattresses are often preferred by people who suffer from allergies. They vary in thickness, firmness, and quality. A mattress of good quality will be about 6 in. (15 cm) thick. It will have some holes or cores in it. The greater the number of cores, the softer the mattress will be.

Mattresses can be filled with almost anything—including water. Water beds conform exactly to body curves and thus provide good, firm support. However, some people find them uncomfortable because the water moves whenever they shift position.

Water beds consist of a heavy-duty plastic water bag, a frame, and a watertight liner between the bed and frame to protect against leaks. They also have a heating device to warm the water.

Water beds are heavy when they are filled. A standard-size bed weighs about 1600 lb. (720 kg). Buildings must have strong foundations to support them. Many leases include a phrase that prohibits water beds in rented dwellings.

Springs. Most beds have springs to support the mattress. Bed springs have three basic forms: *box, coil,* and *flat.* See 9-23.

The most expensive, and the most desirable for most people, are box springs. In these, the coils are attached to a base. The coils are then padded and covered. The coils may vary in number, size, placement, and gauge.

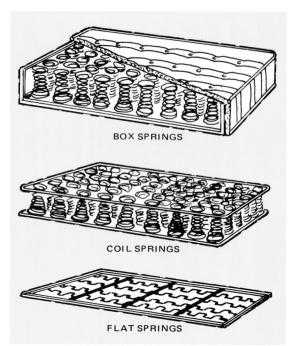

BOX SPRINGS

COIL SPRINGS

FLAT SPRINGS

9-23 Box springs are coil springs that are padded and covered. Coil springs are anchored to a frame and to each other. Flat springs are likely to sag.

When the spiral-shaped springs are without padding and covering, they are called coil springs. In quality and cost, coil springs are between box springs and flat springs.

Flat springs are the least costly. They are lightweight and take up a minimum of space.

Regardless of the type of springs or mattress you choose, they should be bought in matching sets. A common combination is an innerspring mattress and box springs. When they are purchased as a set, the coils in the mattress line up with the coils in the box springs. This makes the bed much more comfortable.

Frames. In some cases, springs (especially flat springs) are built into a bed frame. More often, a sleep set is placed on a simple metal frame. Headboards and footboards can be attached to the frame if desired.

Sleeper sofas

If you need sleep furniture for an occasional guest, you might like to consider a sleeper sofa.

A sofa which converts to a bed can be used in any room you choose. Sofas, like beds, come in several sizes. You can choose them to fit the space you have in a room.

CONSUMER PROTECTION

Buying furniture is a big investment. To help protect your investment, the government has agencies that work for consumers. The Federal Trade Commission (FTC) and the Consumer Product Safety Commission (CPSC) are two such agencies. Federal laws also protect you. The Flammable Fabrics Act prohibits the sale of highly flammable fabrics for apparel and home furnishings. The Textile Fiber Products Identification Act requires that the generic names of fibers appear on labels of all textile products (such as upholstery, carpets, and draperies).

There is also voluntary control of the quality of materials and construction methods used for furniture. Some producers of fibers and manufacturers of fabrics set their own high levels of performance. Some furniture companies have also set high standards for themselves. These companies guarantee the durability and performance of their products after you buy them. Information about superior-quality materials and guarantees is given on the labels of furniture. It is your responsiblity as a smart consumer to read the labels on anything you buy so you will know what to expect from the product.

CHOOSING FURNITURE STYLES

Choosing furniture styles is a matter of taste or personal preference. Your decisions cannot be called "right" or "wrong" by anyone else. However, after studying the various styles, you will have a better idea of which styles you like and how to use each style to its best advantage.

The *style* of furniture refers to design only. It has nothing to do with cost or quality of construction. Any style, from Queen Anne to contemporary, can be made of good or poor materials by good or poor construction methods.

Traditional furniture styles

Furniture styles that were developed in the past are called *traditional* or *period* furniture styles. Each one comes from a different period in history. You can get an idea of the time reference for some traditional furniture styles by looking at 9-24.

Traditional styles from France. While *Louis XIII* was King of France, furniture styles were grand and formal. Rich inlays, carvings, and classical motifs were typical.

Louis XIV, the Sun King, built the magnificent Versailles palace. Its furnishings were extravagent with heavy ornamentation and gold overlays.

During the reign of *Louis XV,* furniture styles became more delicate with smaller proportions. Curved lines and soft colors were dominant.

Just before the French Revolution, *Louis XVI* and Marie Antoinette rulled France. Simple, straight lines and classic motifs such as fluted columns were popular in furniture.

While Napoleon ruled France, he dominated everything—even furniture styles. He made the dignified style called *Empire* popular. The furniture was ornamented with his "N" and military symbols. Egyptian and Roman motifs were also used.

The *Art Nouveau* furniture style was a rebellion against the excessive ornamentation of other styles of the time. The graceful lines of Art Nouveau furniture were based on flower forms.

Traditional styles from England. Jacobean furniture became popular during the reign of James I. The massive pieces of furniture were made of oak wood and often had twisted legs.

Queen Anne furniture is graceful and comfortable. Cabriole legs and carved fans and shells are characteristic of this style. See 9-25.

Several furniture styles became popular during the reigns of the three King Georges. Sometimes these styles are grouped together under the label *Georgian*. See 9-26. At other times, they are labeled according to their designers—Thomas Chippendale, the Adam Brothers, George Hepplewhite, and Thomas Sheraton.

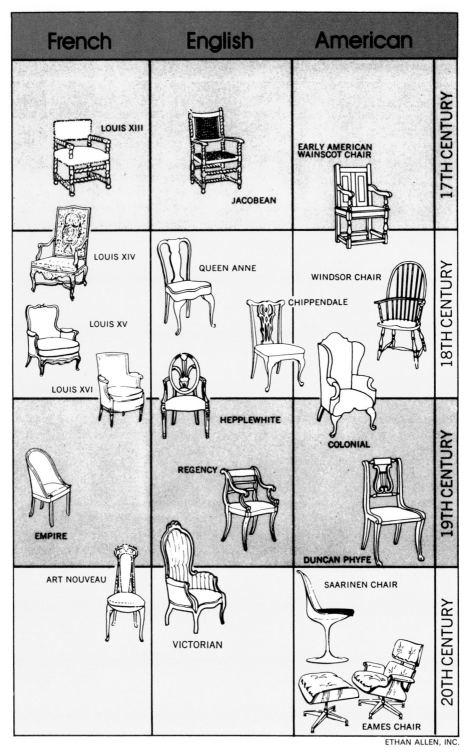

French	English	American	
LOUIS XIII	JACOBEAN	EARLY AMERICAN WAINSCOT CHAIR	17TH CENTURY
LOUIS XIV · LOUIS XV · LOUIS XVI	QUEEN ANNE · CHIPPENDALE · HEPPLEWHITE	WINDSOR CHAIR · COLONIAL	18TH CENTURY
EMPIRE · ART NOUVEAU	REGENCY · VICTORIAN	DUNCAN PHYFE	19TH CENTURY
		SAARINEN CHAIR · EAMES CHAIR	20TH CENTURY

ETHAN ALLEN, INC.

9-24 New styles of furniture are continually designed. Only a few remain popular through the centuries.

9-25 This 18th Century highboy is characteristic of the Queen Anne style of furniture because of its cabriole legs and carved fans.

Gothic and Chinese influences were a part of *Chippendale's* designs. Chippendale was the first person to publish a book of furniture designs, and his designs became popular around the world. Splat-back chairs and curved top edges on the backs of chairs and sofas were typical. Early Chippendale furniture has "s-shaped" legs with claw and ball feet, 9-27. Later, because of Chinese influence, his furniture had straight legs.

Furniture designed by the *Adam Brothers* was classic and symmetrical. The pieces had simple outlines, rectangular shapes, and tapered, straight legs.

Hepplewhite is most famous for his graceful chair designs. The backs of the chairs had shield, oval, and heart shapes.

9-26 Splat-back chairs, straight legs, "s-shaped" legs, and curved top edges on chairs are characteristics of the Georgian style of furniture.

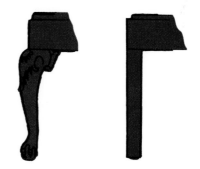

9-27 Curved legs with claw and ball feet were characteristic of early Chippendale designs. His later designs had straight legs.

The *Regency* furniture style is named after the Prince of Wales who reigned as Regent for nine years. The style reflects an interest in the ancient cultures of Greece, Rome, and Egypt. Bold, curved lines were dominant.

Choosing home furnishings   203

During the reign of Queen Victoria, the *Victorian* furniture style became popular. New machines could make detailed pieces of furniture quickly and easily. This led to the excessive use of ornamentation that was typical of the style. Other characteristics were massive proportions and dark colors.

Traditional American styles. The first settlers in America built sturdy, practical furniture. This style was a simplified version of the Jacobean style furniture that was then popular in England. The Wainscot chair is an example.

The colonists used native woods such as maple, pine, and oak. They began making furniture with less massive proportions. Ladder-back chairs and canopy beds were common, 9-28. Windsor chairs also became popular, 9-29. These furnishings were generally called *Early American*.

Later, the *Colonial* style became popular. It was based on England's Georgian style. Graceful lines, "s-shaped" legs and comfortable forms were typical.

After the Revolutionary War, England's influence declined in all areas, including furniture styles. The *Federal* style became popular in America. It combined classic influences with patriotic symbols such as eagles and stars and stripes. *Duncan Phyfe* was a major designer of this period. He is most noted for the lyre motif he used for chair backs. Other characteristics of his designs are brass-tipped dog feed, curved legs, and rolled top rails on the backs of chairs and sofas.

Modern and contemporary furniture styles

Modern furniture is comfortable, convenient and durable. It is designed according to the guideline that "form follows function." Thus, if the function of a chair is for sitting, it should be a comfortable place to sit. If the function of a table is to hold objects, it should be sturdy enough and large enough to hold them.

Unnecessary frills are avoided in modern pieces of furniture. This does not mean, however, that rooms must look boring. Look at the room in 9-30. The colors, fabrics, and accessories add beauty and variety to the room. They enhance the simple lines of the furniture.

ETHAN ALLEN, INC.

9-28 Ladder-back chairs, canopy beds, and braided rugs were typical furnishings of the early colonists.

ETHAN ALLEN, INC.

9-29 Windsor chairs are part of the Early American furnishings in this room.

SUN LAKES DEVELOPMENT CO.

9-30 This room with modern furnishings provides comfortable and convenient living space.

Contemporary furniture styles are the very latest designs. They take advantage of the newest materials and manufacturing methods. Plastics, metals, wood, and glass are used to create an endless range of visual effects.

Pieces of contemporary furniture have simple lines and forms. Geometric shapes such as circles, rectangles, cylinders, and cubes are often used. See 9-31.

The eclectic look

Rooms do not have to be decorated with a single style of furniture. Interesting effects can be achieved by mixing furnishings from different periods and countries. This decorating idea is called the *eclectic* look. See 9-32.

Because a variety of styles is used in furnishing an eclectic room, care must be taken to avoid a busy appearance. Using design

SPIEGEL, INC.

9-31 Unusual, geometric shapes and sleek materials are common for contemporary furniture.

Choosing home furnishings 205

ARMSTRONG WORLD INDUSTRIES, INC.

9-32 The Chippendale style chairs and Early American coffee table combine well with the modern sofa and end table in this eclectic room. Both traditional and modern accessories are also combined.

DECISIONS	RANGE OF AVAILABLE CHOICES
Location	In which room
	For what use
	Out of the way of traffic patterns
	Against which background areas
Form	
Type	Fixed or mobile
	Single-purpose or multipurpose
	Functional or decorative
Style	Traditional
	Modern
	Contemporary
	Eclectic
Materials	Hardwood
	Softwood
	Metal
	Glass
	Fabric
Structural quality	Poor
	Adequate
	Superior
Acquisition	
Process and cost	Initial
	Maintaining
	Replacing
	Financing

9-33 Choosing furniture requires many decisions.

principles is more important when several styles are combined than when furniture of one style is used. But with care, a unified look can be created. The furnishings in an eclectic room should be related in proportion. They should also be related in mood—either formal or informal. Color and texture should be carefully combined and balanced. This will help tie the different parts together so the final effect is a pleasing scheme, not a jumbled collection.

Whether you choose traditional, modern, contemporary, or eclectic settings for a room, you must choose furniture wisely. Decisions concerning furniture are outlined in 9-33.

CHOOSING ACCESSORIES

Accessories are those things which you can live without, but which make life more en-

joyable. The accessories you use in your home are a reflection of your personality. Through your choice of accessories, you can show a preference for such things as seashells, antiques, or Oriental objects. If one of your hobbies is collecting things, you can use the items in your collection as accessories.

Most accessories fit into one of two groups: functional or decorative. *Functional* accessories include pillows, ashtrays, lamps, mirrors, and clocks. *Decorative* accessories vary widely.

ARMSTRONG WORLD INDUSTRIES, INC.

9-34 Functional and decorative accessories are combined to personalize this room. Some pieces, such as the fire screen, are both decorative and functional.

Some examples are plants, flowers, pictures, wall hangings, handcrafted items, and figurines. Functional and decorative accessories are often used together. See 9-34.

Accessories should not be used just to fill up space. Each accessory in your home should be there for a purpose. It may be useful, beautiful, or meaningful to you. If it does not fit any of these purposes, it does not belong in your home.

Accessories can enhance a room if they fit into the overall plan. The design of the accessory should blend with the design of the room in general. Another guideline for the use of accessories is that accessories that are used near each other have something in common. It may be color, style, or purpose. This shared element will help tie the room's furnishings together.

Decisions concerning accessories are outlined in 9-35.

ACCESSORIES

DECISIONS	RANGE OF AVAILABLE CHOICES
Location	In room
	In relation to other objects
Form	
Type	Functional or decorative
Style	Traditional
	Modern
	Contemporary
	Eclectic
Acquisition	
Process and cost	Initial
	Maintenance
	Replacing
	Financing

9-35 Decisions about accessories are usually fun to make.

to Know

box springs . . . butt joint . . . coil springs . . . contemporary furniture styles . . . corner blocks . . . decorative accessories . . . double dowel joint . . . dovetail joint . . . eclectic . . . flat springs . . . foam mattress . . . functional accessories . . . hardwood . . . innerspring mattress . . . knitted fabrics . . . modern furniture styles . . . mortise and tenon joint . . . nonwoven fabrics . . . softwood . . . solid wood . . . tongue and groove joint . . . traditional furniture styles . . . veneered wood . . . wood grain . . . woven fabrics

to Review

Write your answers on a separate sheet of paper.

1. List three ideas to help you get started choosing your own furniture.

2. True or False. Most good furniture is made of solid hardwood.

3. Name four methods that can be used to join wood furniture.

4. What are the two main functions of wood furniture finishes?

5. Most upholstery fabrics are:
    a. Woven.
    b. Nonwoven.
    c. Knitted.

6. Furniture that is popular for outdoor use is most often:
    a. Fine hardwood.
    b. Upholstered.
    c. Glass.
    d. Metal.

7. Compare flat springs and coil springs in upholstered furniture. Consider both comfort and cost.

8. Which one is NOT a traditional furniture style?
    a. Louis XV.
    b. Chippendale.
    c. Colonial.
    d. Saarinen.

9. Furniture styles that take advantage of the latest materials and manufacturing methods are called _____.

10. Describe an eclectic room.

to Do

1. Examine wood furniture in your home to find out how many different types of joints are used.

2. Collect samples of fabric suitable for upholstery. Label them as woven, nonwoven, and knit. Divide them into subclasses such as plain weave, twill weave, satin weave, and pile weave. List characteristics of fibers they contain.

3. Find and label pictures of various furniture styles.

4. Choose a furniture style and write a report about it. Include illustrations.

5. List some of the accessories in your home. Note which ones are functional and which ones are decorative.

6. Look through magazines and find rooms with the eclectic look.

7. Plan a study trip to a furniture store. Prepare a list of questions to ask your tour guide about furniture construction and furniture styles.

10

Equipping and maintaining the home

After studying this chapter, you will be able to:
- Choose household appliances to fit your needs.
- List the basic cleaning and maintenance needs of a typical household.
- Take steps to make your home safe and secure.

Making a home attractive is only part of the inside story. To meet needs and personal priorities, a home must also be functional. Appliances such as refrigerators, freezers, ranges, washers, and dryers help people meet their primary needs for food and clothing. Performing maintenance helps keep a home clean and safe. Such an environment promotes well-being and self-esteem.

CHOOSING MAJOR APPLIANCES

Major appliances account for a large part of a housing budget. This is especially true when you completely equip a home, 10-1. If you rent a home that has major appliances in it, part of your rent goes toward the cost of the appliances.

Careful planning will help you choose the appliance that is best for your needs and your budget. First, decide if you really need the appliance. Will you use it frequently? Does it have all the features you want? Does it have extra features you do not need? Extras will add to the price.

Consider the size of your living unit. How large should the appliance be? Which size will satisfy your living unit now and in the near future? Will the appliance fit the space where it is to be placed? Can it be brought up stairways and through doors to reach the place where it will be used?

Does the appliance meet safety standards? Electrical appliances should have the *Underwriters' Laboratories* (UL) symbol. If the symbol is on the body of the appliance, all parts of the appliance meet the UL standards. Gas appliances should be approved by the *American Gas Association*. Their Blue Star certification seal means that the appliance meets standards of safety, performance, and durability.

Do you have the proper electrical or gas connections to use the appliance safely? Major electrical appliances should have a three-prong plug. The third (round) prong is the grounding plug. This prevents electrical shock and should never be removed.

What is the average yearly energy cost of operating the appliance? Most major

10-1 A fully equipped kitchen is a convenient, but costly, part of housing.

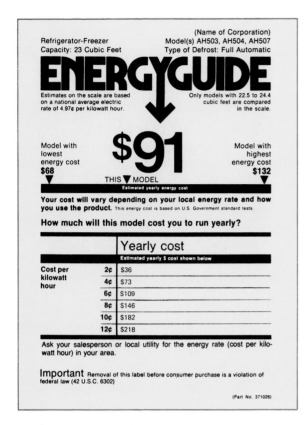

10-2 This EnergyGuide label is for a refrigerator-freezer.

appliances have *EnergyGuide labels* which enable you to compare average cost estimates for similar appliances, 10-2. This helps you determine which appliance would be the most energy efficient and least costly to operate.

Do you like the color of the appliance? Will it look good with the other furnishings in the room? See 10-3.

Is the appliance well-constructed? Is it from a reputable manufacturer? Is the instruction book thorough and easy to understand? Is after-sale service offered?

Does the appliance have a full or limited warranty? Under a *full warranty,* you may have the item repaired or replaced free of charge (at the warrantor's option). You cannot be asked to do anything unreasonable to have it repaired or replaced. Under a *limited warranty,* you can be charged for repairs. You may have to mail the item back to the warrantor or take other steps to get repairs.

What is covered by the warranty—the entire product or only certain parts? Are labor fees included? How long does the warranty last?

Does the appliance fit your budget? The purchase price of an appliance is only part of its true cost. If you pay for it on an installment

10-3 Before you choose an appliance, measure the amount of available space and check the color scheme of the room.

Equipping and maintaining the home 211

plan, you will also pay a finance charge. Other "hidden" costs include an installation charge, repair bills, and bills for either gas or electricity.

Refrigerators

Refrigerators are available in many sizes, styles, and colors. A one-door refrigerator is designed to keep food cold, not frozen. It may have a small section that is colder than the rest, but its use is limited. It provides only very short-term storage for commercially frozen foods, and it keeps ice cubes.

A variation of the one-door refrigerator is the compact refrigerator. It is suitable for rooms in college residence halls or small apartments. It can be purchased or rented at a fairly low price. It does not require any special wiring. It may be capable of freezing ice cubes, but it is not suitable for storing frozen foods.

Most refrigerators made today are two-door models with a separate freezer section. See 10-4. The temperature in the freezer section remains at about 0 deg. F (−17.8 deg. C). The freezer section may be above, below, or at the side of the refrigerator.

When shopping for a refrigerator, you should consider how much storage space you need. Think about whether or not you need a separate freezer section. Space inside a refrigerator is measured in cubic feet or liters. A basic guideline is that every adult needs about 4 cubic feet (113 L) of refrigerator space and about 2 cubic feet (57 L) of freezer space. These amounts are for persons who shop once a week for food. If you shop more often, you will need less storage space.

Another consideration is the amount of kitchen space you have for a refrigerator. Measure the height, width, and depth of the space you have. Take the measurements with you when you shop.

Notice which way you want the refrigerator door to open. It should open away from your best counterspace so you can add or remove food quickly and easily.

Refrigerators vary in the amount of defrosting they require. Some models must be defrosted by hand. Some defrost automatically. Others are frostless — frost does not accumulate. The frostless models are convenient, but

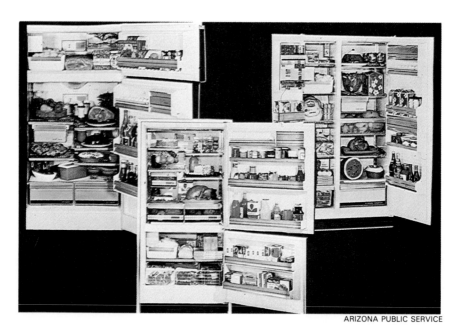

10-4 You can choose from three types of two-door refrigerators. Each model has a separate freezer section.

they cost more. They also use more electricity.

Other special features of refrigerators include meat compartments with separate temperature controls, adjustable shelves, and ice and water dispensers in the door. A checklist for refrigerators is shown in 10-5.

CHECKLIST FOR REFRIGERATORS

____ Does the refrigerator require defrosting?

____ Are interior and door shelves adjustable for more flexible use of space?

____ Is space available for heavy and tall bottles?

____ Is interior well lighted?

____ Does the refrigerator have a porcelain interior —best for durability and resistance to scratches, rust, and stains?

____ Are shelves made of strong, non-corroding, rust-resistant materials?

____ Are all interior parts easily removable and/or accessible for cleaning?

____ Are door shelf retaining bars strong and securely attached?

____ Does the meat pan have adequate ventilation and does it maintain proper cooling temperature?

____ Is crisper space adequate?

____ Is crisper tray designed to keep moisture in?

____ Is the freezer section easy to reach, use, clean, and organize?

____ Do the exterior doors have magnetic gaskets on all edges?

____ Is refrigerator easy to move for cleaning?

____ Does refrigerator have switch to turn off door heater when not needed to prevent condensation?

____ Is refrigerator's energy consumption figure available?

SEARS CONSUMER INFORMATION SERVICES

10-5 Consider these points before choosing a refrigerator.

Freezers

If a refrigerator-freezer does not provide enough storage space for frozen foods, you may want to buy a separate *freezer*. It can help you save money if you use it to store food purchased at low prices.

The size you need depends on the size of your living unit. A basic guideline allows about 6 cubic feet (170 L) for each person.

The two styles of freezers are *chest* and *upright*. Large, bulky packages are easier to store in a chest model, 10-6. Chest freezers use less electricity because less cold air escapes when the door is opened. One disadvantage of chest freezers is that they require more floor space. Another is that food must be lifted when it is removed.

Food is easier to see and remove in upright freezers. Only a small amount of floor space is needed, but upright freezers cost more to operate.

You can choose a freezer with either a manual defrost or frostless system. Frostless models are convenient, but their purchase and operation costs are higher.

A checklist for freezers is shown in 10-7.

WHIRLPOOL CORP.

10-6 Chest freezers provide energy-efficient storage space for frozen foods.

CHECKLIST FOR FREEZERS

____ Will model fit your floor space and weight limitations?

____ Will the type of opening be convenient in its location?

____ Are shelves and/or baskets adjustable?

____ Are all sections readily accessible?

____ Is the interior well lighted?

____ Does it have a safety signal light to let you know that power is on?

____ Is the freezer frostless? If not, does it have a fast-defrost system?

____ Does it have easy-to-read and accessible controls?

____ Does it have magnetic gaskets to seal cold air in more completely?

____ Does it have a power-saver switch to allow for lower use of energy when activated?

10-7 Consider these points before choosing a food freezer.

Ranges

Many changes have been made in ranges. These changes have been due to advances in technology and growing concern about energy conservation. You will have many factors to consider before choosing a range.

Your first decision concerns fuel. Your choice of either electricity or gas depends on the availability and cost of each.

Electric ranges have coils of wires through which electric current flows. This current provides the heat. The heating units are sometimes hidden under a smooth surface of glass-ceramic material. The smooth surface makes the range-top easy to clean.

The heat in *gas ranges* is produced by the combustion process between gas and the oxygen in the air. The heat is controlled by regulating the flow of gas through a valve. More gas means higher flames and hotter temperatures.

Styles of ranges. Ranges come in many styles and sizes, 10-8. Your choice depends on the capacity you need and the space you have.

Free-standing models are the most common. They offer the most options in sizes, colors, and features. They may have an oven below

10-8 You can choose from several styles of ranges.

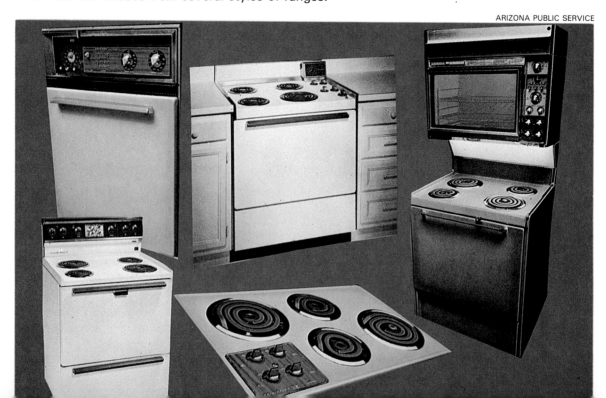

the cooking surface, at eye level, or both. They may stand alone or be between counters for a built-in look.

Slide-in (or drop-in) models fit snugly between two base cabinets. Chrome strips are often used to cover the side edges and provide a built-in look. The oven is below the cooking surface.

Built-in models separate the cooking surface from the oven. This allows flexible kitchen arrangements. The surface units are installed in a countertop. The oven is installed in a wall or specially made cabinet. See 10-9.

Special features. Both gas and electric ranges are available in split-level styles with a microwave oven on top. Some electric ranges have a single oven that works as both a conventional and a microwave oven, 10-10.

Induction heat ranges cook by creating heat in the cookware and not in the range surface. The heat is then transferred to the food. A magnetic attraction transfers the heat from coil to pan, so all cookware must be ferrous metal such as cast iron or steel. Cleanup is easy because spills do not burn and the coils are covered with smooth glass. An induction rangetop is shown in 10-11.

Hoods are a useful part of any range. They are used over the cooking surface to help vent heat and odors from the kitchen.

Self-cleaning ovens can be set at extremely high temperatures to "burn" soil away. Only a little ash remains to be wiped clean. Because such high temperatures are reached during cleaning, these ovens have extra insulation. This helps to save energy during normal baking periods. The self-cleaning feature adds to the price of the range. But the cost of operating the cleaning cycle is less than the cost of chemical oven cleaners.

Continuous cleaning ovens have a special coating on the oven walls. Food spatters on the walls are oxidized over a period of time during the normal baking process. These cost less than self-cleaning ovens. However, most people find them less effective. Also, these ovens do not have extra insulation.

Other special features to consider include clocks, timers, and programmed cooking

QUAKER MAID KITCHENS

10-9 This convenient kitchen has a built-in oven and rangetop. A microwave oven is also in the kitchen.

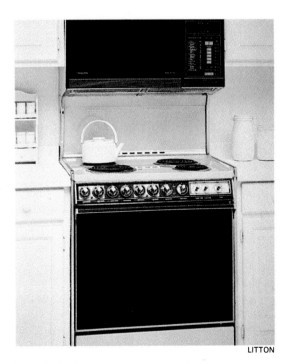

LITTON

10-10 This two-oven range features a microwave oven on top and a combination conventional and microwave oven below.

Equipping and maintaining the home 215

cycles. Some ranges have thermostatically controlled surface units or oven rotisseries. Others have surface units that can be replaced with grills, griddles, or cutting boards.

Study the checklist for ranges in 10-12.

Convection ovens

To save time and energy, convection ovens are being used more and more in home kitchens. These ovens can cut cooking times by about one-third and fuel consumption by almost one-half when compared to conventional ovens. The diagram in 10-13 shows how a convection oven works. Foods are baked and roasted in a stream of heated air. A fan or blower inside the oven keeps the heated air in constant motion. Because heated air is forced directly onto foods and is constantly in motion, foods cook faster at lower temperatures.

Although convection ovens are available by themselves, they are usually found in combination with conventional or microwave ovens, 10-14. The combination models allow you to use two different cooking methods.

Microwave ovens

Microwave ovens can cook, defrost, and reheat foods in a fraction of the time required for conventional ovens. Microwave cooking can also save up to 75 percent of the energy used by conventional ovens when cooking certain foods.

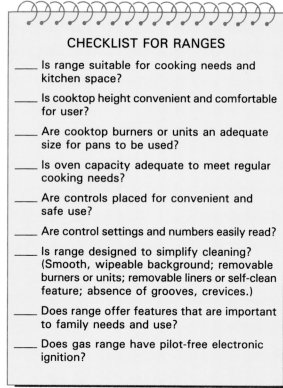

CHECKLIST FOR RANGES

____ Is range suitable for cooking needs and kitchen space?

____ Is cooktop height convenient and comfortable for user?

____ Are cooktop burners or units an adequate size for pans to be used?

____ Is oven capacity adequate to meet regular cooking needs?

____ Are controls placed for convenient and safe use?

____ Are control settings and numbers easily read?

____ Is range designed to simplify cleaning? (Smooth, wipeable background; removable burners or units; removable liners or self-clean feature; absence of grooves, crevices.)

____ Does range offer features that are important to family needs and use?

____ Does gas range have pilot-free electronic ignition?

SEARS CONSUMER INFORMATION SERVICES

10-12 Consider these points before choosing a range.

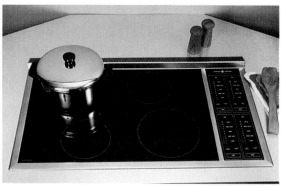

GENERAL ELECTRIC

10-11 Induction rangetops use magnetic energy to heat pans.

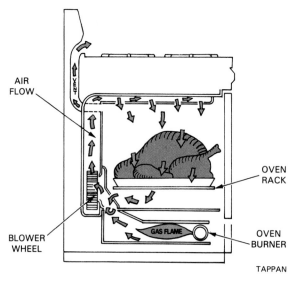

AIR FLOW

OVEN RACK

BLOWER WHEEL

GAS FLAME

OVEN BURNER

TAPPAN

10-13 In a convection oven, heated air is recirculated inside the oven.

216

10-14 This is a convection/conventional combination wall oven.

JENN-AIR

Food is cooked in a microwave oven by high frequency energy waves called microwaves. As food absorbs microwaves, the molecules within the food vibrate against each other. The friction that is produced creates the heat that cooks the food.

The time required to cook foods depends on the type of food being cooked and the power level used. Most microwaves have at least four or five power levels, 10-15. Low power levels are needed for cooking "delicate" foods such as eggs, cheese, meats, and sauces. High power levels can be used for most other foods.

Oven-proof glass, paper, and plastic can be used as cooking containers because microwaves pass through them. Metal containers should not be used since they reflect microwaves.

Styles of microwave ovens. Several styles of microwave ovens are available: countertop or freestanding models, microwave ovens with exhaust hoods, upper microwave ovens of two-oven ranges, combination ovens, and mounted or space-saving ovens.

Countertop models are the most popular and offer the greatest choices of features. They can be placed on a countertop, table, or cart.

Microwave ovens with exhaust hoods are made to be attached to the wall and cabinet above a range. This model is similar to a countertop model. However, it may have less capacity, less cooking power, or fewer special-feature options.

Upper microwave ovens of two-oven ranges are available with gas and electric ranges. These ovens are also similar to countertop models but may have fewer options.

Combination ovens combine the microwave oven with a conventional oven or with a convection oven. Combination ovens are available in range and countertop models.

Mounted ovens go on the wall or under a cabinet. Many of these ovens are smaller models. Because they may have less power, they may require longer cooking time.

Special features. With the various models and styles of microwave ovens available today, there are also various features from which to choose. These include automatic programming, automatic settings, browning elements, the temperature probe, and turntables.

A microwave oven with *automatic programming* automatically shifts power levels at preset times. This feature allows you to program the oven to defrost, cook, then keep warm in one step.

AMANA

10-15 A microwave oven with at least four or five power levels allows you to program the right amount of power for the right length of cooking time.

Automatic settings determine cooking times and correct power levels for you. You just set the controls for the type and sometimes the amount of food, and the oven does the rest.

Browning elements are electric heating coils on the ceiling of the oven. They give added top browning and crispness to food following microwave cooking.

A *temperature probe* (sometimes called a food sensor) helps you control cooking by turning off the oven automatically when food reaches a preset temperature or by keeping the oven at a set temperature when food reaches a preset temperature. Temperature probes are helpful when cooking roasts, casseroles, soups, and stews.

Study the checklist for microwave ovens that is given in 10-16.

Dishwashers

The size of your living unit and the amount of time you have help determine your need for a dishwasher. This appliance can save you time and energy.

Another advantage of a dishwasher is that it can get your dishes cleaner than you can by hand. It uses hotter water and stronger deter-

KITCHENAID, INC.

10-17 This built-in dishwasher is attractive and convenient.

gents. It can also dry dishes so they don't have to be wiped with towels that may carry germs.

Most dishwashers are built-in styles as shown in 10-17. Other models are portable. They are on roller casters so they can be moved easily from storage to the sink.

Dishwashers work in cycles. For instance, a normal cycle for average loads usually consists of a prerinse, one or more washes and rinses, and a drying period. The cycles vary in different dishwashers.

Special features. Look for a dishwasher with an adjustable upper rack. This makes it possible to wash large or odd-size items.

Newer models offer energy-saving features such as a cool drying cycle. This can save up to one-third the electricity used in a normal drying cycle.

Study the checklist in 10-18 before choosing a dishwasher.

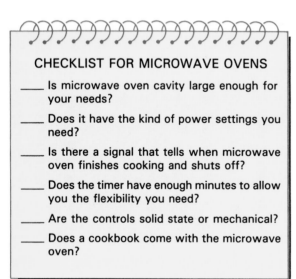

CHECKLIST FOR MICROWAVE OVENS

_____ Is microwave oven cavity large enough for your needs?

_____ Does it have the kind of power settings you need?

_____ Is there a signal that tells when microwave oven finishes cooking and shuts off?

_____ Does the timer have enough minutes to allow you the flexibility you need?

_____ Are the controls solid state or mechanical?

_____ Does a cookbook come with the microwave oven?

SEARS CONSUMER INFORMATION SERVICES

10-16 Consider these points before choosing a microwave oven.

Trash compactors

Trash compactors compress household trash to about one-fourth of its original volume. The trash is put into heavy-duty paper bags that are lined with plastic.

Compactors are available as free-standing and built-in models. They will handle almost any kind of trash such as bottles, tin cans, plastic cartons, and food scraps. They will *not* handle highly flammable materials and aerosol cans. These should be discarded separately.

Food waste disposers

The smell and mess of food scraps are easily eliminated by a *food waste disposer,* 10-19. This appliance fits below a sink. It catches and grinds all types of food scraps. It is connected to the city sewer or drained into a septic tank.

Both "batch-feed" and "continuous-feed" models are available. In "batch-feed" models, the food is placed in the grinding chamber.

MAYTAG

10-19 Food waste disposers have sharp blades which grind soft foods and small bones into tiny particles.

Then cold water is turned on and the lid is put in place. When the food has been ground, the water is turned off and the lid is removed. In "continuous-feed" models, food is added to the disposer as it is running.

Automatic washers

Size is one of the most important variables in automatic washers. If your living unit is small, a compact machine may be best for you, 10-20. Some are permanently installed, and others are portable. Some have only the basics: washing, rinsing, and spin-drying. Others have the features of full-size machines.

To suit a variety of fabrics, washers have several different cycles such as regular, permanent press, and delicate. All cycles have the same basic steps: fill, wash, rinse, and spin.

CHECKLIST FOR DISHWASHERS

_____ Are the tub and door lining materials made of porcelain enamel?

_____ Does the wash system have two levels? (A single system takes a great deal of care in loading.)

_____ Will it hold at least 10 place settings? Pots and pans?

_____ Does it offer more than one cycle, such as rinse/hold or prerinse cycle?

_____ Is an automatic wetting agent dispenser provided?

_____ Is the dishwasher insulated to eliminate excessive noise and heat?

_____ Does it have forced air drying? A no-heat drying cycle?

_____ Does it have an energy saver where the heating element is partially or completely off during some cycles?

SEARS CONSUMER INFORMATION SERVICES

10-18 Consider these points before choosing a dishwasher.

GENERAL ELECTRIC

10-20 Compact washers and dryers are great for small living units or for people with limited space.

They vary in the length of time, speed of agitation, water temperature, and number of rinses.

A cutaway drawing of an automatic washer is shown in 10-21. It shows you the basic structure of the appliance.

Special features. Some washers save water by letting you choose from two or more water levels, according to the load size. Another feature that saves water is called the "suds-saver." It retains the wash water so it can be reused. (The rinse water is always fresh.)

Deluxe models have dispensers which release detergent, bleach, and fabric softeners into the wash water at the right time.

Use the checklist in 10-22 when buying an automatic washer.

Dryers

Automatic clothes dryers are often bought at the same time as washers. They are usually available as a matching set.

Dryers can be operated by either gas or electricity. Compare installation and operating costs as well as purchase prices before you buy.

The dryer you choose should be large enough to dry a full load from your washer. Some construction features you should consider are shown in the cutaway drawing in 10-23.

Special features. Basic dryer models have a pre-set temperature which is safe for most fabrics. The drying time is the only variable.

More expensive machines have both time and temperature settings. You can set the temperature at high, medium, low, permanent press (which allows clothes to tumble without heat at the end of the drying time), and air-only (which has no heat and is used to fluff items).

Deluxe models have a moisture-sensing system. You set the control for the degree of dryness. The dryer shuts off when clothes reach the selected dryness.

Another feature of deluxe models guards against wrinkles. If you do not unload the dryer as soon as the cycle ends, it tumbles the clothes without heat for a few seconds every few minutes.

Look at the checklist for dryers in 10-24.

Water heaters

Unless you are building a house, your choice of a water heater will already be made for you. Water heaters are operated by either gas or electric heat. The type of water heater you have depends on the heating system in your home.

If you are in the market for a water heater, you will need to consider the size of water heater you need. This will depend on the amount of hot water you use. The more people living in your home, the more hot water you are likely to use and need.

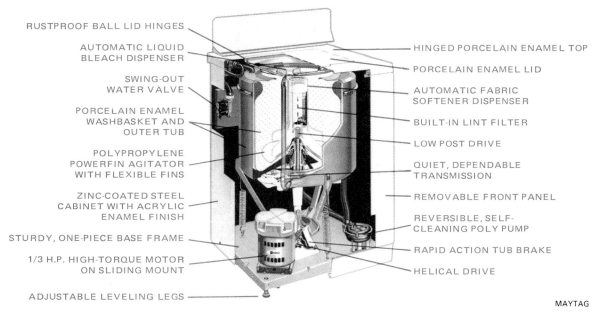

RUSTPROOF BALL LID HINGES

AUTOMATIC LIQUID
BLEACH DISPENSER

SWING-OUT
WATER VALVE

PORCELAIN ENAMEL
WASHBASKET AND
OUTER TUB

POLYPROPYLENE
POWERFIN AGITATOR
WITH FLEXIBLE FINS

ZINC-COATED STEEL
CABINET WITH ACRYLIC
ENAMEL FINISH

STURDY, ONE-PIECE BASE FRAME

1/3 H.P. HIGH-TORQUE MOTOR
ON SLIDING MOUNT

ADJUSTABLE LEVELING LEGS

HINGED PORCELAIN ENAMEL TOP

PORCELAIN ENAMEL LID

AUTOMATIC FABRIC
SOFTENER DISPENSER

BUILT-IN LINT FILTER

LOW POST DRIVE

QUIET, DEPENDABLE
TRANSMISSION

REMOVABLE FRONT PANEL

REVERSIBLE, SELF-
CLEANING POLY PUMP

RAPID ACTION TUB BRAKE

HELICAL DRIVE

MAYTAG

10-21 Automatic washers are complex appliances. Good quality construction is important.

An insulating jacket is another consideration concerning a water heater. This jacket is made of a flexible insulating material. It can be installed at any time. A water heater wrapped in an insulating jacket requires less energy to heat water. Since the heating of water is a high energy cost in a home, it is wise to make sure your water heater is properly insulated.

Other appliances

Several household appliances have been discussed in this chapter, but there are many

CHECKLIST FOR AUTOMATIC WASHERS

____ Will the washer fit your space limitations?

____ Does the washer have a self-cleaning lint filter?

____ Is a water level selector provided?

____ Is a water temperature selector provided?

____ Is more than one cycle available including a presoak cycle? A permanent-press cycle? A knit cycle? A delicate cycle?

____ Does it have an off-balance switch that stops machine and signals when load is unbalanced?

____ Are bleach, fabric softener, and detergent dispensers offered?

____ Is an optional second rinse selector provided?

____ Has porcelain enamel been used for the tub and lid?

____ If a portable compact model, does it have an agitator and single tub for wash, rinse, and spin cycles?

____ If a portable compact model, does it connect to sink faucet for automatic filling?

10-22 Consider these points before buying an automatic dishwasher.

more. The procedures for choosing them are much alike. The first step is always to determine your needs and your resources. Then do some comparison shopping. Compare construction details, warranties, and prices. Learn about all the latest features. New developments are always being made, even in "standard" appliances such as vacuum cleaners. For instance, central vacuum systems with hose attachments are available. See 10-25. Decide which features you want and can afford. Then you can be confident that your final choice will be a wise one.

MAINTAINING A HOME

Maintaining a home involves keeping it clean and safe. It also involves making sure that equipment, electrical and plumbing systems, and other parts of the home are in proper working order. Maintenance is needed to keep the home environment secure and comfortable. You will use the decision-making process to choose how and to what level you will maintain your home.

CHECKLIST FOR DRYERS

____ Is lint trap conveniently placed for ease in removing, cleaning, and replacing?

____ Is there an automatic pilot light or electronic ignition on gas dryer?

____ Is control panel lighted? Interior lighted?

____ Is there a finish signal—buzzer or bell at end of drying period?

____ Is there a safety button to start dryer?

____ Does dryer offer one heat setting meant for use on most fabrics?

____ Does it have an automatic sensor to prevent overdrying?

____ Does it offer a wrinkle-guard feature? An air-only no-heat setting?

____ Does it give a touch-up cycle to remove creases in dry clothes?

SEARS CONSUMER INFORMATION SERVICES

10-24 Consider these points before choosing a dryer.

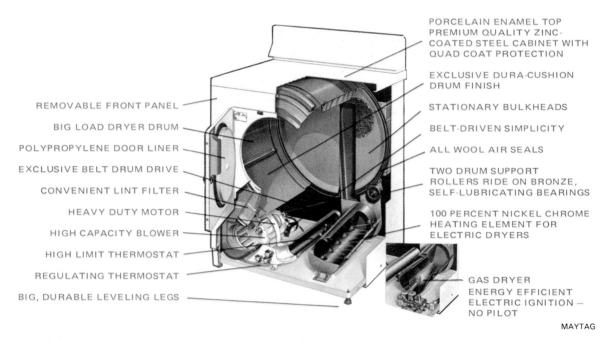

PORCELAIN ENAMEL TOP
PREMIUM QUALITY ZINC-COATED STEEL CABINET WITH QUAD COAT PROTECTION

EXCLUSIVE DURA-CUSHION DRUM FINISH

STATIONARY BULKHEADS

BELT-DRIVEN SIMPLICITY

ALL WOOL AIR SEALS

TWO DRUM SUPPORT ROLLERS RIDE ON BRONZE, SELF-LUBRICATING BEARINGS

100 PERCENT NICKEL CHROME HEATING ELEMENT FOR ELECTRIC DRYERS

GAS DRYER
ENERGY EFFICIENT ELECTRIC IGNITION — NO PILOT

MAYTAG

REMOVABLE FRONT PANEL
BIG LOAD DRYER DRUM
POLYPROPYLENE DOOR LINER
EXCLUSIVE BELT DRUM DRIVE
CONVENIENT LINT FILTER
HEAVY DUTY MOTOR
HIGH CAPACITY BLOWER
HIGH LIMIT THERMOSTAT
REGULATING THERMOSTAT
BIG, DURABLE LEVELING LEGS

10-23 You cannot see construction details of an appliance that you buy. But those details determine the appliance's quality.

NUTONE DIV. OF SCOVILL

NUTONE DIV. OF SCOVILL

10-25 This central cleaning system is ducted to the outside. It is quiet and convenient to use. The heavy machinery stays in one place. Only the hose and end pieces are carried from room to room where they are connected to special outlets.

Keeping the home clean

Everyone has different standards of cleanliness. One person may want every part of a room spotless with each object in its place. Another person may not mind some clutter. When people share a home, they should come to an agreement on acceptable cleaning standards. The standards should be realistic so that everyone can work together to meet the standards.

A certain minimum of standards is needed for the health and safety of family members. Garbage needs to be contained and removed from the dwelling regularly. Garbage can attract rats, roaches, and other insects. Any items which cause odors should be removed or properly stored. This will help to keep the air fresh.

Decide how much time you can devote to cleaning. Your decision will affect your choices in home furnishings. For instance, if you don't want to spend much time cleaning, you would choose a resilient floor covering rather than a thick, plush carpet. Also, you would not choose furniture and accessories that require much care. These would include items which tarnish and those made of fine woods.

Setting up an agenda of cleaning tasks will help you organize your cleaning time. A checklist of common tasks is shown in 10-26. You may divide tasks among household members.

To help make cleaning easier, keep needed cleaning items on hand in an organized area. See 10-27. Your supply of cleaning items will depend on your needs.

Cleaning tools can be broken into two main types. The first type is tools used to remove loose dust and dirt. They include the following:

- A broom and dustpan for sweeping hard floors and steps.
- A dust mop for picking up dust on hard floors.
- A vacuum cleaner with attachments for

carpets, hard floors, woodwork, furniture, upholstery, and curtains.

- Cloths for dusting and polishing.

The second type of cleaning tools includes those used to remove soil that is stuck to surfaces. These items are included:

- A pail to hold cleaning solutions.
- A wet mop for cleaning floors.
- Sponges for washing walls, woodwork, and appliances.
- A toilet bowl brush.

- A stepladder or stool for reaching high places.

Cleaning agents and waxes and polishes are also needed for cleaning. Several of these are listed in 10-28. Always read labels on cleaning products to make sure they will not damage a surface. Follow directions carefully to avoid injury or damage. Also, do not mix different cleaning products. Mixing two or more safe products can result in dangerous chemical compounds.

CHECKLIST FOR CLEANING

Daily cleaning tasks

_____ Make bed.

_____ Straighten up bedroom, bathroom, living and eating area.

_____ Wash dishes.

_____ Wipe kitchen counters and cooking surface, clean sink.

_____ Sweep kitchen floor.

_____ Empty wastebaskets, ashtrays, and other garbage containers.

Weekly cleaning tasks

_____ Change bed linens.

_____ Do laundry and mending.

_____ Wash kitchen garbage pail or change liner.

_____ Wash kitchen floor.

_____ Clean bathroom sink, tub, and toilet.

_____ Wash bathroom floor.

_____ Dust accessories.

_____ Dust and polish furniture.

_____ Vacuum lampshades.

_____ Vacuum carpet.

_____ Shake out small rugs.

Monthly cleaning tasks

_____ Vacuum and turn mattress.

_____ Wash mattress pad.

_____ Remove old wax and rewax hard floors.

_____ Vacuum drapes, wipe blinds.

_____ Vacuum upholstered furniture.

_____ Wash windows and mirrors.

_____ Clean and wax furniture.

_____ Clean kitchen shelves.

_____ Clean refrigerator (defrost if needed).

_____ Clean range, including oven.

_____ Wash bathroom walls.

Bi-yearly cleaning tasks

_____ Clean closets.

_____ Dry-clean or wash bedding.

_____ Clean drapes thoroughly.

_____ Wash seldom-used glasses and dinnerware.

_____ Clean silverware.

_____ Replace shelf paper.

_____ Wash all walls.

_____ Clean woodwork.

10-26 Doing these cleaning tasks will help keep your home clean and comfortable.

10-27 Storing cleaning supplies neatly in one place helps make cleaning easier.

Keeping the air clean

Clean air in the home is more of a concern than it has been in the past. This is partly because people are making houses more energy efficient. To save energy used for heating and cooling, houses have become more air tight. Air tight houses create some new problems.

One problem created is increased inside air pollution. Few people realize that the air inside the average home may be polluted. In some homes the situation is critical. Inside pollution comes from many sources. Fuels such as wood and gas emit polluting chemicals. Insulating materials contain pollutants. Radioactive waves from television sets, microwave ovens, and other sources cause pollution.

The most dangerous of all indoor pollutants probably is radon. *Radon* is a natural radioactive gas found in the earth. If a house is sitting on a radon-rich site, the gas will enter the house and be trapped inside it.

Personal and household cleaning products add to the indoor pollution problem. Even stagnant water left in containers like vaporizers and humidifiers pollutes the air.

Usually no single source creates a great pollution problem. The problem arises when all the sources are combined and locked in an air tight house. The air may become so polluted that it affects health. People may develop allergies, become very ill, or feel tired and listless. This is more likely to happen when houses are kept tightly closed. Possible pollution problems and solutions are shown in 10-29. Perhaps you can determine if your home is too air tight.

There are solutions to polluted inside air. For instance, you could move to another location. But most people are not ready to move when they realize their inside air is polluted. They are willing to take other measures that reduce pollution levels.

Ventilation reduces pollution levels. Rooms need to be ventilated to allow an exchange of fresh and stale air. So do the attic and the crawl space under the floor. If your house did not have vents built in, they can be installed. Exhaust fans can be added to increase ventilation. If ventilation is planned, air will be exchanged at a good rate.

Air pollution can be reduced by using fewer chemicals in the house. Learn the effects of the chemicals in your house. Eliminate or reduce the use of those that are the most polluting. For instance, don't use aerosol sprays which contain fluorocarbons. *Fluorocarbons* are chemicals that stay in the air when they are sprayed. Large amounts in the air make breathing difficult.

House cleaning procedures affect the pollution level. For instance, using a feather duster merely moves dust around. The dust is still in the air. The best cleaning device is probably a system that uses *aerodynamics* (air in motion) and *hydrodynamics* (water in motion). Such a vacuum cleaner draws air through a compartment containing water. The air is "washed" before it returns to the room. See 10-30.

A central vacuum system is also better than a standard model. Air is filtered to the outside rather than through a dirt-filled bag.

CLEANING PRODUCTS

CLEANING AGENTS (USED TO REMOVE SOIL FROM SURFACES.)	
Agent	**Method of action**
Water	Dissolves and flushes away dirt.

Alkalies
   soaps
   washing sodas
   some general purpose cleaners
	Break down surface tension of water, allowing water to penetrate and pick up dirt better.

Synthetic detergents	Relieve surface tension more than soaps to clean and cut grease better. Unlike soaps, detergents do not react with minerals to form scum deposits.

Acids
   ammonia
   vinegar
   lemon juice
	Cut grease; act as a mild bleach.

Fat solvents	Dissolve soil held by grease.

Fat absorbents
   fuller's earth
   talcum
   bentonite
   cornmeal
	Dry materials are sprinkled over oily soil. Agents absorb the oils; oils are brushed away with the absorbent.

Abrasives
   silver polish
   scouring powder
   steel wool
   soap pads
	Rub dirt away with a scraping or polishing action. Used dry or with water depending on type.

WAXES AND POLISHES (USED TO PROTECT AND ADD SHINE TO SURFACES.)	
Agent	**Method of action**

Solvent-base cleaning waxes
   liquid wax
   paste wax
	Used on hard floors. Loosen soil. Remove old coats of wax. Form new coating of wax.

Water-base cleaning waxes
   emulsion wax
   solution wax
	Used on hard floors other than wood or cork. Lift out soil. Form new coating of wax. Do not remove old coats of wax; must use remover to strip floor occasionally.

Furniture polishes
   aerosol spray
   creamy liquid
   paste polishes
	Lift out soil. Remove old coats of wax. Form new coating of wax.

Multipurpose cleaner waxes	Used on counter tops, tile, appliances, paneling, furniture, cabinets. Lift out soil. Remove old coats of wax. Form new coating of wax.

10-28 Using the proper cleaning agent for the job is important.

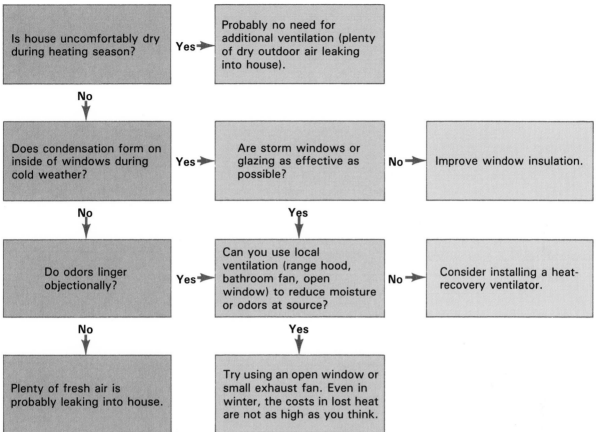

DIAGNOSING A TOO-TIGHT HOUSE

**You can make your own rough diagnosis of the ventilation rate in winter
by looking for a few key syptoms.**

Is house uncomfortably dry during heating season? **Yes→** Probably no need for additional ventilation (plenty of dry outdoor air leaking into house).

No

Does condensation form on inside of windows during cold weather? **Yes→** Are storm windows or glazing as effective as possible? **No→** Improve window insulation.

No / **Yes**

Do odors linger objectionally? **Yes→** Can you use local ventilation (range hood, bathroom fan, open window) to reduce moisture or odors at source? **No→** Consider installing a heat-recovery ventilator.

No / **Yes**

Plenty of fresh air is probably leaking into house.

Try using an open window or small exhaust fan. Even in winter, the costs in lost heat are not as high as you think.

10-29 If you spot problems with ventilation in your house, you can correct them with a few simple steps.

Safety measures

There are hazards in every home. These can be reduced by taking some practical safety measures. These guidelines will help you keep your house safe:
- Follow instructions when using electrical appliances. Read the information and keep a file.
- Be careful about using electricity near water. Electrical shock can be fatal.
- Disconnect electrical cords from the outlet first, then from the appliance. Grasp the plug to disconnect.

- Store dangerous chemicals out of the reach of children. Some products that are hazardous are household cleaning products, colognes, and lotions. Food extracts, liquor, medicine, and vitamins are also hazards.
- Read labels. Use products as directed. Do not combine cleaning products.
- Keep emergency telephone numbers by the telephone. Have household members learn the numbers. 911 is used for emergency nationwide.
- Install smoke alarms and a fire alarm. Plan and practice using an escape route.

REXAIR

10-30 This vacuum cleaner uses aerodynamics and hydrodynamics to keep dust in the vacuum cleaner.

- Understand terms like flammable and inflammable. These words are not opposites. They both mean that something will burn easily.
- Use fabrics with UFAC hangtags for upholstery and other decorating purposes. UFAC stands for Upholstered Furniture Action Council. Fabrics with the label are resistant to burns. See 10-31.
- Burn only seasoned (dry) wood in wood burning heaters and fireplaces. Green wood can cause creosote build-up. Creosote causes chimney fires.
- Care for wood burners and fireplaces properly. Chimneys need regular sweeping (cleaning). Spark arrestors should be used to prevent sparks from flying out chimneys and starting fires.
- Learn the rules of pool safety—for care as well as use. Practice them in your own pool if you have one.

Home security

Whether you own or rent, you can take measures to safeguard your home against intruders. Many measures are merely common sense. For instance, you should not publicize your absence when you are away from home. Make arrangements so that your home looks lived-in even when you are away.

Do not let strangers in your house. In doors that visitors use, install a peep hole with a wide angle lense. This will help you see people without opening the door. If a stranger asks to make a phone call, make the call for him or her.

Make your home's exterior as visible as possible. Install a system to light exterior doors and the yard. Use monitors so that lights are on from dusk to dawn, 10-32. Trim shrubs so

10-31 Look for this label to find fabrics that are burn-resistant.

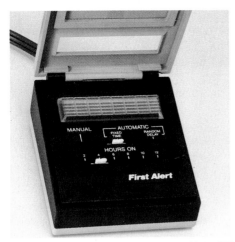

FIRST ALERT

10-32 A timer can be used to turn lights on at dusk and shut them off at dawn.

that doors and windows can be seen from the street. If shrubs are growing under windows, make sure that they are thorny or that they cannot be used as a shield for an intruder.

Make doors as secure as possible. Install dead bolt locks on exterior doors, 10-33. Use the kind that require a key to unlock the inside as well as the outside. This type of lock is called a *double cylinder lock*. Change lock cylinders when you move into a new place. (Cylinders are less expensive than complete locks.) This change prevents entry by those who may have a key.

Keep doors and windows locked. If there is a door between the garage and the house, keep it locked too. Do not leave keys inside locks. Also do not hide keys near the home. Intruders can usually find these. Make sliding doors and windows secure with extra locks and other measures. See 10-34.

Use exterior doors with solid wood cores or made of heavy material such as heavy duty metal. (Many doors are so weak that they can be broken down with a strong kick.) Hang doors so that hinges are on the inside. Otherwise, burglars can remove the pins in the hinges and open the door. Place a sheet of heavy plastic, such as acrylic, over the inside of a glass paned door.

THERMA TRU CORP.

10-33 Dead bolt locks help keep doors more secure.

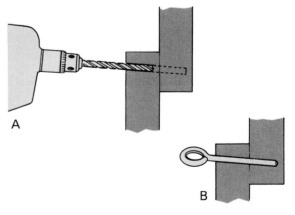

10-34 To make sliding doors and windows more secure, drill a hole through both frames where they overlap (A). Then place a pin in the hole (B).

Equipping and maintaining the home 229

Mark valuables with an indentification number. Your local law enforcement agency may loan you the marking equipment. Marking valuables does not protect them from being stolen. But if they are stolen, the identification number makes items easier to trace. Keep valuable items such as jewels and savings bonds locked away. You may store them in a home safe, a private security vault, or a safe-deposit box at your bank.

You should have some system to warn of and deter intruders. You may keep a dog to bark when someone is outside of the home. (Some dogs are trained to protect their owners.) Or a security system can be installed. Another choice is to live in a place that has security guards.

Your personal priorities will affect the way you choose to keep your home secure. For instance, some people feel safe with a security guard nearby. Having a guard may make other people feel as if they are giving up some freedom. No matter what your priorities are, you will probably want to take some security measures. Choose those that make you feel as comfortable and safe as you can within your home.

Repair work

Keeping appliances and utilities in good repair helps keep your home safe and comfortable. Sometimes, you will need to hire a professional to do repair and maintenance work. But you can do some repairs with the right tools and some basic knowledge. Keeping a home repair kit will help. The basic tools for a kit and their uses are shown in 10-35. You will need some maintenance supplies other than tools. Some helpful supplies are listed in 10-36.

Tools and equipment can be expensive. But you should buy quality tools because they will last longer than very inexpensive ones. Build your supply by buying tools as you need them. To get the right tool for your job, ask for help at the hardware store.

Plumbing. One of the most common plumbing problems is clogged drains. Drains tend to clog when grease, hair, and other particles settle in the pipes. Sometimes, simply running hot, soapy water will dissolve the clog. Otherwise, try a commercial drain cleaner. These contain strong chemicals designed to dissolve clogs. They may be in dry or liquid form. Read the directions and safety information before using.

A *force cup,* or plunger, can be used to move some clogs. To use, make sure that enough water is standing to cover the cup. Fit the cup over the drain opening. Work the handle up and down many times. This will move the water in the drain and loosen the clog.

If none of these methods work, you can use special tools to clean the drain. A *cleanout auger* can be used in most drains. *Closet augers* are used in toilets. These tools are designed to reach through the pipe and break apart the clog.

Installing screws and nails. To install a screw in a wall or a piece of wood, use a nail to start a slight hole. If the surface is hard, drill a hole using a drill bit slightly smaller than the screw. Use the proper type of screwdriver (Phillips or standard) for the screw. Try to match the size as closely as possible. Using the wrong size makes the task more difficult and can damage the screw head.

To drive nails, use one hand to hold the nail in place. Tap the nail a few times to start the nail into the surface. Then drive the nail holding the hammer at the end of the handle for more power. When the nail is secure, you should be able to let go of it and finish driving it in with the hammer.

If you are placing nails or screws in walls, location on the wall is important. To secure heavy objects, fasteners should be placed where a stud is behind the wall surface. See 10-37. You can find studs by tapping on the walls lightly. You will hear a hollow sound between studs. When you tap a stud, the sound will be lighter and more solid. After you find one stud, you can find others by measuring 16-inch (41 cm) intervals to the left or right.

Fuses and circuit breakers. Electrical circuits in a house or apartment are monitored by a service entrance panel. See 10-38. The panel may contain fuses or circuit breakers. If any circuit in your house is overloaded with appliances or other electric items, the *fuses* or

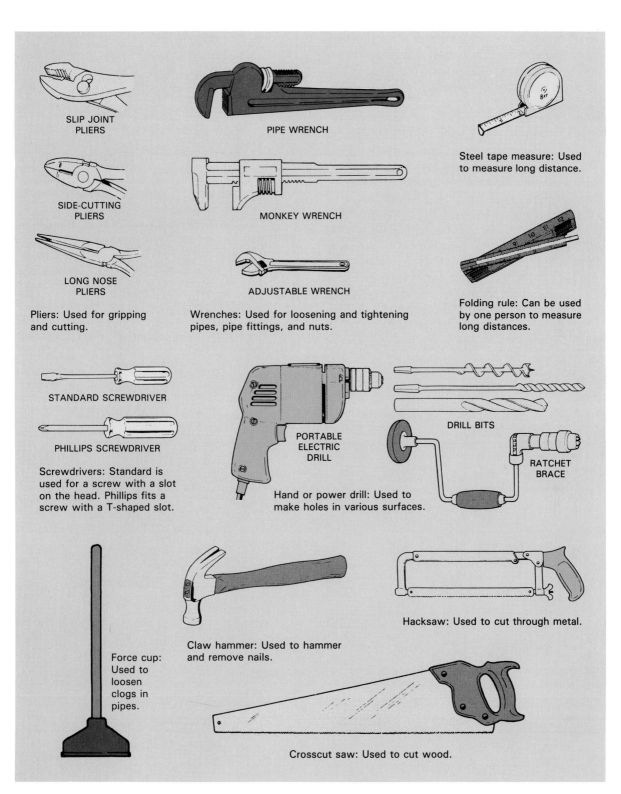

SLIP JOINT PLIERS

PIPE WRENCH

Steel tape measure: Used to measure long distance.

SIDE-CUTTING PLIERS

MONKEY WRENCH

LONG NOSE PLIERS

ADJUSTABLE WRENCH

Pliers: Used for gripping and cutting.

Wrenches: Used for loosening and tightening pipes, pipe fittings, and nuts.

Folding rule: Can be used by one person to measure long distances.

STANDARD SCREWDRIVER

PHILLIPS SCREWDRIVER

Screwdrivers: Standard is used for a screw with a slot on the head. Phillips fits a screw with a T-shaped slot.

PORTABLE ELECTRIC DRILL

DRILL BITS

RATCHET BRACE

Hand or power drill: Used to make holes in various surfaces.

Hacksaw: Used to cut through metal.

Force cup: Used to loosen clogs in pipes.

Claw hammer: Used to hammer and remove nails.

Crosscut saw: Used to cut wood.

10-35 These basic tools will help you handle many household maintenance tasks.

circuit breakers cut off the power. This prevents damage to wiring and possible electrical fires.

When an overload happens, you must either replace a fuse or reset a circuit to restore power. Fuses screw into the entrance panel like light bulbs. The fuse has a clear window at the bottom with a metal strip across it. The metal strip is called a fuse link. You can detect a blown fuse by a broken strip or a darkened window. To replace the fuse, first disconnect the main fuse. (This will disconnect all power, so have a flashlight ready.) Take out the blown fuse and put in a new one. To avoid electrical shock, be sure that you are standing on a dry surface. Your hands should also be dry.

A circuit breaker does not need to be replaced when it shuts off. It disconnects power by swinging to an "off" position. To restore power, simply switch the circuit breaker to an "on" position.

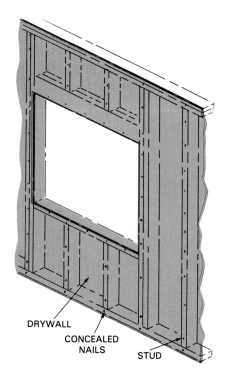

10-37 Studs are placed 16 inches apart behind walls. Find a stud before hanging anything heavy on the wall.

HELPFUL MAINTENANCE SUPPLIES

FASTENERS	LUBRICANTS
Nails Tacks Screws Bolts Nuts Washers	Oils Chemical lubricants
ADHERING AGENTS	**SURFACE SMOOTHERS**
Glues Cements Solder Soldering paste	Sandpaper Steel wool

10-36 Some supplies other than tools are needed for maintenance work.

SIEMENS ENERGY & AUTOMATION, I-T-E

10-38 The service entrance panel monitors the electrical system for the house.

232

to Know

aerodynamics . . . American Gas Association . . . circuit breaker . . . continuous cleaning oven . . . double cylinder lock . . . electric range . . . EnergyGuide label . . . fluorocarbons . . . food waste disposer . . . force cup . . . full warranty . . . fuse . . . gas range . . . hydrodynamics . . . induction heat range . . . limited warranty . . . microwave oven . . . radon . . . self-cleaning oven . . . Underwriters' Laboratories . . . ventilation

to Review

Write your answers on a separate sheet of paper.
1. Name two symbols that assure you that an appliance has met safety standards.
2. Explain the difference between a full warranty and a limited warranty.
3. Which style of freezer is more energy efficient?
   a. Upright.
   b. Chest.
4. Of what kind of material must cookware used on an induction range be made? Why?
5. Describe how a convection oven works.
6. How is heat produced in a microwave oven?
7. Describe four styles of microwave ovens.
8. List two special features that are available on some automatic washers.
9. (True or False) Brooms and vacuum cleaners are the best tools for removing soil that is stuck to surfaces.
10. Name some health problems that may result from inside air pollution.
11. List some chemicals found in the home that are considered hazardous.
12. List five measures you can take to make your home more secure.
13. When hanging a heavy painting, place the nail where a _____ is behind the surface.
14. A blown fuse can be detected by a _____ or a _____.

to Do

1. Do some comparison shopping for major appliances. Compare sizes, features, energy costs, and prices. Use the checklists given in this chapter. Compare your findings with those of other students.
2. Find a warranty and instruction booklet for a major appliance. List the kinds of information that it gives.
3. Set up a cleaning agenda for your home. Use the checklist in 10-26 as a guideline. Then list the cleaning tools and supplies needed to perform the tasks on your agenda.
4. Find and read two or three magazine or newspaper articles on inside air pollution. Report your findings to the class.
5. Design a brochure that gives guidelines for safety in the home.
6. Invite a police officer to speak on home security. If possible, have the officer demonstrate how to mark identification numbers on valuables.
7. As a class, visit a hardware store and have the manager describe some of the tools and supplies. Have the manager demonstrate how to use some basic tools.

VENTARAMA SKYLIGHT CORP.

With careful planning, you can find decorating and redecorating bargains to make your home comfortable and attractive.

Bargains in home decorating and design

After studying this chapter, you will be able to:

■ Describe the difference between a bargain and a low price.

■ Explain ways that planning and shopping can help you find decorating and redecorating bargains.

■ List ways to organize storage and save space in a dwelling.

■ Explain how to find bargains in remodeling.

Anyone may profit by using money-saving ideas. You may want to "stretch" your housing dollars for many different reasons. Perhaps you are not yet high on your career ladder. Your take home pay may not seem to cover all you need and want.

If you rent or expect to move soon or often, you may not want to invest much in the place where you live. You are likely to fill your living space with items that can be taken with you when you leave. Or you may want to decorate inexpensively so that you don't mind leaving your bargains behind when you move.

If the number of members of your living unit increases, your housing costs will also increase. So "cutting corners" may continue to be important to you as you move through the life cycle.

Bargains may or may not cost a great deal of money. Some bargains may be less costly than similar items, but they may require more time or effort. For instance, a store fifty miles away may have carpeting for 20 percent less than a nearby store. The bargain may be worth the extra driving time to some people, but not to others.

No matter what the cost, a product is not a bargain for you unless it fits into your life-style. No "bargain" is worthwhile if you don't need it or if you cannot afford it. Neither is it a bargain if you really would rather have something else. A true bargain must improve the quality of life.

BARGAINS IN DECORATING

Decorating does not have to be expensive to be attractive. Good design that fits your life-style and tastes is more important than cost.

See 11-1. Some background treatments and furnishings are less expensive than others. If they fit into your decorating scheme and do not have hidden expenses, they are bargains for you. Other background treatments and furnishings are bargains because they are durable and classic in design. These items will not need to be replaced in a couple of years because they are worn or out of fashion.

Planning

Before you begin decorating, you need to have a plan. When you are shopping for bargains, you may be tempted to buy items that won't fit into a good room design. Having a plan before you start shopping will help you buy only those items that you can really use.

The first step in planning is to decide how much money you can spend on decorating. All of the members of the household should have some say in the amount to be spent. Make a

KIRSCH CO.

11-1 This furniture is inexpensive, but it is attractive and fits well in this attic apartment.

budget for redecorating and stay within the budget. Overspending is not likely to give you the same satisfaction as spending only what you can afford.

Next, decide what you want. Determine your priorities. Discuss housing priorities with the others in your household. Look for ideas and pictures in books and magazines. Window shop to see what is available and to become aware of decorating trends.

Once the members of your household have discussed your ideas, you can make a plan. Make decisions that will help all of you to satisfy your priorities. Plotting your plan on paper will make it easier to visualize. This helps to avoid misunderstandings.

As you make your plan, use the principles of design. Remember that good design is always good design. Fads do not always last.

Always consider storage when making your decorating plans. Having enough storage helps you make the most of your housing. See 11-2.

Well-organized storage helps make living easier. It keeps your living spaces from becoming too cluttered.

Once you agree upon a plan, write down all the information you will need for shopping. List room dimensions and sizes of windows and doors. Gather color, fabric, wood, or other samples that match what you want. As you purchase decorating items, add information about them to your list. This will help you choose only those items that will fit into your decorating scheme as you shop.

Interior designers. You may choose to use professional services to help you decorate. An interior designer can help you plan, make purchases for you, and see that the work is done. A designer can save time and help you avoid costly mistakes. A designer also has contacts that you cannot make on your own.

When you use an interior designer be sure to know what you want and communicate your desires to the professional. You will be the one

FORMICA CORP.

11-2 The well-designed storage space in this bedroom allows a person to use the room as an office as well.

living with the decisions. Get what you want and what you can afford.

The top interior designers are members of the *American Society of Interior Designers (ASID)*. Members of the organization are required to have a high level of preparation and training. You may want to ask a designer about professional training and membership before using their services.

You can decide how much help you want from a designer and how much decorating you want to do on your own. Most designers expect to do the bulk of the planning and let the client do some of the purchasing and work. Decide how much work you want the designer to do according to your priorities.

Getting the right price

You may have heard people say, "Let the buyer beware." This is especially true when you are shopping for bargains. Sale items and less expensive items are priced that way for a reason. It's up to the buyer to find out why and decide whether or not the lower price is worthwhile.

Some sales are held just to get people to come into the store. These are called *loss leader* sales. The store management hopes that once you are there, you will buy other items that aren't on sale. If you shop these kinds of sales, be careful to buy only what you want and need at the price you want. For instance, you may find that a chair is on sale, but the matching sofa is not. If you only buy the chair, it may be a good bargain. But if you want a chair and sofa that match, you may be able to get a better deal somewhere else.

Other sales, called *seasonal sales,* are held so that stores can get rid of stock to make room for new items. For instance, air conditioners are often on sale in August so that the store can make room for heating systems. Many high quality products are discounted during seasonal sales, 11-3. But finding such bargains may mean waiting longer than you wanted to decorate.

Many stores mark down prices on items that are slightly damaged. Make sure you know where and how bad the damage is. A desk with a surface scratch may be worthwhile if the price

BARGAIN MONTHS

January	February	March
Appliances, blankets, carpets and rugs, furniture, home furnishings, housewares, white goods.	Air conditioners, carpets and rugs, curtains and drapes, furniture, home furnishings, housewares, storm windows.	Laundry appliances, storm windows.
April	**May**	**June**
Gardening specials.	Blankets, carpets and rugs, linens, television sets.	Building materials, fabrics, furniture, lumber, television sets.
July	**August**	**September**
Air conditioners, appliances, carpets and rugs, fabrics, freezers and refrigerators, stereos, white goods.	Air conditioners, bedding, carpets and rugs, curtains and drapes, fans, gardening equipment, home furnishings, housewares, summer furniture, white goods.	Appliances, paint, television sets.
October	**November**	**December**
China and silverware.	Blankets, housewares, home improvement supplies.	Blankets, housewares.

11-3 You can find good bargains if you wait for seasonal sales.

is good enough. But if the drawers don't work, you may not think of the desk as a bargain.

Other sales are held on discontinued lines or special purchases. These sales may offer high quality goods at unusually low prices. But once those items are gone, you will not be able to purchase matching items. You may find wallpaper that is discounted for this reason. If there is enough for you to finish the whole area that you want to paper, it is a bargain. But know that you will not be able to find matching paper later.

Discount houses often sell products at lower prices than retail stores. At these stores, you will probably give up service for the lower price. You may have to wait a long time for assistance or to receive your purchase. Delivery service for large items may not be available. And if you have a problem with a product, you may not be able to get service from the store. If you are willing to give up these conveniences, discount houses may have bargains for you.

Garage sales, auctions, and flea markets can provide great bargains if you have the time. Some items you find there may need repairs or refinishing. You can decide whether the price is low enough to be worth the extra cost.

Backgrounds

The backgrounds in your decorating scheme set the stage for the furnishings you choose. Although they do not need to be costly, they do need to be carefully planned.

Floor treatments receive more wear than other background treatments. And they are usually more expensive. Unless you plan to replace a floor treatment within a couple of years, choose one that is durable. (Chapter 7 contains information that will help you choose durable products.) Also, try to choose a color and style that allows you to change your decorating scheme in the future.

By using the same floor covering throughout a dwelling, you can make it seem larger and more unified. This can be important if your house or apartment is small.

Choosing a *classic* wall treatment can save you the cost of changing your wall treatment

as styles change. Classic treatments continue to be in style year after year. Off-white paint is a popular classic wall treatment. Off-white permits you to use a great variety of colors and designs in a room. It also helps rooms appear more spacious and airy. See 11-4. Other classic wall colors include light beige, pale blue, and pale yellow.

PRESLEY DEVELOPMENT CO.

11-4 Off-white walls give this room a spacious appearance.

You can use bold, bright wall treatments to give a room a dramatic look. Wallpaper with bold patterns and painted graphic designs or murals make colorful focal points. Bold treatments tend to make a room look smaller, so use them carefully, 11-5. Be sure to choose furnishings for the room that do not compete with the wall.

The most common wall treatment is paint. It is also the easiest to use and the least expensive. Choose the right paint for the right job. Washable paints are important for rooms such as kitchens and children's rooms. If the paint can be cleaned, repainting will not be needed as often. High-gloss and enamel paints are easier to clean than flat and satin finish paints.

Bargains in home decorating and design   239

11-5 Bold wall treatments tend to make rooms seem smaller.

Wallpaper comes in many types and designs. Some designs have matching fabric that can be used to make coordinating accessories. See 11-6. Many styles are inexpensive, especially if you apply them yourself. If you hang your own wallpaper, think about using prepasted paper. This often costs a little more than unpasted paper. But working with unpasted paper is not easy for the novice. The time and effort saved makes prepasted paper a better bargain for most people.

Sheets or fabric can be glued to walls like wallpaper. They can be coordinated with curtains and accessories made with matching fabric or sheets.

Great looking window treatments can make a room look great. The right ones can help disguise flaws in design that would be costly to fix. If windows are of different sizes or unevenly spaced, window treatments can help. Certain treatments can camouflage windows that are not in proportion with the rest of the

11-6 Window treatments made from fabric that matches the wallpaper give this kitchen a stylish look.

11-7 If you use sheets as dining room curtains, you can make matching tablecloths and accessories.

room. For instance, you can use matching curtains and wallpaper on the same wall. If your windows are old or loose, insulating window treatments can help.

Sheets can be used as inexpensive curtains. The hems work as casings for curtain rods. You can match the sheets in a bedroom with curtains made of sheets. Or you can use sheets to make living room or dining room accessories to match curtains, 11-7.

Furnishings

Furniture is often your biggest decorating investment. To get the most value from fur-niture, choose pieces that are durable and have classic designs. The appearance of furniture with simple lines and colors can be changed easily by changing accessories. Also, more complex furniture is often more expensive than simpler furniture. Carving, latticework, and other extras add to the cost of furniture, 11-8.

You can begin furnishing your living room, dining area, or family room by using outdoor furniture, 11-9. This can be helpful if your budget does not allow you to purchase the quality of furnishings you want. As your budget allows, you can replace the furniture and decorate your patio at the same time.

11-8 Many factors affect the price of furniture. Both of these dining room sets are of high quality. But the set on the left has much detailed carving. The china cabinet has latticework on its glass doors. Because of the extra craftwork involved, this set would be more expensive than the set on the right.

11-9 Outdoor furniture can be used inside until you can afford to replace it with indoor furniture.

Outdoor benches make good coffee tables and end tables. They also can be used for indoor seating. Picnic tables and lawn chairs can be used inside. You can dress them up with tablecloths and cushions.

Flat-topped trunks and chests can be used as end tables and coffee tables. At the same time, they can be used for storage. Paint, stencil, or cover them for decoration. You can make a trunk into portable storage for shirts and blouses. Turn a trunk on end. Mount it on rollers and insert a rod for hangers.

Plastic or wooden cubes can be used for shelves, tables, desks, and seats. See 11-10. Some cubes are divided to provide shelf space or so that drawers can be added. Plastic cubes come in many colors. Wooden ones can be painted to coordinate with your decorating scheme.

Accessories. Accessories add a personal touch to a room, 11-11. They make a statement about the personalities of the people living in a home. And they help bring together the other parts of a room to make a unified design.

Pillows and cushions can add splashes of color to a room, 11-12. Make your own from material that coordinates with other room furnishings. Or decorate pillows with stichery or paint designs. You can use them as throw pillows, back rests, and cushions for chairs.

Quilts can be used as wall hangings or displayed on quilt racks. You can make your own, use a family heirloom, or purchase one at a rummage or garage sale. A heavy quilt can

11-10 Cubes can be arranged in many ways to help you furnish your living space.

ARMSTRONG WORLD INDUSTRIES, INC.

11-11 The wall hangings, books, and other accessories in this den give the room a personalized look.

be hung over an unused window or door for added insulation. Quilts can also be used in place of headboards or displayed on beds.

Many types of displays can be used to decorate a room. Any kind will work if it blends with the rest of the room. Display family photos on a wall or on shelves. Or you can display crafts that you do. Just about anything you collect can be displayed—even cookware.

You can use plants to fill empty spaces and brighten rooms. But be sure you are willing and able to care for them. Hang them or place them on tables or stands. Put large plants on the floor. Group them or use them individually. Choose plant containers that fit the room decor.

BARGAINS IN REDECORATING

Some time after you have decorated for the first time, you will probably want to change your decorating scheme. Parts of your home may look out of fashion. Some furnishings may be worn. Or you may just be tired of a room and ready for a change. As your life situation changes, so will your priorities. In turn, you may redecorate part or all of your home to meet your priorities.

Redecorating is different from decorating because you already have a base from which to start. If you decorated wisely the first time, there should be several items that you will want to keep when you redecorate. Old and new items do not need to match. They only need to agree, 11-13.

Use the same steps in planning to redecorate that you used to decorate. Planning is important if you are to find new items that blend with the old. Determine what you want to keep and what you want to replace. Evaluate why you want to get rid of items. You may find that some can be kept with a few changes. For in-

244

11-12 Making pillows is an inexpensive way to brighten a room. The other parts of this decorating scheme are neutral. The whole look of this room can be changed later just by changing the pillows.

stance, your couch may be sturdy, but you may not like its color or pattern. Reupholstering may satisfy your redecorating needs at a lower cost than replacing the couch.

You may redecorate in a single stage. Or you can redecorate in a series of stages spread over time. Time and money limits may cause you to take this approach. After you decide what you want to change, you can divide your project into stages. For instance, to redecorate the living room, you may replace the carpet as one stage. Changing the curtains may be another stage. And replacing some of the furniture and accessories could be another stage. Your priorities and budget will help you determine the order of the stages.

SOLVING SPACE PROBLEMS

If your home is small, you need to make the most of your space. Having organized storage

11-13 New and old can be blended when you redecorate.

Bargains in home decorating and design   245

helps you make more room in your living spaces. It also makes finding stored items easier.

You can reorganize closets in many ways, 11-14. These can help make using your storage space easier.

Adding shelf space above the hanging rod in a closet is helpful. In most closets there is only one shelf and it is about half the width of the closet. To triple your shelf space, get two more boards cut to the size of the existing shelf. Fit one in place just in front of the one already there. You may need to extend the frame or base on which it rests. The other shelf can be placed between the first shelf and the ceiling. You will need to put a base in place for it. The shelves need not be nailed in place. If you move, the boards can go with you.

Other movable boards can be cut to fit the space above a shower or tub. Place a plastic liner on the shelf to prevent moisture buildup. You can enclose these shelves by hanging a curtain on an expandable rod. Or if you are skilled in carpentry you can add doors. Shelf units can be placed in other parts of the bathroom for added storage, 11-15.

MARILYN BRANDOM,
PHOTO BY PHILIP BARTHOLEMEW

11-15 This wicker shelf unit can be used for extra storage even in a small space.

Space under a stairway or at the end of a hall or room can often be converted to storage, 11-16. You can buy ready-to-use shelves for this space. They can be purchased in components so you can adapt them to the space that exists. Or you can build your own shelves.

ARMSTRONG WORLD INDUSTRIES, INC.

ARMSTRONG WORLD INDUSTRIES, INC.

11-14 Storage areas can be organized in many ways to best meet your needs.

11-16 Ready-made storage pieces like these can turn unused space into an efficient storage area.

Often utility rooms and garages have poorly organized storage space. Shelves can make storage in these areas more efficient. Some types of shelves can be attached to the *ceiling joists* (wood boards that support the ceiling). See 11-17.

Shelves can also be placed in window nooks and over radiators. Shelf arrangements on bare walls provide open storage for displays.

Cardboard storage boxes come in many sizes and styles. Many have drawers or doors. Some fit under beds; others will fit in small spaces throughout the house. They also can be used to organize closet storage. Boxes can be painted, papered, or covered with fabric to match room decor.

Hooks and poles can be used for some types of storage. They are popular for hanging coats.

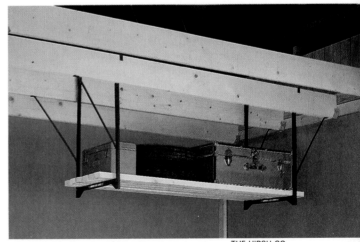

11-17 Shelves like this add storage space to garages and work areas.

Bargains in home decorating and design 247

They can be used in bathrooms to hang towels and bathroom supplies. (The supplies can be placed in buckets or plastic bags with handles.) Hooks can also be used to hang plants or other objects from the ceiling.

Space savers

Many furniture pieces are designed to help save space. Sofa beds and daybeds are two such pieces. They double as couches and beds, 11-18. This saves room if you don't have space for both.

Wall beds (sometimes called Murphy beds) are stored against the wall for extra floor space when the bed is not used. Wall beds are attached to the floor, the wall, or both. For this reason they may not be the right choice if you

rent or plan to move soon. A wall bed has an advantage over a sofa bed. A standard mattress can be used in it. Because it is not folded, the mattress retains firmness and box springs can be used. Wall beds can be purchased from twin to king sizes.

You can replace your regular bed frame with a platform that has drawers. This provides storage and sleeping space in the same area. Or you can use stacking beds in a children's room to save space, 11-19.

Stacking chairs and folding chairs are other types of space-saving furniture. Padded chests used for seating and storage also save space.

A drop leaf table takes up little space when the leaves are down. But it can be easily expanded when extra space is needed. You can

11-18 To save space, daybeds can double as couches.

GEORGIA-PACIFIC CORP.

11-19 Stacking beds allow people who share a room to have more space for daytime activities.

build a hinged table surface or desk that is attached to the wall. It can have legs that fold out or a hinged support that swings out from the wall. The table lays flat against the wall when it is not being used. Other household furniture and equipment can be mounted to the wall to save space. See 11-20.

NUTONE/SCOVILL

11-20 An ironing center can be stored neatly and out of the way. It is easy to set up for use.

In the kitchen, lost space can be regained by using small appliances that are installed on the wall or hung under kitchen cabinets. Many smaller appliances are available to be used where space is a premium, 11-21.

BARGAINS IN REMODELING

Remodeling is usually more expensive than redecorating. This is because it involves changes to the structure such as adding a wall or a room. But there are times when remodeling is more of a bargain than moving or trying to live in your home the way it is.

OSTER CORP.

11-21 This under-the-cabinet can opener is a convenient appliance that does not take up any counter space.

Bargains in home decorating and design   249

Remodeling may improve what is already there, like redoing the kitchen or basement, 11-22. Or usable space such as a family room or a garage may be added. You may enclose a porch or build a patio. Some kinds of remodeling increase the market value of your home, 11-23. Other remodeling gives you more satisfaction but does not increase the value of the home.

The cost of remodeling is measured in many ways. You need to ask yourself if the cost of remodeling is a better value than moving or keeping your living space the same. Will remodeling increase the quality of life in your home? Will the process cause too many inconveniences for the members of your living unit? Adding a room is not likely to be as inconvenient as remodeling the kitchen or bathroom. Will you remodel, then realize that you need to move anyway?

You also need to decide whether to use professionals or do the work yourself. You can save about half the money by remodeling yourself. But the work could take you twice as long or longer. If your project is not too complex and you know what you are doing, remodeling yourself may be worthwhile. But if tasks like rewiring and adding plumbing are involved, you may be better off hiring a professional. You may choose to do some tasks yourself and hire people for others. Or you may have a remodeling service do the whole job.

Getting your money's worth

Do your homework before you start a remodeling project. This will help you avoid making changes that cost you more than they are worth. Start by researching information about remodeling products, trends in design, and financing. Get estimates on how much your

GEORGIA-PACIFIC CORP.

11-22 This family has increased their living space by remodeling their basement.

remodeling project will cost. Find out trends in relationship to regaining remodeling costs when you sell your house. If you need a home improvement loan, shop to find the best rate.

If you decide to use a contractor to do your remodeling, select carefully. Find out answers to these questions:

1. Is the contractor licensed? By whom?
2. How long has the contractor been in business?
3. How have other clients felt about the contractor's work? (Ask the contractor for references or find names of clients at the local building department.)
4. Will the contractor show you a similar completed project?
5. Does the contractor have insurance coverage for all workers?
6. Will the contractor give you *lein wavers* to show that suppliers and subcontractors used for the project have been paid? (A lein waver prevents you from being held liable if your contractor does not pay for items used to remodel your house.)

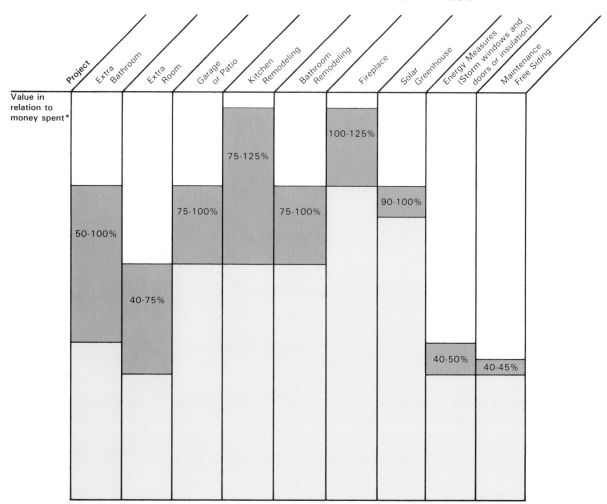

HOME IMPROVEMENT AND INCREASED HOME VALUE

*This means you can regain this much of your costs if you sell your house. There will be some loss in value as the house becomes older.

11-23 Remodeling improves your home. It can also increase your home's value.

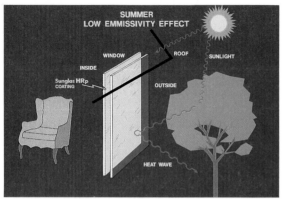

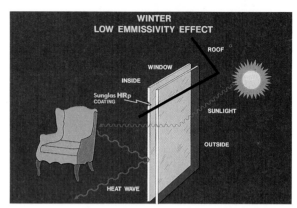

FORD GLASS DIV. FORD GLASS DIV.

11-24 A special coating on this insulating window keeps heat to the warm side of the glass.

Do not pay for the entire remodeling project until all of the work is finished the way you want it. The best arrangement is to pay 25 percent of the total fee before work starts. Pay the rest after the project is finished and you have inspected all the work. Contractors are more likely to complete a project the way you want it if they are waiting to be paid.

As you make your remodeling plan, keep your neighborhood in mind. Keep your improvements in line with nearby houses. Try not to raise the value of your home more than 20 percent over the value of neighboring homes. If you do, you may not be able to get the full value when you sell your house.

Consider adding features that conserve energy when you remodel. Such features are bargains because they lower your monthly energy bills. They also increase the resale value of your home. You may remove a drafty window and replace it with a wall or with an *insulating window*. See 11-24. Insulating windows provide a view, but they insulate better than standard windows. You may add insulation to your walls or replace old doors with insulating doors as you remodel. See 11-25. Or you may replace older appliances with other models that use less energy.

Trends in remodeling

House fashions change as do clothing fashions. The trend in housing today is toward high quality and open floor plans. Entertainment has also become a big housing concern.

New technology has improved the quality of housing materials. More and more components are standardized. This means that better quality products can be made at a lower price.

Computers of different types are also improving the quality of housing. Many programs

THERMA TRU CORP.

11-25 A fiberglass door with a polyurethane core has a much higher insulative value than a regular wood door.

ARMSTRONG WORLD INDUSTRIES, INC.

11-26 Open floor plans make living spaces seem bigger than they really are.

are designed to help plan a home that is as energy efficient as possible. Some help you find the best quality at the lowest price. Others help you design the most efficient floor plan to meet household members' needs.

Computers are also used within the home. Microcomputers control automatic garage door openers. Computers can be used to monitor lighting. They can also monitor heating and cooling systems. These functions make homes safer, more energy efficient, and more comfortable.

Floor plans are changing. Houses are more open. Rooms are less likely to be divided by walls, 11-26. This is especially true in smaller homes. For instance, the dining room, living room, and kitchen may really be one large room. Plants, shelves, or stairs may be used to divide the space into separate areas. But since you can see beyond one room into the next, each room seems more spacious.

Large window areas are also being used to make homes seem bigger. Picture windows, sliding glass doors, and bay windows all provide panoramic views. They lead the eye beyond a room. Skylights make rooms seem lighter and brighter. They also create a feeling of drama. Skylights are popular in kitchens, baths, and hallways. See 11-27.

VENTARAMA SKYLIGHT CORP.

11-27 Adding skylights to a room makes it seem brighter and more open.

Bargains in home decorating and design 253

Entertainment has become a big part of many people's lifestyles. A growing concept in housing is the media center. A media center may contain a stereo system, compact disc player, television, video recorder, and a personal computer. The media center can be in the living room or family room. Sometimes it is a part of a bedroom. More and more, the center is placed in a room of its own.

These trends should be considered if you are planning to remodel. They can help you make plans that will keep your living space modern. They can help you make the most of the space you have. If they increase your comfort and are within your budget, they can be a bargain for you.

to Know

American Society of Interior Designers . . . classic . . . insulating window . . . lein waver . . . loss leader sale . . . seasonal sale

to Review

Write your answers on a separate sheet of paper.

1. Which statement is always true about a bargain?
   a. It is less expensive than a similar item.
   b. It can be purchased nearby.
   c. It improves the quality of life.
   d. It does not need any repairs.
2. Name a possible drawback to using each of the following price reductions:
   a. Loss leader sales.
   b. Seasonal sales.
   c. Damaged goods sales.
   d. Discontinued line sales.
   e. Discount house price.
3. Changing furnishings and accessories is easier if you choose backgrounds that are _____.
4. Furniture that is a good value has:
   a. A low price.
   b. Simple lines.
   c. Bright floral fabric.
   d. Wood carvings.

5. _____ add a personal touch to a room's decoration.
6. (True or False) To redecorate, you should change all of the backgrounds, furnishings, and accessories in a room.
7. Name five places where you can add shelves to increase storage space.
8. Explain why a person might choose a wall bed instead of a sofa bed to save space. Explain why a person might choose a sofa bed over a wall bed.
9. (True or False) Remodeling is usually more expensive and complex than redecorating.
10. Give three guidelines to follow when remodeling.
11. Describe two methods that can be used to make small homes seem more open.

to Do

1. Divide into groups of three to five students and make a decorating plan for a living room. Include a budget, a rough sketch, samples of colors and dimensions needed, and prices from nearby stores.
2. Look for decorating articles on how to make small rooms look big. Clip pictures and record the kinds of background treatments that are used in the rooms.
3. Compare prices on a piece of furniture such as a couch or dining room table. Go to different stores or find different models in the same store. Try to find out why similar pieces have different prices. A salesperson may be able to help you. Share your findings with the class.
4. Make a bulletin board that shows how inexpensive items can be used to decorate a room. If possible, include prices of items used.
5. Make a list of guidelines to follow when you are planning to redecorate.
6. Make a model of a well-organized storage closet.
7. Make a list of remodeling projects that you think are good do-it-yourself projects. Make a list of those you would want to turn over to a professional.
8. Write a report on how computers are being used in homes.

Using bargains to remodel can increase your satisfaction with your house.

Bargains in home decorating and design 255

part 4

Progress in housing

Tony Cascade was a hotel manager in a large city. But when he got tired of the crowds and pollution, he built a small resort hotel in the middle of these natural surroundings. Before building, Tony consulted an architect. The architect designed a contemporary structure that blends well with the surroundings. Engineers were also consulted so that the structure would use natural resources as efficiently as possible.

Tony is content to live where nature is not crowded out by buildings, cars, and other manufactured goods. His concept of progress in housing is for people to spread out more. He feels that houses that do not waste natural resources are important for the future.

Not all of Tony's guests agree with his concept. Brenda Jones, an architect from New York, likes to visit Tony's resort for one week each year. But she would never give up life in the city. She enjoys living close to other people. She likes having facilities such as shopping centers and theaters nearby. Brenda's idea of progress in housing is to build more efficient multifamily units. She wants all people to be able to enjoy the kinds of natural surroundings that Tony does. But she thinks that city living is needed for industry and business. One of her goals as an architect is to design structures that make city living more pleasant.

What does progress in housing mean to you? What do you think can be done to make housing better for now and for the future?

Modern architectural styles have evolved from many styles of the past.

12

Evolution of exteriors

After studying this chapter, you will be able to:
- Recognize several different exterior house styles of the past and present.
- Discuss the background of these styles and the possibilities for future styles.
- Make a wise decision when choosing an exterior style for your house.

Each national or racial group has a *cultural heritage.* Because the United States has such a large mixture of peoples, it is rich in cultural heritage. Throughout the history of this country, ideas from many cultures have influenced the exterior designs of dwellings.

American Indian

Cultural influence can be seen in the dwellings of Indian tribes. The Navajos of the Southwest live in eight-sided *hogans* that are usually made of logs and mud. The door of a hogan always faces east because of religious belief. In Taos, New Mexico, Pueblo Indians live in an apartment-type community. See 12-1. The basic design used in their *adobe* dwellings is copied in houses throughout the country. The boxy construction, flat roof, and projecting roof beams are typical characteristics.

Spanish

The *Spanish* house style is pictured in 12-2. It is widely used in the South and Southwest where the climate is warm and dry. The overall design is asymmetrical. Other characteristics are a red tile roof, an enclosed patio, arch-shaped windows and doors, wrought iron exterior decor, and stucco walls. (Stucco is a type of plaster applied to the exterior walls of a house.)

Swedish

The "All-American" *log cabin* was actually created in Sweden. It was a popular style for those who traveled to the American frontier. It is still popular in underdeveloped wooded areas.

The typical log cabin is built of unfinished logs. It is a one-story, rectangular building with few windows. It has a gable roof. (Roof styles are pictured in 12-3.)

Dutch

Early Dutch settlers left their mark on colonial architecture with what is known as the *Dutch Colonial*. See 12-4. This style was not copied from houses in Holland. The Dutch created it after they came to America. The first Dutch Colonial houses were built in Pennsylvania and New York. They were often built of fieldstone or brick, but sometimes wood was used. They had a gambrel roof with eaves that

12-1 Pueblo Indians live in these dwellings built of adobe or baked mud.

THE GARLINGHOUSE COMPANY

12-2 This modern version of a Spanish style house copies many features of old mission churches and houses of southern California.

260

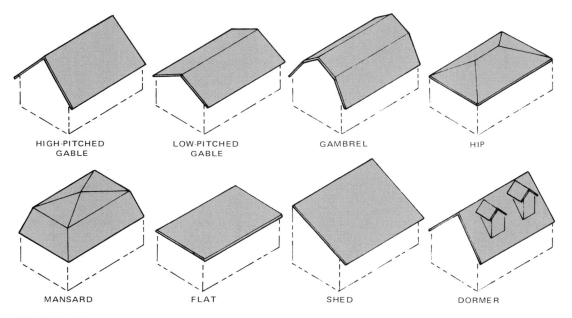

HIGH-PITCHED GABLE LOW-PITCHED GABLE GAMBREL HIP

MANSARD FLAT SHED DORMER

12-3 Roof styles have a great effect on the exterior design of buildings.

flared outward. Sometimes the flared portion extended out over an open porch. It became known as the "Dutch kick."

Other characteristics of the Dutch Colonial are a central entrance, a chimney that is not centered, dormers in the second story, and windows with small panes.

French

The French influence is seen in many structures. The *Mansard* roof, a variation of the gambrel roof, was designed by a French architect. When used on detached single-family dwellings, the roof continues all around the house. When used on commercial buildings, the Mansard roof may be used only on one or two sides. Dormers often project from the steeply pitched part of the roof.

French influence is also seen in the house style called *French Provincial*. See 12-5. This style was introduced to New Orleans and became popular all over the country.

12-4 The outstanding characteristic of the Dutch Colonial house is a gambrel roof which flares at the bottom.

12-5 French Provincial houses are usually symmetrical with a formal appearance.

A French Provincial house can be as tall as two-and-one-half stories. it has a delicate, dignified appearance and is usually symmetrical. The windows are a dominant part of the design. The tops of the windows break into the eave line. A modern adaptation of the French Provincial is shown in 12-6.

MASONITE CORP.

12-6 This modern house has many characteristics of the French Provincial style.

English

Although exterior house designs were influenced by many cultures, England's influence was the greatest. This is because the history of the United States is so closely tied to England. During the decades that England ruled the colonies, its influence was felt in all phases of life, including housing. English influence is so closely related to the colonists' own ideas that separating house styles into "English" and "American" groups is difficult. Studying them together is easier.

English/American

When the first settlers arrived in America, they lived in crude caves and huts. As soon as they had the needed resources, they built dwellings that satisfied more of their needs and priorities. Because of the harsh climate, they found they needed dwellings that had sturdy walls and steep roofs with shingles to shed rain and snow. They also needed large chimneys to accommodate large fireplaces and small windows to help keep heat inside. The historic reconstruction at Plimoth Plantation near Plymouth, Massachusetts, duplicates some of the early dwellings. See 12-7.

Most of the people in the early history of America were farmers. The life-style of these people was simple. This was reflected in their housing. Houses, especially those in New England, were small and far apart. Living units sometimes consisted of more than one generation, so the small houses would be crowded.

These houses were alive with change. Families did not move because they needed a larger or better house. They adapted their house to fit their new situation. Thus, the house changed often to reflect the growth, success, and attitudes of its owners.

The earliest homes were simple one-room buildings with a wooden or stone chimney at one end. As the family grew larger and/or prospered, additions were built. The first addition to be made was a second room, as

12-7 This view of Plimoth Plantation shows the reconstructed village of the early colonists.

large as the first. It was added next to the wall with the chimney. See 12-8. This is how the *Cape Cod* house design was created.

As shown in 12-9, the traditional Cape Cod is a small, symmetrical, one-and-one-half story house with a gable roof. It has a central entrance and a central chimney with several fireplaces. The eave line of the roof is just above the first-floor windows. The windows usually have shutters.

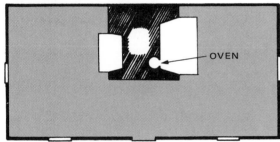

12-8 Colonists would make their houses larger by adding a room on the other side of the chimney.

12-9 The Cape Cod is a one-and-one-half story house with a gable roof and central entrance.

When more space was needed, the loft area of the Cape Cod was expanded and made into finished bedrooms. Openings were cut in the roof for the construction of dormers which added light and air to the second story.

Another way to extend the space of the basic Cape Cod design was to add a lean-to section to the back. See 12-10. This created the *salt box* house design pictured in 12-11. The name salt box comes from the shape of the boxes in which salt was stored at that time.

A salt box house is two or two-and-one-half stories high. It has a steep gable roof that extends down to the first floor in the rear. A large central chimney and large windows with small panes of glass are typical characteristics.

A later development was the *garrison* house, 12-12. The name comes from early garrisons or forts. Like the houses named after them, they had an overhanging second story. The overhang allowed extra space on the second floor without having to dig larger foundations. It also had a supporting effect so that second story floor joists did not sag in the middle. (Joists are the beams that are set on edge to support flooring.)

The overhang is always on the front of the house and sometimes extends to the sides and rear. Carved drops or *pendants* below the

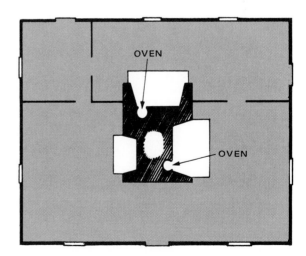

12-10 With a lean-to section added to the rear of the house, the basic Cape Cod became a salt box house.

overhang provide ornamentation. Other characteristics of the garrison house are a symmetrical design, a steep gable roof, and windows that have small panes of glass.

Later developments. As colonial life prospered, better houses were built. A popular style was the *Georgian*. It was adapted from English architecture. It is called Georgian because it was popular during the era when the Kings George I, II, and III ruled England.

Two Georgian houses are shown in 12-13 and 12-14. They have simple exterior lines, a dignified appearance, and a symmetrical design. The windows have small panes of glass.

WESTERN RED CEDAR LUMBER ASSOC.

ACORN STRUCTURES, INC.

12-11 Pictured are the traditional salt box house and a modern version of the same style.

12-12 The garrison style house features an overhanging second story.

264

12-13 Georgian houses have simple, dignified lines. Ornamentation is found under the eaves.

12-14 A symmetrical design and tall chimneys at each end are often features of Georgian houses.

The roof style is either hip or gable. The hip roofs are sometimes topped by a flat area with a *balustrade* (railing). This area is called a captain's walk or a widow's walk.

Georgian houses usually have a tall chimney at each end of the roof. Most of them have some ornamentation under the eaves. As the style developed, it became more elaborate. More ornamentation was given to doors and windows. The style also changed according to where it was built. Wood was used in New England. Stone was used in the Mid-Atlantic region. In the South, brick was used, and a wing was added to each side of the main house.

When the American colonists began to pull away from English influence, the *Federal* style became popular. See 12-15. The Federal style house has a box-like shape. It is at least two stories high and has a symmetrical design. The roof is flat and is surrounded by a balustrade. *Pediments,* 12-16, are usually over the doors and windows. Sometimes a small *portico* is added to the main entrance. (A portico is an open space covered with a roof that is supported by columns.)

Greek Revival

The next major step in the evolution of exteriors was called the *Greek revival.* During

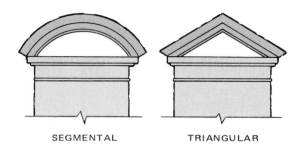

SEGMENTAL   TRIANGULAR

12-16 Pediments are used over doors and windows to add interest to a design.

this stage, the architecture of ancient Greece became popular. Thomas Jefferson was a great promoter of this style. He was a skilled architect and designed his famous home, Monticello, in the Greek revival style. See 12-17. He also designed some government buildings in this style, thus setting a pattern for many of the official buildings in America.

The main characteristic of the Greek revival style is a two-story portico. (A portico is a covered area in front of a house.) The portico is supported by Greek columns and has a large triangular roof called a pediment. Houses of this style are large and impressive.

An offshoot of the Greek revival style is the *Southern Colonial.* In the South, people owned

12-15 The large, boxy Federal style is suitable for single-family and multifamily dwellings.

12-17 Thomas Jefferson's home, Monticello, is typical of the Greek revival style.

12-18 Mount Vernon is a good example of a Southern Colonial house.

ROLOC

large amounts of land. Large numbers of people were needed to run the plantations. At least 200 and sometimes as many as 500 people lived on a single plantation. Large houses seemed a natural part of the Southern culture.

Mount Vernon, the home of George Washington, is typical of the Southern Colonial style, 12-18. The two-story columns are much like those of the Greek revival style. But these columns extend across the entire front, and they are covered by an extension of the roof. The Southern Colonial is a large, two or three-story frame house. The design is symmetrical. The roof style is hip or gable. Dormers (windows that extend from the roof), shutters, and a *belvadere* are often included. (A belvadere is a small room on the roof of a house used as a lookout.)

English influence returns

Following the Civil War, the *Victorian* house style became popular. It is named after Queen Victoria of England. The main characteristic is an abundance of decorative trim. See 12-19. Other characteristics are high porches, steep gable roofs, tall windows, and *turrets* or towers.

As the style developed, owners tried to outdo one another in the amount of decorative trim on their houses. Quantity became more important than quality. Jigsawed wood trim in scrolls and designs appeared under eaves and around windows and doors. This decoration came to be known as "gingerbread."

Inside, Victorian houses had high ceilings, dark stairways and long halls. This style came to be associated with the "haunted" houses of horror movies.

Traditional, modern, and contemporary

The house styles previously described in this chapter are called *traditional* styles. They are the best of the designs that were created in the past. They have survived the test of time. They have distinct characteristics that set them apart from other styles.

Modern house styles are relatively new. They have been accepted by many people and have a good chance of surviving. The ranch and the split level are the two major modern house styles.

Contemporary house designs are the very latest ones. They are controversial. Some people like them; some do not. The designs are

12-19 Excessive ornamentation is found on houses of the Victorian style.

surprising. They look "strange" because people are not used to seeing them. Listing their characteristics is impossible because they vary so widely in shape, detail, and materials. Only time will tell which of the contemporary designs are good enough to last.

Ranch

The *ranch* style, 12-20, began in the West. Informal life-styles, large plots of land, and a warm climate made the ranch style ideal for that region. A ranch house is a one-story structure, but it often has a basement, 12-21. It has a low-pitched roof with a wide overhang. Large windows and sliding glass doors that open onto a patio are common.

The ranch style has become popular throughout the country. The building materials and the number of energy-saving features used vary according to the region.

The one-story structure without stairs makes the ranch house easy to maintain and easy to

walk through. However, because it covers a large area, it is expensive to build. The large foundation and roof are costly. Another disadvantage of the long, rambling structure is that it is less energy-efficient than other house styles.

12-20 Indoor and outdoor living areas are easily integrated in a ranch house.

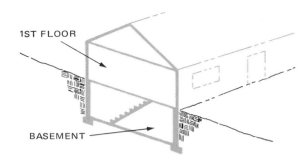

12-21 Some ranch houses have basements which can be used as living space.

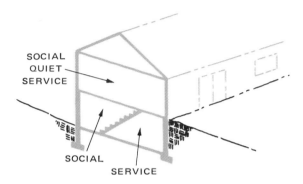

12-22 Part of the basement of a hillside ranch is above ground level.

A variation of the ranch is the *hillside ranch,* 12-22. As its name implies, the house is built on a hill. Part of the basement is exposed. Depending on the layout of the lot, the exposed part may be anything from a living area with a beautiful view to a garage. See 12-23.

Another variation of the ranch is the *raised ranch,* 12-24. (It is sometimes called split entry.) It is like the ranch except that the top part of the basement is above ground. This allows light to enter the basement through windows. The basement living area can be very pleasant if it is well-insulated and waterproof. A disadvantage is that some stairs must be climbed to get anywhere in the house. This can be a problem for children, handicapped persons, and the elderly.

Split level

The *split level* house style, 12-25, was developed for sloping lots. This is where it looks best although it is sometimes used on flat lots. A split level house has either three or four levels. The levels can be arranged in many ways, as shown in 12-26.

An advantage of the split level is that separating traffic to the social, quiet, and

12-23 The exposed part of the basement of this hillside ranch is used as a garage.

service areas is easy. Also, there are only a few stairs to climb to get from one level to another. On the other hand, some stairs must be climbed to get from one area to another which is difficult for some persons.

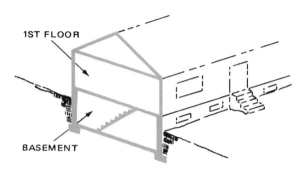

12-24 The top part of the basement of a raised ranch house is above ground. This makes the basement livable.

When comparing houses with the same amount of living space, ranch styles are more costly to build, heat, and cool than split level styles. However, split level houses are more costly to build, heat, and cool than two-story houses. A two-story house is economical and energy-efficient, 12-27.

Contemporary house designs

Contemporary designs cannot be described as easily as traditional or modern ones. They do not fit into nice, neat categories.

The one identifying trait of a contemporary design is uniqueness. Most of them use simple lines with little ornamentation. The exterior design is often important to the dwelling as a whole. It encloses some areas to provide privacy, yet indoor and outdoor spaces are integrated in other areas.

Roof styles and building materials vary widely. For instance, an A-frame house has a

12-25 Split level houses have three or four levels that help separate the social, quiet, and service areas.

270

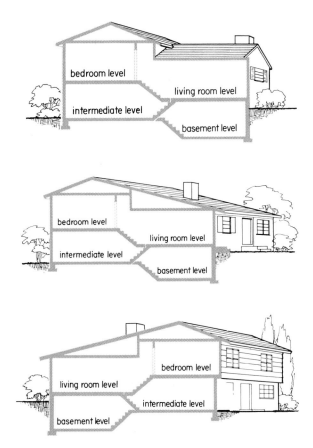

12-26 Changing the arrangement of levels in a split level house changes its outside appearance.

very steep gable roof which extends to the ground. Most of the exterior is either roof or window. On the other hand, a "plastic" house has a molded shape made of fiberglass or a plastic material. Windows are small and unimportant to the design. Look at 12-28 to see some contemporary house designs.

Housing designers

The most noted architect of modern times is Frank Lloyd Wright who lived from 1869 to 1959. He is called the "father of modern architecture." In the early years of his career, his influence was greatest in Europe, but it spread throughout the world. Contemporary housing designers are influenced by his work, especially those working in the United States.

Long before the idea became widely accepted, Wright realized that many changes were taking place in family life. He designed houses to accommodate those changes.

Wright's beliefs about housing were contained in a speech he gave to the Association of Federal Architects in 1938. He said, "Every decent design for any building should be a design for better living, a better design for a richer, fairer way of life . . ."

He also gave his prescription for a modern house. "First, a good site. Pick one at the most difficult spot – pick a site no one wants – but pick one that has features making for character; trees; individuality . . . That now means getting out of the city. Then standing on that site, look about you so you can see what has charm . . . Build your house so that you may still look, from where you stood, upon all that charmed you and lose nothing of what you saw before the house was built but see more."

He further noted that the architecture is right only if it "accentuates the character of the landscape."

Frank Lloyd Wright valued economy. He tried to use materials that were close at hand – those found in the near natural environment. Although his houses were unique, beautiful, and functional, they often cost less than other houses of equal size that were built at the same time. One of the houses he designed is shown in 12-29.

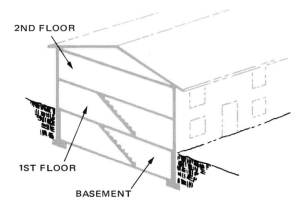

12-27 The two-story house is an economical house design.

12-28 Contemporary house designs vary in size, shape, and building materials.

12-29 This house in Phoenix, Arizona, was designed by Frank Lloyd Wright.

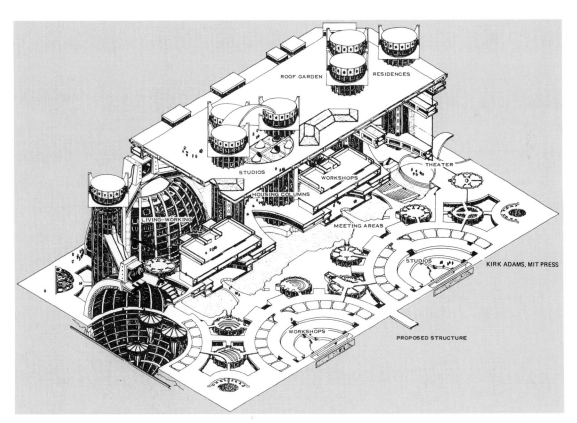

ROOF GARDEN
RESIDENCES

STUDIOS

WORKSHOPS
THEATER

HOUSING COLUMNS

LIVING-WORKING

MEETING AREAS

STUDIOS

KIRK ADAMS, MIT PRESS

WORKSHOPS

PROPOSED STRUCTURE

12-30 Modular structures make it possible for the entire city of Arcosanti to be built on only seven acres of land.

Paolo Soleri was a student of Frank Lloyd Wright. His first experimental dwellings are found near Taliesin West, the Frank Lloyd Wright School of Architecture. Soleri has designed cities for as few as 3000 and as many as 170,000 people. A sketch of one of these cities, Arcosanti, is shown in 12-30. In 12-31, you can see one of the structures being built.

SALLY CLEVENGER

12-31 This is a model of a multifamily dwelling being built at Arcosanti.

Soleri's idea is to build his structures from the cheapest durable materials that are close at hand. His structures are of concrete made with sand and gravel taken from a nearby riverbed. His architecture students do the building themselves. They learn the basic building crafts—laying brick, building forms, and casting concrete.

His designs are modular. The large structures are repetitions of a basic module that are stacked 30 high. But unlike modular complexes of other designers, Soleri's modules are irregular or angular shapes rather than rectangles. Beds and bookshelves of plywood are built in.

Another contemporary architect, Moshe Safdie, designed *Habitat*. This multifamily housing project was on display at Montreal's Expo -67. Like Soleri's Arcosanti, Habitat is an entire city located on just a few acres. Public facilities for recreational and cultural opportunities are built in.

Contemporary architects like these know that humans can adapt their environment to meet their changing needs and priorities. They also know that the environment can be damaged if humans use it unwisely. The challenge they face is to design satisfying dwellings in a controlled environment. If this challenge is met, people of today as well as people in the future will have the opportunity to live in surroundings that help them meet their highest needs and personal priorities.

to Know

adobe dwelling . . . balustrade . . . belvadere . . . Cape Cod . . . contemporary . . . cultural heritage . . . dormer . . . Dutch Colonial . . . Federal . . . French Provincial . . . flat roof . . . gable roof . . . gambrel roof . . . garrison . . . Georgian . . . Greek revival . . . hogan . . . hillside ranch . . . hip roof . . . log cabin . . . Mansard roof . . . modern . . . pediment . . . portico . . . raised ranch . . . ranch . . . salt box . . . shed roof . . . Southern Colonial . . . Spanish . . . split level . . . traditional . . . turret . . . Victorian . . . Frank Lloyd Wright

to Review

Write your answers on a separate sheet of paper.
1. A red tile roof, an enclosed patio, and arch-shaped windows and doors are characteristics of:
   a. Adobe dwellings.
   b. Spanish house.
   c. Dutch Colonial.
   d. French Provincial.
2. The log cabin is the result of _____ influence.
3. Draw sketches of a low-pitched gable roof and a high-pitched gable roof.
4. An overhanging second story is a characteristic of what house style?

5. Which house style had its beginning as a one-room dwelling?
   a. Spanish house.
   b. French Provincial.
   c. Cape Cod.
   d. Southern Colonial.
6. Which architectural style was promoted by Thomas Jefferson?
7. Describe a portico.
8. List four characteristics of a Victorian house.
9. Name one advantage and one disadvantage of the ranch house.
10. What kind of lot is best suited to the split level house style?
11. Who is known as the "father of modern architecture?"
12. Which of the following words would best describe Paolo Soleri's Arcosanti?
   a. Steel.
   b. Rectangular.
   c. Expensive.
   d. Modular.

to Do

1. As a group activity, make a collage of sketches and photographs of house styles. Divide into teams. Write stories about the lifestyles of people who lived when the styles were first popular.
2. Take pictures of different house styles in your community. Work together as a class to identify them.
3. Go to the library and do some research on architectural styles. Report to the class on some of the factors that influenced each style.
4. Read real estate ads in the newspaper. Note the styles mentioned and the way they are described.
5. Collect news items about contemporary architects and/or contemporary house designs.
6. Give a report on one of the following:
   a. Frank Lloyd Wright.
   b. Paolo Soleri.
   c. Moshe Safdie.

Fulfilling needs for housing without creaing new problems is a
challenge in today's world.

13

Housing needs today

After studying this chapter, you will be able to:
- ■ Describe the rapid growth of cities during the Era of Industry.
- ■ Explain how slums are created and describe some slum clearance projects.
- ■ Discuss the pros and cons of suburbs.
- ■ Discuss the rapid changes taking place in the Era of Automation.
- ■ List some of the ways you can control your housing environments.

Many of today's housing needs have been brought about by the rapid population shift of the 20th century. It brought families from agricultural areas into the cities. This created housing problems that still confront most, if not all, major cities.

THE ERA OF INDUSTRY

As the United States began to mass produce more goods, factories attracted a large labor supply. People came from scattered farms and concentrated in small areas. Agriculture became a way of life for fewer and fewer people. Now, less than five percent of

American people farm for a living. This dramatic shift took place in less than a single lifetime. It caused many changes, including some related to housing.

The new city life

In the city, small social groupings that had existed gave way to a new city life. Money was earned outside the home, so the home was no longer a family work center. It became a place to eat, sleep, and spend leisure time.

The sudden and rapid growth of city populations caused a rush to build houses. A confusing number of house styles came into being. Too little control of surroundings brought problems. Construction was often of shoddy quality and designs were poor. Too many people were jammed into too little space.

The creation of slums

Row houses and apartments can be good places to live. (Row houses are a continuous group of houses connected by common sidewalls.) But in early cities, too many were built in too little space. Too little consideration was given to building satisfying housing. As a result, *slums* were created.

Congress defines a slum as an area in which most of the buildings are harmful to health, safety, or morals. Poorly built shacks, tenement houses, and once good homes that are in bad repair are all types of slum housing.

Whole areas become slums for many reasons. The cause may be neglect, overcrowding, poor arrangement of living space, or lack of ventilation, light, and sanitation. Buildings in these areas become targets for arson and other crimes that affect health and safety. Factories and junkyards are close to slums. They often pollute the air. Children must play on streets or in crowded and equally unsafe public play areas. Other problems of substandard housing are listed in 13-1. Living conditions like these do not always satisfy even the primary needs of people, much less their secondary needs and personal priorities.

Slums affect everyone

Slum conditions, no matter how close or far, touch you in some way. Your community may pay the cost of welfare and fire, police, and health protection for a slum area. Since the federal government shares some of these costs with local governments, the costs are spread to taxpayers everywhere.

Slums are also costly in terms of human resources. People living in slums may not have the chance to develop their full potential. Society loses the chance to gain from their intelligence, creativity, and skills.

PROBLEMS IN SUBSTANDARD HOUSING

NONHUMAN	HUMAN
Rats and other vermin	Violence to persons
Poisons	assault
Fire and burning	fighting and beating
Freezing and cold	rape
Poor plumbing	Violence to possessions
Dangerous electrical wiring	things thrown or dropped
Trash (broken glass, cans, and so forth)	stealing
Heights that are not protected	Verbal abuse
Poorly designed or deteriorating structures	from own family
walls too thin	from neighbors
ceilings coming down	from caretakers
doors that will not close or lock	from outsiders
rickety stairs	

Adapted from: Rainwater, Lee. "Fear and the House-As-Haven in the Lower Class." Symposium on the Social Psychology of Low-Income Housing: Policy and People, American Psychological Association. Los Angeles, CA.

13-1 How would you feel if you had to face these problems?

Slum clearance projects

Federal, state, and local agencies have taken action to eliminate slum conditions. Laws have been passed to protect the nation's housing. In addition, some communities have made progress toward better housing as a result of group effort. Some of the many projects that have been undertaken are:

1. In Cleveland, Ohio, a guide on saving declining neighborhoods was developed and published.
2. A real estate board in Norristown, Pennsylvania, inspected all the property in town. They notified owners whose houses needed to be improved. As a result, 50 units were torn down, and 500 were improved.
3. A nonprofit foundation for slum clearance was formed in East Chicago, Indiana. Purdue University and several industrial companies took part in the project.
4. The city of New Orleans developed a program to enforce housing standards. All houses were to be inspected within 10 years. In the first year, 2000 homes were improved to meet the city's housing standards.
5. A nationwide project called ACTION (American Council To Improve Our Neighborhoods) was established. The purpose of the council is to help groups of citizens with projects. See 13-2.
6. The Community Block Grant Program has been used for a variety of purposes. Members of a community determine their housing needs and apply for federal funds. The program has assisted low and moderate income families.

The move to the suburbs

Suburbs are cities, towns, or villages that are clustered around the borders of a larger city. They sometimes extend into farm lands.

Suburbs were formed as people moved away from the inner city. They wanted to escape the crowding, noise, and crime. They wanted to live in newer, better homes that they could own.

Improved transportation made the move to the suburbs possible. Before the Industrial Revolution which started the Era of Industry, good transportation was not available. There were no systems of roads, trains, or buses to get people from one place to another. People had to live a short distance from their jobs.

When rail and bus transport systems were developed, they linked the suburbs to the city. Transportation became convenient and cheap. The popularity of the family car also helped solve the problem of transportation.

Many people then combined the use of their car and the mass transit systems to get from their suburban homes to their jobs in the city. As the transport systems developed people could spread out even further. In 13-3, you can see a huge transportation network to move people to and from the suburbs by rail. A similar network of highways and expressways moves people to and from the city by car.

Pros and cons of suburbs

People who moved to the suburbs did escape many of the city's problems. Generally, they

Put these things together and they spell ACTION— for your home, neighborhood, community, country.

Alert your neighbors to the opportunity of community improvements. Arouse their interest.

Clear up your own housing and neighborhood deficiencies first.

Talk to community leaders. Get them to join you and help.

Insist on a start being made right away, no matter how small. Tackle at least one manageable project as a focus for organized activity.

Organize the widest possible participation from every part of your community.

Never give up. Keep prodding local officials. If one course of action fails, try another.

13-2 These are the goals of the American Council To Improve Our Neighborhoods. Together, these goals could have a great impact on housing.

System Map

Legend

● Red Line · Glenmont/Shady Grove
● Orange Line · New Carrollton/Vienna
● Blue Line · Addison Road/National Airport
● Green Line · Branch Avenue/Greenbelt
○ Yellow Line · Franconia-Springfield & Huntington/Mt Vernon Sq-UDC

⇔ Parking

⊚ Transfer station

Station in service

Future station

13-3 A network of mass transit lines connects Washington, D.C. with the surrounding suburbs.

felt more safe and secure. They lived in nicer homes that were closer to schools, parks, and shopping centers. However, suburbs have created new housing problems. Those who live along transportation routes between cities and suburbs often complain of noise and fumes. Generally, such residential properties are less costly because of the nuisances. The priorities of the residents determine whether they choose to accept the nuisances or to move to an area with more costly housing.

Another problem of suburbs is a sense of sameness and dullness. Neighborhoods are full of houses that are similar in design and value. Many suburbs lack the excitement of having a variety of things to see and do.

Still another outcome of life in the suburbs has been the emergence of neighborhoods similar in class. Distinct social classes in the suburbs have brought with it problems that are related to segregation and integration.

Segregation means setting apart. In relation to housing, it means that groups of similar people are set apart from others. Thus, people in the lower class are often grouped together in the inner city. People of the middle class dominate the suburbs. Upper-class people usually live on large estates or in plush downtown apartments.

Integration means combining. In integrated housing, groups of people are mixed. People of different ethnic backgrounds, races, religions, educations, and socioeconomic levels live next to each other. See 13-4.

The topic of integration has caused a great deal of unrest and disagreement. It has been an issue in schools and on jobs. This problem is closely related to housing decisions. Some laws have been made to deal with the problems. Open housing ordinances make it illegal to deny equal housing opportunities. People of any race, religion, age, or other group cannot be denied housing in a neighborhood.

Do you recall any problems with integration in your community? Were they solved, or do they still exist?

GEORGE GALE

13-4 Some housing projects integrate low and middle-income families. This neighborhood has some houses in a lower price range.

Rural housing

Many rural people have beautiful and comfortable homes as shown in 13-5. However, rural areas have housing problems just as urban areas do. In fact, studies show that the *rural poor* are some of the most neglected people in the United States. Their housing is often substandard as shown in 13-6.

Another neglected group are *migrant workers.* These are seasonal workers who move from farm to farm as they are needed. They sometimes must live in substandard housing such as that pictured in 13-7.

Many of the rural poor and migrant workers do not have sanitary conditions in their homes. Some are without hot water, flush toilets, and places to bathe or shower. So far, most housing improvement projects have been directed toward substandard housing in urban areas. Because the buildings are more concentrated there, the problems are more noticeable. Both urban and rural areas need attention.

ERA OF AUTOMATION

In just one lifetime, the country's main economic support changed from agriculture to industry to automation. Today, machines are

CAROL RIGGS

13-6 The rural poor live in substandard housing.

performing tasks once done by humans. The pace of life has become faster than it once was.

In his best seller, "Future Shock," Alvin Toffler tells us that change was so slow in past history that it was hardly noticed. One could live an entire lifetime and not feel the impact of the changes taking place. He reminds us that of the last 800 lifetimes, humans spent 650 of them as cave dwellers. Only in the last two

MASONITE CORP.

13-5 Many farm families live comfortably in good housing.

13-7 At certain times of the year, migrant workers must live in housing like this. Little community assistance is available for these people.

lifetimes has anyone used an electric motor. And in the last lifetime alone, most of the objects we take for granted in everyday life have been developed, 13-8. Future shock is the term Toffler uses to describe these fast-moving changes.

Housing a changing people

You are living in a time of change. The rate of change is so rapid that sometimes people have difficulty knowing where they are or what they need. Watching the changes occur is like seeing a movie with the projector running at high speed. You cannot tell very much about what is taking place.

These rapid changes can be discussed in terms of objects, places, and people. They all affect housing.

Objects related to housing. Objects are available in many forms and from many types of materials. If you were to list the objects in a typical home, which ones could you cross off as not being needed? How many are needed?

Today, many objects are mass-produced to minimize cost. Buying a replacement for something is sometimes cheaper than repairing it. Objects are made for short-term use because newer models will be available soon. We have become a "throw-away" society. Have you ever noticed the items that are taken to city dumps?

Have you seen some that could still be used? What "throw-away" objects are used in your home? Do you use paper towels or napkins?

Only a few generations ago, people bought sugar and flour in large cotton sacks that were recycled. They were made into dish towels, pillow cases, clothing, or some other item. Then they were probably recycled again as cleaning rags. What kind of containers are used for food

13-8 Most young people expect to see computers in schools and homes. But they were not so common just one generation before.

Housing needs today   283

products today? What happens to the containers?

Place related to housing. Most people today move quickly from one place to another. Jobs, vacation plans, and other aspects of living cause people to travel a great deal. The average car owner travels 10,000 miles (16 000 kilometers) each year. Some people belong to the "jet set." They frequently travel long distances by air. Add these to the other methods of transportation, and the picture is clear that today's society is made of mobile people.

Mobile people move the location of their housing too. One family out of five will move from one home to another within a year. The number of two-home families is increasing. These families spend part of their time in one place and part in another.

People related to housing. Because objects and places change, people must also change. And because people change, their housing needs and priorities change.

One such change is in the pattern of home ownership. Home ownership was once very important to most Americans. But since people now move more often, they may choose not to own their homes.

People of today have different life-styles than have been common in the past. Many households consist of a single person or a single-parent family. Others consist of couples who do not have children. With smaller living units, less space is needed.

Not only do people as individuals change, but the total number of people in America has increased. More people have caused a need for more housing units than were ever needed before.

Housing and the economy

Housing performs better than most parts of the economy. In fact, housing has led the way according to economic indicators. The contribution of the housing industry to the *Gross National Product* (GNP) is shown in 13-9. (The GNP is the total value of the goods and services produced in the United States during a time period.)

THE ECONOMY AND HOUSING

Quarter	Change in housing industry	Change in GNP
IV 84	− 10.8%	+ 0.6%
I 85	+ 1.7	+ 3.7
II 85	+ 7.1	+ 1.1
III 85	+ 8.5	+ 3.0
IV 85	+ 5.7	+ 0.7
I 86	+ 9.7	+ 3.2

Copyright 1986, Builder magazine, Hanley-Wood, Inc., Washington, D.C., Reprinted with permission.

13-9 This chart shows that the housing industry has an effect on the nation's economy. Much of the money spent on housing is used to employ all of the people involved in manufacturing and selling houses. They then have more money to spend. In this way, growth of the housing industry improves the economy.

Many people are employed in the building industry. Others are in related fields. Can you name some of the careers and jobs available in constructing a house? In securing a loan to buy a house? In the furnishings and decorating of a home? Probably no one can identify all of the employment areas that are involved in housing.

Mortgage interest rates and tax advantages are factors related to growth in the housing industry. Another factor is the need for housing by the "baby boomers" who were born during and immediately after World War II. They continue to need housing into the 1990s.

Changes in the types of housing that are considered to be popular, less expensive, or best suited for the changing life styles of people affect the economy also. The mobile home industry boomed a number of years ago. Manufactured housing of various types continue to be popular. Multifamily units and other types of attached housing meets the need for those needing less expensive housing. First time home-owners, singles, and the elderly require less space and often have less of their income to spend on housing.

Our mobile society requires changes in housing. Those who desire to or must rent affect the economy in one way. Homeowners have a different effect. Many homeowners want to "trade up" in their housing. That means they desire to improve their standard of living by securing a better or bigger house or by changing neighborhoods.

Computer-matched housing

In this Era of Automation, many decisions are made for people. They do not question the decisions. In fact, people often take them for granted. People expect carpet and draperies to be furnished when they move into a house. Large pieces of equipment such as the kitchen range and refrigerator are there. There may be many shelves, drawers, and a snack bar that are already built-in. People do not have to make decisions about size, color, brand, or price of items unless they want to change them.

You will always make some housing decisions, but they are becoming easier. Nationwide real estate companies now rely on computers to provide them with information about available housing. The real estate agent can enter into the computer the type of living unit you have or want, and your living unit can be "matched" to a new home. When you move into your new home, everything will be ready for you. You will bring few items with you. Most of the usable things you have will be left behind for the next living unit that is "matched" to your old dwelling.

Life will probably continue to move at a fast pace, so you should prepare yourself to make new types of housing decisions. To do so requires being aware of changes and of the effects changes have on people and the environment.

CONTROLLING HOUSING ENVIRONMENTS

For decades, the great American dream was to own a single-family dwelling. When a family reached that point in life, they were considered "successful." The creation of suburbs is proof that Americans sought that dream.

As suburbs developed, sites for dwellings became smaller. The houses were built closer together. The streets and highways became con-

gested. The new housing environment did not satisfy a great number of the people. They had to learn to control their environment so they could maintain its satisfying qualities.

Micro and macroenvironments

Your *microenvironment* is your near surroundings. It affects you greatly because you interact with it so much. The dwelling in which you live is one part of your microenvironment. The yard or site on which your dwelling rests is another part.

Your larger surroundings are called your *macroenvironment*. It includes:
1. A transport system including roads, railways, and airports as well as individual vehicles.
2. Community facilities such as shopping centers, churches, schools, hospitals, and fire and police protection.
3. The housing industry.
4. Private and government agencies, some of which are listed in 13-10.

GROUPS CONCERNED WITH HOUSING

American Association of Retired People
American Bankers Association
American Public Health Association
Building Products Institute
Department of Agriculture—especially
   Farmers Home Administration (FmHA)
Department of Health, Education and Welfare (HEW)
Department of Justice
Department of Labor
Environmental control agencies at national, state, and local levels
Federal Equal Housing Opportunity Council
Federal Housing Administration (FHA)
Housing and Urban Development (HUD)
Housing Authority at state and local levels
Manufactured Housing Institute
National Association of Home Builders
National Association of Real Estate Boards
National Commission in Urban Problems
Planning Commissions at state and local levels
Veteran's Administration (VA)

13-10 These are some of the groups that influence your macroenvironment.

You are already in the habit of making decisions about your microenvironment. If you are to control your total housing environment, you must also become involved in the decision-making that affects your macroenvironment. Are you aware of the housing decisions being made in your community? Do the people living there want to become a part of the decision-making process? Are they encouraged by housing agencies and other groups to become involved?

Types of environments

As you think about controlling your housing environment, you should be familiar with the three different types of environments:
1. The natural environment.
2. The constructed environment.
3. The behavioral environment.

The *natural environment* is that which is provided by nature, 13-11. Land, water, trees, and solar energy are examples of resources of the natural environment.

The *constructed environment* is the natural environment after it is changed by human effort. A constructed environment is created whenever a dwelling is built, whenever trees and bushes are planted around the dwelling, and whenever heat pumps, heaters, or air conditioners are used to change the indoor climate.

Together, natural and constructed environments can provide pleasing surroundings as shown in 13-12. A highway through the mountains makes the beautiful scenery accessible to people. Buildings located along beaches allow people to enjoy a view of the water, 13-13.

The *behavioral environment* is the interaction among people. Human resources such as intelligence, skills, energy, and attitude are part of this environment. Feelings such as happiness, loneliness, love, and anger are another part of it.

CALIFORNIA REDWOOD ASSOC.

13-11 Much of the beauty provided by nature surrounds this house.

13-12 Dwellings and the objects put in and around them are part of the constructed environment.

CALIFORNIA REDWOOD ASSOC.

13-13 This building allows people to relax while enjoying a view of the ocean.

13-14 The cooperation of people who are making the most of their human resources is an example of a good behavioral environment.

The behavioral environment overlaps with the other types of environments, 13-14. It is found wherever people interact with each other—in child care centers, schools, shopping centers, neighborhoods, and homes.

The environment affects the environment

One type of environment affects another type, causing chain reactions, 13-15. As an example of how this happens, consider a certain community which has a limited amount of land (part of the natural environment). In this community, houses are built close together. The constructed environment covers almost all the land. No land is set aside to preserve part of the natural environment.

The people who live in this community create the behavioral environment. The behavioral environment is full of conflict because the constructed and natural environments are not satisfying. The people are crowded too close together. They do not have the space they need nor the beauty of nature they want. Because they did not control their environments, they cannot satisfy all their needs and priorities.

People and the environment affect each other

Once a constructed environment is started, it seems to keep growing. When a housing area is developed, streets, schools, shopping areas, and other constructed elements appear. They are added because people want them.

As the dwellings are being completed, people start visiting the models that are open. Not everyone who visits moves into the new development, but some people do. They use the recreation and shopping facilities. People created the constructed environment, and it fulfills their needs.

People affect people

If you know and understand the needs and priorities of others, you are more likely to agree with their ideas. Suppose that some people want to make changes in the neighborhood park. If you understand the reasons for the changes being proposed, you are more likely to support them.

If you have the ability or skill to help carry out plans, people look to you because of that resource. When they want help with a project, they will come to you. If you agree with their ideas, you will help them achieve the changes they want. The chain continues. People are influencing each other, and they are changing the environment.

A REVIEW OF HOUSING NEEDS

There are some needs to consider when planning future housing. To meet these needs, the ideas should fit into an overall plan. To achieve an effective housing environment, the plan will include the following aspects:

1. Understanding the different types of environments.
2. Using the resources provided by each type of environment.
3. Determining the needs and priorities of the people involved.
4. Knowing how people react to each other under certain conditions.
5. Considering how housing fits into the environmental picture.

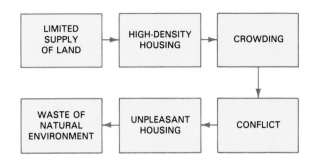

13-15 One type of environment affects another type. The result is a chain reaction.

6. Making housing decisions that provide lasting satisfaction for people.
7. Making housing decisions that conserve and develop an environment that encourages human growth.
8. Taking action once the decisions are made.

Meeting these needs is a challenge for the future.

BRICK HOUSING INSTITUTE OF AMERICA

Modern housing must be designed to meet many needs.

to Know

behavioral environment . . .
constructed environment . . .
Gross National Product . . . integration . . .
macroenvironment . . . microenvironment . . .
migrant workers . . . natural environment . . .
rural poor . . . segregation . . . slums . . . suburbs

to Review

Write your answers on a separate sheet of paper.

1. What was the main cause of the dramatic population shift from rural to urban areas?
2. Why might a housing area become a slum?
3. Name two ways slums affect you.
4. Describe three slum clearance projects.
5. Give two reasons people moved from cities to suburbs.
6. Describe two housing problems created by the move to the suburbs.
7. Differentiate between integrated and segregated housing.
8. Two groups of people in rural areas who often live in substandard housing are the _____ _____ and _____ _____.
9. What is meant by the term "future shock?"
10. Give one example of how each of the following influences housing trends:
    a. Objects.
    b. Place.
    c. People.
11. List three ways that housing affects the economy.
12. Your near surroundings are your _____; your larger surroundings are your _____.

13. After the natural environment has been changed by humans, it is called a:
    a. Behavioral environment.
    b. Constructed environment.

to Do

1. Ask some older persons to tell you about how their housing has changed throughout their lifetime. How did their life-style and housing affect each other? You might tape the interviews and share them with the class.
2. Get brochures from housing developers and builders of several types of homes. List the advantages they give for the type of home they promote. Tell how the advantages are related to the following:
    1. Natural, constructed, or behavioral environment.
    2. Microenvironment or macroenvironment.
    3. Objects, places, or people.
3. Collect articles from newspapers and magazines that tell about housing needs today.
4. Find out about plans for integration in your community. Tell how they are related to housing.
5. Describe a suburb with which you are familiar.
6. Find out about all the major housing acts since 1930. Give the year of each act and its major provisions.
7. Check the houses in your neighborhood to see how many have changed occupants in the last year.
8. List some of the things you own. Write "1" beside those you have had less than one year. Write "5" beside those you have had more than five years.

14

Housing
for tomorrow

After studying this chapter, you will be able to:
- Describe a planned community and list some of the elements it should include.
- Discuss some new sources of living space.
- List some new building materials and methods.
- Describe the importance of controlling the environment.

How can people have better housing for tomorrow? No one knows just what the future holds. But by learning from the past and watching for new developments, people can make tomorrow's housing better.

Housing of the future should be designed and constructed for the people who are to use it. People do not want to plan future slums. Needs and priorities of people should be considered. Housing must allow for the changes taking place in the lives of people. It should also take advantage of new technologies. But at the same time, care must be taken to protect the environment.

Government leaders have been aware of the need for planning in housing. In the United States, congress has passed many acts to help shape the future of housing. Legislation has been passed to cover many concerns, from slums to mortgage loans to energy conservation. Before making changes in housing, check legislation to find out whether any laws affect you.

PLANNED COMMUNITIES

Planned communities are one answer to today's housing problems. Instead of just "happening" one building at a time, these communities are designed to meet present and future needs. Careful consideration is given to the use of resources and to the needs and priorities of humans. Arcosanti, designed by Paolo Soleri, and Habitat, designed by Moshe Safdie, are two examples of planned communities. (Refer to Chapter 12.)

Columbia, Maryland

Columbia, Maryland, is a community that was planned by architect James W. Rouse. It is located on 15,000 acres (6070 hectares) of land between Baltimore and Washington, D.C. About 3200 acres (1295 hectares) are set aside for such things as parks, lakes, and a golf course.

The city of Columbia is really a group of seven villages. They are built around an urban downtown. In this arrangement, the villages are called *satellite communities*.

The total number of residents in Columbia can reach 110,000. It is planned as an integrated community for people from different backgrounds. The homes are in a wide range of prices and styles. Some can be purchased, and some can be rented.

Included in the planning of Columbia were specialists from many fields: architects, sociologists, educators, religious leaders, and doctors. They tried to answer the question, "What should be included in a well-planned community?" They considered the following factors:

1. The desired life-styles of the occupants must be considered.
2. The occupants must be able to afford the housing.
3. The neighborhood must be arranged so people have easy access to schools, churches, stores, and health facilities.
4. Recreational facilities should be provided for all age groups from the very young to the very old.
5. A community should be broken up into neighborhoods by the use of green belts, parks, and playgrounds.
6. A public transportation system should be provided to move people where they need to go without great expense.
7. There should be opportunity for employment for all who need work.
8. Educational opportunities should be available for all at the level they need.
9. There should be health facilities that provide care (both to prevent and remedy poor health) at a cost people can afford.
10. There should be a communication system so that people will know about each other and community activities.

Millennium City

Millennium City is another new concept of city life. An Austrian, Hermann J. Fraunhoffer, is the designer. He is interested in meeting the housing needs of all people, especially children and the elderly.

In this city of the future, buildings are in the shape of disks or rings, 14-1. Each ring provides housing for about 100,000 people. The rings reach a diameter of one mile (1.6 kilometers) and are 400 feet (122 meters) high. They contain housing units ranging in size from 300 to 2200 square feet (27 to 198 square meters). Durable building materials such as glass, steel, and concrete are used. The structures are expected to last 500 years. A close-up view is shown in 14-2.

Traffic patterns in Millennium City follow the outlines of the rings. They can be compared to the traffic pattern of a skating rink. The circular flow of traffic makes traffic control simple.

A mass transit system (a monorail), bicycle paths, and walkways provide easy access to all areas of the city. Since each structure is in the form of a circle, everything is close together.

14-1 Perhaps cities of the future will resemble Millennium City.

A person can get to any place within the circle in a minimum amount of time. People of any age can travel anywhere in the city easily. Parking space for personal vehicles is provided. However, cars are needed only for transportation away from the city.

Each ring is designed to include shops, schools, and churches. These and other community services occupy the bottom levels of the rings. Inside the rings are open areas. They include features such as lakes, zoos, and golf courses.

Power is produced within each ring. For instance, the mass transit system can be fueled by gases from recycled human waste. Solar energy is trapped and used to heat and cool buildings. Other resources are wisely used, and pollution is controlled.

Millennium City is a fresh alternative to the "cereal box" designs of many multifamily dwellings of today. Fraunhoffer claims the city is realistic. One of the concepts used in his design is that of *cluster housing*. Clustering provides the best use of space. It creates high density housing, but the land that is saved can be used for gardens and parks. These "green spots" make high density housing more satisfying.

14-2 A close-up view of Millenium City shows the monorail and landscaping.

Housing for tomorrow 293

SPACE AND HOUSING

Many of today's housing problems relate to space. About 75 percent of the people in the United States are living on less than ten percent of the land. Yet space for housing is difficult to find. It is also expensive. To solve this problem, some new sources of living space are being explored.

Housing in outer space

Do "condominiums in space" sound like architectural science fiction? Dr. Gerard O'Neill, a noted physicist, does not think so. He believes that before long, thousands of people will be living "out there."

One proposal is for a giant space capsule to contain 10,000 people. The capsule is planned to be a self-contained world. It has its own grass, fields, streams, and animals. Residents live in small communities. Motor vehicles travel the highways. Climate, use of resources, and pollution are all controlled.

Another way outer space may affect housing is through the use of satellite power stations.

The stations would supply energy for use on Earth, so we would never have an energy shortage. Energy would always be available at low prices.

Housing under the ground

Some people think living space could be extended downward. Caves, cellars, and basements all have their place in the story of housing. But the idea of building whole communities underground has not yet been tried.

Paolo Soleri's first home in Scottsdale, Arizona, is an "earth house." It has been occupied for a number of years. You can walk on the roof without realizing that there is a dwelling underneath. Only when you approach the entrance are you aware of the underground dwelling.

No doubt Soleri carried out the idea expressed by his teacher, Frank Lloyd Wright. Wright said, "No house should ever be on a hill or on anything. It should be of the hill, belonging to it, so hill and house can live together, each the happier for the other." A dwelling that fits Wright's description is shown in 14-3.

WESTERN WAYS FEATURES

14-3 This dwelling seems to belong with the hill.

HOME BUILDING PLAN SERVICE

14-4 Earth sheltered homes are protected from the elements.

Another concept related to housing under the ground is *earth sheltered housing.* An earth sheltered home is one that is partially covered with soil, 14-4. The shelter of the soil helps protect the home from the elements and climate extremes. A number of earth sheltered homes are designed with active and/or passive solar collectors and are powered in part by solar energy.

Housing on and under the water

Living space may be found on and in bodies of water. The SS United States, once the world's fastest ocean liner, has been converted into a seagoing condominium. The prices of its 282 housing units are very high.

Less costly seagoing living quarters are available. Some are on ocean sites, and others are on smaller bodies of water. Most of them are houseboats which are used as second homes, 14-5. However, the same idea may be used in the future to lessen the shortage of space for housing.

Captain Jacques-Yves Cousteau is an ocean explorer. He predicts that one day people will live in cities under the surface of the water—perhaps on the ocean floor. These cities might be somewhat like the housing capsules planned for outer space.

Some of these housing predictions may not come true. Some may just be science fiction.

It will be interesting to see which directions housing of the future will take. What do you expect to happen during your lifetime?

MATERIALS AND METHODS FOR HOUSING

In Richmond, Virginia, there is a four bedroom house that looks like many of the others in the area. But it is different.

Nearly everything in the house is made from recycled materials. From the roof down, the materials have an unusual story. They have come from many sources and have been changed into building materials. The following is a partial list of the materials and how they were obtained:

California—Glass bottles from the parks were crushed into rock-like pieces. They were used for brick, concrete blocks, driveway pavement, and floor tile.

Florida—Aluminum beverage cans were picked up along the beaches. Termite-proof material was produced and was used for the frame of the house.

Mississippi—Discarded auto tires were melted and mixed with some of the crushed glass for the driveway surface.

Missouri—The Environmental Research Department of the University of Missouri developed the formula for the pavement.

14-5 Houseboats are popular as second homes. They can be used for year-round housing, too.

New Jersey—Old newspapers were made into hardboard. It was used for subflooring and wall paneling.

New York—Garbage was processed and became *compost* (fertilizer) for the outside yard.

North Carolina—Leftover fibers from carpet factories were remade into new yarn for carpets.

West Virginia—*Fly ash* (solid, airborne particles from burned fuel) was collected from the polluted air to become 20 percent of the cement used to make concrete.

Many other materials were recycled and used in the structure. The house is a project of about 20 organizations. They worked with the Reynolds Metals Company. The idea was to show that recycled products can be used to construct houses. Such houses look as good and are as durable as those made with common building materials.

Many people believe that our country can recycle on a large scale. Then recycled materials can be used to build homes. The demonstration home did not cost more than similar houses nearby. If you recheck the list, you can see that products were brought from a great distance. If recycled materials become more widely available, the cost will be even less.

Materials and methods are closely related. Old materials are being put to new uses, and new materials are being developed. These factors open the door to new building methods. One of these new methods involves the use of curved lines. Instead of the straight walls and right-angle corners of many designs, curved lines can be used more. Some studies show that the use of curved lines may have a calming effect on people. The building in 14-6 shows how curved lines can be used in building designs.

Reducing waste in housing

To reduce waste in housing, long term housing goals should be considered. What type of housing is popular today? If you look around you, you will see that houses are temporary. This calls for more buildings to replace them. It means that materials will be wasted unless they are recycled.

PPG INDUSTRIES

14-6 The curved part of this structure adds interest and may have a calming effect on people.

On the other hand, if all dwellings were built to last 500 years, how long would they remain practical? Would builders be able to take advantage of growing human knowledge? How permanent should housing units be?

Structures that are built to allow for flexibility can conserve resources. Suppose the outside shell of a building is built independently of the inside partitions or walls. The interior space could be reorganized to meet the changing needs and priorities of living units.

High tech and housing

The period in which we live is one of *high tech* (high level of technology). Many advances are possible in housing because of high tech. It has already become a part of traditional housing. High tech may soon allow you to be able to control the operation of home appliances outside the home. Reverse microwave ovens are another product of high tech. They rapidly chill food. The kitchens and baths of the future may arrive as units to be set in place and attached to a utility hookup. Kitchens may blend with media centers. Media centers will house computers, television sets, video, and stereo systems. The "Smart House" is an experimental house that uses high tech in many ways. See 14-7.

14-7 The "Smart House" uses high tech to make living more pleasant and safer. For instance, electrical outlets will only supply power to an electric device with the proper wattage needs. This means that if fingers or appliances that would overload the circuit contact the outlet, no current will reach them.

Housing for tomorrow 297

ENVIRONMENTAL CONTROL

Ecology is the relationship between all living things and their surroundings. You harm the ecology each time you put some undesirable items into your surroundings. Look at 14-8 to see the many types of pollution that can harm your surroundings.

Humans have made many demands on the environment. But they cannot continue "taking" without "giving." If the environment is to continue to satisfy so many human needs, people must care for it.

The need for fuel

Fuel provides heat, and people need heat to live. You need heat inside your body. You also need heat in your microenvironment and macroenvironment.

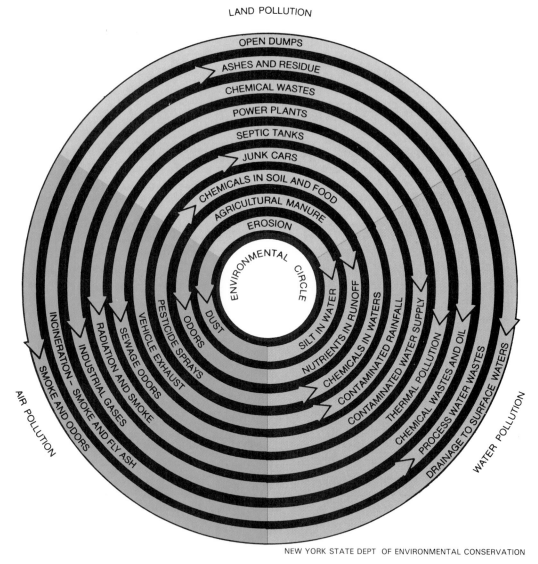

LAND POLLUTION

OPEN DUMPS
ASHES AND RESIDUE
CHEMICAL WASTES
POWER PLANTS
SEPTIC TANKS
JUNK CARS
CHEMICALS IN SOIL AND FOOD
AGRICULTURAL MANURE
EROSION

ENVIRONMENTAL CIRCLE

SILT IN WATER
NUTRIENTS IN RUNOFF
CHEMICALS IN WATERS
CONTAMINATED RAINFALL
CONTAMINATED WATER SUPPLY
THERMAL POLLUTION
CHEMICAL WASTES AND OIL
PROCESS WATER WASTES
DRAINAGE TO SURFACE WATERS

WATER POLLUTION

SMOKE AND ODORS
INCINERATION— SMOKE AND FLY ASH
INDUSTRIAL GASES
RADIATION AND SMOKE
SEWAGE ODORS
VEHICLE EXHAUST
PESTICIDE SPRAYS
ODORS
DUST

AIR POLLUTION

14-8 This environmental circle shows many kinds of pollution. Notice that each kind can affect land, air, and water.

Like all forms of energy, fuel begins as solar energy (energy from the sun). Nature converts solar energy to raw materials such as oil and coal. The conversions take millions of years to complete. The raw materials are then refined and used as fuel for cooking; for heating, cooling, and lighting buildings; and for running machines.

The supplies of common sources of fuel are being depleted. Researchers are working to find new sources that will supply enough fuel for the future.

Since 1974, laws have been passed to encourage conservation of energy. These include acts to encourage research on making solar energy more useful. They also include rulings to give grants to low and moderate income families to improve the energy efficiency of a home. Tax credits are also given for adding energy saving features to homes.

Garbage as energy. Some regions are working on systems to recycle garbage. The energy created from the garbage is used to provide heat and electrical power for homes and businesses. St. Louis, Missouri, was one of the first cities to recycle its garbage. New York is promoting the "3 Rs" by asking citizens to "recover, recycle, and reuse" garbage.

The garbage in most communities is simply burned or buried. In places where garbage is recycled, it is sorted. The *combustible* (burnable) materials are used as fuel for operating power plants or for heating. Metal cans and glass are sent back to industries to be reused. Scientists are trying to find more ways of recycling garbage.

Wind as energy. Some regions of the United States have strong, shifting winds that can be used for power. Windmills can convert air motion to electrical energy. They use specially designed generators to harness the wind. Some of the electricity that is produced is fed into storage systems. The systems keep the power flowing even when the air is still.

Geothermal energy. Geothermal energy comes from steam, hot water, or very hot rock stored deep beneath the surface of the earth. It can be reached by drilling extremely deep holes through lava (a type of volcanic rock).

Reykjavik, Iceland, is the first city in the world to become almost entirely heated by geothermal energy. Approximately half a million people in California, Mexico's Baja, and the Mexicali Valley have their fuel needs met with geothermal energy. Other geothermal projects are being developed in the United States.

Solar energy. Many houses are being designed to use solar energy. See 14-9. There are two types of systems: active and passive.

14-9 This house uses both active and passive solar systems to heat it.

Active solar systems have equipment to capture the sun's energy and to put it to use. *Solar collectors* soak up the heat. Then water or air carries the heat to a storage area or to where it will be used.

A *passive solar system* has no working parts. It includes any design or construction material that makes maximum use of sun, light, or wind for heating and cooling. A passive solar system might include breezeways, skylights, and large areas of windows. It might include cement pipe columns or dark-colored walls that would absorb heat from the sun and then gradually transfer the heat inside.

14-10 "Solar One" was the first house to use only sunlight for energy. It has both active and passive solar systems. The house was built for the Institute of Energy Conversion.

The building in 14-10 is the first house designed to operate on solar energy. It was designed to produce heat as well as electricity for lights and appliances, 14-11. Thus, it has an active solar system. Much of the south side of Solar One is enclosed in glass. Thus, it also has a passive solar system.

Solar energy could supply a majority of the energy needed to heat and cool buildings throughout the United States, 14-12. Solar heating systems are expensive to install. However, utility bills are greatly reduced when solar energy is used. In the long run, solar heating systems usually cost less than conventional systems.

Some solar systems are designed to supply more energy than is needed. The excess is sold to a utility company. A *photo-voltaic system* converts light to electricity. See 14-13.

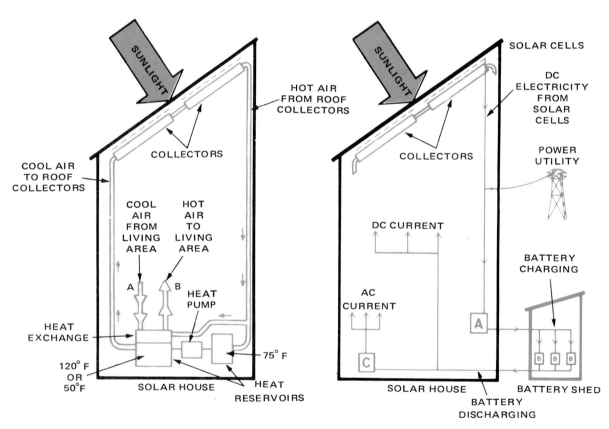

14-11 The heating system for "Solar One" is shown on the left. The electrical system is shown on the right. Solar cells are able to convert sunlight directly into electricity.

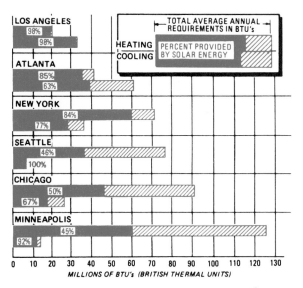

CALIFORNIA REDWOOD ASSOC.

14-12 This chart shows the amount of heating and cooling that could be done with solar energy in some major cities of the United States.

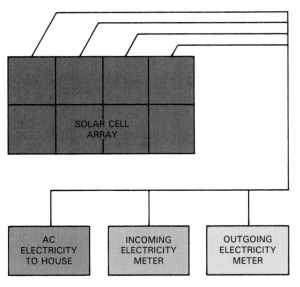

14-13 In a photo-voltaic system, silicon chips are joined by electrical wires to form solar cell arrays. The arrays collect solar energy. The amount of energy depends on the season, the time of day, and the cloud cover.

14-14 This manufactured house has windows placed to take advantage of passive solar heating. It uses a fireplace/stove as its main heat source. The water heater is placed behind the fireplace to save energy that would otherwise be needed to heat the water.

Conserving energy

Dwellings can be built to conserve energy. In cold climates, windows can be placed mainly on the south side of the house. Floor plans can be designed in a way that conserves the energy needed to circulate warm or cool air. Fireplaces or stoves can be used as a main heat source. The house shown in 14-14 was designed to conserve energy.

Properly insulating attics and outer walls helps to conserve energy. The amount of insulation needed depends on climate. Homes in colder climates need more insulation. The efficiency of insulation is shown by its R-value.

An *R-value* is a number assigned to insulating materials. Higher R-values indicate a better insulating ability. The map in 14-15 shows five different heating zones in the United States. Also shown are recommended R-values for home insulation in each zone.

Tech House was built by NASA's Langley Research Center at Hampton, Virginia. It is designed for a family of four. It uses only about a third of the kilowatt hours of energy of the conventional home. Moreover, it recycles much of the water which it uses.

Homes that are already built can also be changed to conserve energy. Changing a structure to make it more energy efficient is called *retrofitting*. These changes may be simple such

Recommended R-Values

Heating Zone	Attic Floors	Exterior Walls	Ceilings Over Unheated Crawl Space or Basement
1	R-26	R-Value of full wall	R-11
2	R-26	insulation, which is	R-13
3	R-30	3½" thick, will depend	R-19
4	R-33	on material used.	R-22
5	R-38	Range is R-11 to R-13.	R-22

R- Values Chart

	Batts or Blankets		Loose Fill (Poured In)		
	glass fiber	rock wool	glass fiber	rock wool	cellulosic fiber
R-11	3½"-4"	3"	5"	4"	3"
R-13	4"	4½"	6"	4½"	3½"
R-19	6"-6½"	5¼"	8"-9"	6"-7"	5"
R-22	6½"	6"	10"	7"-8"	6"
R-26	8"	8½"	12"	9"	7"-7½"
R-30	9½"-10½"	9"	13"-14"	10"-11"	8"
R-33	11"	10"	15"	11"-12"	9"
R-38	12"-13"	10½"	17"-18"	13"-14"	10"-11"

14-15 This map shows the five different heating zones in the United States and the recommended R-values for home insulation in each zone.

as adding weatherstripping. Or the changes may be major such as building a solar room to collect heat for the entire home. For a small fee, utility companies will evaluate a home and suggest changes that can be made to make it more energy efficient. Other energy-saving ideas are listed in the Appendix.

Noise pollution

Noise is often ignored as a pollutant, but it can make your environment unpleasant and even harmful.

Unwanted sound is *noise.* Within dwellings, it comes from appliances and active family members. Outside dwellings, it comes from cars, airplanes, and neighbors.

Sound is measured in *decibels.* The quietest sound that can be heard is rated at 0 decibels. A whisper is 30 decibels. Normal conservation is about 60 decibels. Continued exposure to noise louder than 60 decibels can be harmful. The sound levels of household appliances are given in 14-16. The U.S. Environmental Protection Agency has set noise standards for home products. If you listen before you buy, you can choose quiet products.

14-17 With careful planning, natural beauty can remain a part of today's environment.

Researchers are trying to learn more about the effects of sound on unborn babies. Even they can be harmed by noise.

Acoustical (sound deadening or absorbing) materials such as ceiling tile and fiberglass insulation reduce noise in a house. Draperies and carpeting also help to absorb sound. Pleasant sounds can drown out undesirable noise. Music playing within the dwelling, for example, can shut out the sound of traffic on the street.

Visual pollution

Visual pollution hinders your psychological well-being. It occurs in many forms. Signboards and destruction of natural surroundings are examples of visual pollution.

Some landscapes are disfigured by overhead power lines. Some communities require underground utilities in new housing developments.

While Lady Bird Johnson was First Lady of the United States, she began a campaign against visual pollution. Many improvements have been made. An example is the beautiful surroundings of the home shown in 14-17. However, much work still needs to be done.

Fighting pollution is one way to control your environment. A healthy environment will help make tomorrow's housing better.

HOUSEHOLD NOISEMAKERS

APPLIANCE	SOUND LEVEL IN DECIBELS
Floor fan	38 to 70
Refrigerator	40
Washing Machine	47 to 78
Dishwasher	54 to 85
Clothes dryer	55
Hair dryer	59 to 80
Vacuum cleaner	62 to 85
Sewing machine	64 to 74
Food disposal	67 to 93
Electric shaver	75
Electric lawn edger	81
Home shop tools	85
Gasoline-powered mower	87 to 92
Gasoline-powered riding mower	90 to 95
Chain saw	100
Stereo	up to 120

14-16 These sound levels are for someone who is close to or operating the appliance.

to Know

acoustical . . . active solar system . . .
"cereal box" designs . . . cluster housing . . .
cluster unit . . . combustible . . . compost . . .
decibel . . . earth sheltered housing . . .
ecology . . . fly ash . . . high tech . . .
noise pollution . . . passive solar system . . .
photo-voltaic system . . . planned communities . . .
retrofitting . . . R-values . . .
satellite communities . . . solar collectors . . .
visual pollution

to Review

Write your answers on a separate sheet of paper.
1. Describe a planned community and name two examples.
2. Explain the transportation system of Millennium City.
3. What is the advantage of cluster housing?
4. How might outer space affect housing of the future?
5. Which of the following building materials might we find in houses of the future? (Check all that might be used.)
    a. Brick, block, and stone.
    b. Earth and sod.
    c. Materials not yet invented.
    e. Recycled trash such as cans, bottles, paper, and garbage.
    f. Wood.
6. Comment on this statement: "It is not practical to have houses that would last 500 years. They would be out of style and useless long before they wore out."
7. _____ is the relationship between living things and their environment.
8. How can wind be used as an energy source?
9. Briefly describe how solar energy is captured and used.
10. A _____ system supplies enough energy to sell.
11. _____ refers to changing a structure that is already built to make it more energy efficient.
12. Compare the terms sound and noise.
13. The unit of measure for sound is a _____.

to Do

1. As a small group activity, make a list of questions to ask people about their housing. Include some questions about the types of housing they expect in the future.
2. Bring news items and magazine articles about housing of the future to class.
3. Find out more about the people who are concerned about housing of tomorrow. You may choose from this list or find others:
    a. Rouse, James.
    b. Fraunhoffer, Hermann.
    c. Soleri, Paolo.
    d. Safdie, Moshe.
    e. Cousteau, Jacques-Yves.
4. Write a "science fiction" story about housing of tomorrow.
5. Survey your class or school to find which types of fuel or energy are used in the homes of students and teachers.
6. Collect articles from the local newspaper related to pollution that affects your environment. Report to the class.
7. Check your home for sources of sound. Include both indoor and outdoor sounds. Ask family members which ones they consider noise.
8. Report on the noise standards that have been established by the U.S. Environmental Protection Agency.
9. Work with other members of your class to determine ways you can conserve energy.
10. Check the buildings in your community to see how many have active solar systems and how many have passive solar systems.
11. Find magazine articles that describe ways in which high tech influences housing. Report your findings to the class.

15

Careers
in housing

After studying this chapter, you will
be able to:
- Describe several careers that are
  related to the field of housing.
- Explain which job skills and
  personal qualifications are
  required for housing careers.

The number of living units in the United
States is growing. About two million new housing units are needed each year to accommodate
them.

The needs of living units change as units
become larger. Needs also change as the people
in the living units grow older and pass through
the different stages of their life cycle. According to the Associates Building Industry, 13 different types of living units seek housing, 15-1.
The young and adult singles and the compact-
ing families are the most active in the housing
market.

Who provides housing?

No one person can expect to provide adequate
housing. The efforts of people from many
career areas are combined to provide housing
that satisfies people of all life-styles, 15-2.

People who work in the building industry are
perhaps the first ones that come to mind when
thinking about who provides housing. They are

an important part of housing, but they do not provide all that is needed in a good housing environment. People who work for health agencies and other community improvement groups contribute to housing environments. Fire fighters and police officers help you feel secure. Garbage and refuse collectors help keep your environment clean, safe, and beautiful. People who work for the telephone company make it possible for you to contact plumbers, carpenters, family members, and friends. All these people are not in "housing" industries, but they make housing environments more satisfying.

CAREER CLUSTERS

Since careers related to housing are so varied, they do not all fit in one category. Instead they are grouped into several smaller categories. Jobs or careers that are closely related make up a *career cluster*. In 15-3, you can see how the career cluster related to housing design and interior decoration can be broken down into individual careers according to the jobs that need to be done. Sometimes a career cluster is

MASONITE CORP.

15-2 Many people from different career groups were involved in building, selling, and furnishing this house.

called a *career web*. Look at 15-4 to see why this name is appropriate.

One cluster of careers in the building industry is with the Manufactured Housing Institute. They represent about 25,000 firms and businesses in the United States and Canada. They

TYPES OF LIVING UNITS

LIVING UNIT	DESCRIPTION
Young single	Does not want to bother with problems of upkeep; probably lives in a rented apartment.
Adult single	Over 30 years old; is practical, often wants to buy larger home than needed because it is likely to go up in value.
First home buyers	Younger family moving out of apartment into first house; economy and room to grow are important.
Family moving up	Has growing needs as well as income; may be planning to have more children.
Established family	Stable needs, income; size of family will remain constant for many years.

LIVING UNIT	DESCRIPTION
Single adult family	Only one adult (unmarried or formerly married); children still growing.
Compact family	Only one child.
Compacting family	Has children who have already left or soon will.
Never nested	Have no children and never plan to.
Empty nesters	Middle-aged couple whose children are all on their own.
Active retirees	May not work but definitely are not sedentary.
Nonactive retirees	Does not move about much any more; needs can be met in limited housing.

15-1 Every type of living unit has its own housing needs.

CAREER CLUSTER	SUBCLUSTERS	JOBS
Housing design, interior decoration	Design and decoration	House designing and planning Interior decorating Counseling on house design and decoration
	Furnishings selectivity	Selecting paint and finishes Selecting furniture styles, draperies and slipcovers Selecting and combining home accessories Selecting household equipment
	Refurbishing and refurnishing	Upholstering Refinishing furniture Repairing furniture
	Product testing	Serviceability testing of furnishings Comparative testing of household equipment Counseling on home furnishing and equipment Demonstrating home furnishings and equipment

U.S. OFFICE OF EDUCATION

15-3 The career cluster related to housing design and interior decoration offers several distinct types of jobs.

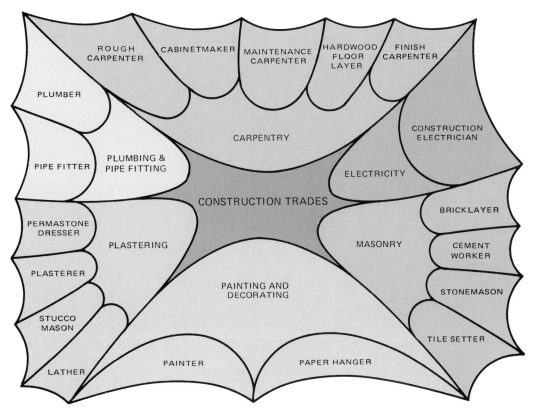

15-4 A career web for construction trades shows related areas of work and kinds of workers needed.

identify five subclusters within their career cluster. These are listed in 15-5. Each subcluster can be divided into individual jobs. The jobs offered in the subcluster of mobile home parks are listed and described in 15-6.

Look at 15-7, 15-8, and 15-9. These illustrations show career clusters in other areas related to housing.

CAREER CLUSTER	SUBCLUSTERS
Manufactured housing	Manufacturers—more than 900 manufacturing plants in USA and Canada
	Mobile Home Trade Associations (National and State)—more than 60 Associations in USA and Canada
	Manufactured house suppliers—more than 1000 major suppliers in USA and Canada
	Manufactured house dealerships—more than 10,000 dealers in USA and Canada
	Mobile Home Parks—more than 13,000 rated parks in USA and Canada

15-5 The career cluster related to the manufactured housing industry has five subclusters and many job opportunities.

Career information

Many kinds of careers are a part of the housing industry. Special skills and training are needed to carry out the assigned tasks of each one. When you think about possible future careers, you need to know what qualifications are needed for the different kinds of jobs. You also need to know what the job is like and what would be expected of you if you had the job.

Usually school counselors can provide you with job descriptions and a list of qualifications that are needed for the jobs. Sometimes this information can be obtained from a vocational teacher. Libraries are another source of career information. They have many publications dealing with careers. Two such publications are the *Dictionary of Occupational Titles, Vols. I and II.* (Washington, D.C., U.S. Dept. of Labor) and the *Occupational Outlook Handbook* (U.S. Dept. of Labor, Bureau of Labor Statistics). Most libraries have many additional sources of career information. They may have sets of job guides or career briefs that tell about specific jobs. These may include information such as:
- Definition of the job title.
- List of duties.
- Personal qualifications needed.
- Education and training needed.
- How and where to receive the education and training needed.
- Future outlook on employment.
- Earnings.
- Opportunities for advancement.
- How and where to find a job.
- Related careers.

Ask your librarian for help in finding the career information you need.

JOB DESCRIPTIONS

The biggest questions when considering careers are "What is available?" and "What is that job like?" *Job descriptions* provide the answers to those questions. The following job descriptions are related to housing.

Architects

An architect's job is to design buildings that satisfy people. Such buildings must be safe, attractive, and useful. But there is more to the job than design. Architects must be sure that the proper materials are used and that the builder follows the plans.

Architects tend to be payed well. But they must take much care to be sure that their work is accurate. Architects also have a long training period. Five years are required to attain a bachelor's degree. Then a two-day examination must be taken to receive a license. Becoming established often takes many years of hard work and experience.

POSITIONS IN THE SUBCLUSTER OF MOBILE HOME PARKS

JOB TITLE	WHAT PERSON DOES
Developer	Obtains satisfactory zoning. Leases or buys land in order to build a mobile home park. Hires land planners, architects, and engineers to design a park. Installs water and utility connections. Builds streets, foundations, service, and recreational buildings. Prepares site for each home.
Park manager	Supervises all functions of park operation. Maintains services and contact with home owners. Collects rent. Plans activity program for residents in a "service" or retirement park.
Social director	(Sometimes position is combined with that of park manager.) Plans activity program for park residents.
Office administration clerk/typist	Does clerical work, typing and filing.
secretary	Takes dictation, does typing, filing, and perhaps purchasing of supplies.
accountant	Controls all accounting systems and procedures including payroll, accounts receivable, accounts payable, insurance. Prepares tax report and financial statements.
Maintenance manager/ groundskeeper	Keeps lawns and grounds clean. Maintains service buildings such as community pool, laundromat, and office. Assists home owners in certain home repairs.
Advertising and public relations manager	Found in large parks only. In most instances, the job is probably combined with the park manager's. Determines advertising program and media to use in cooperation with manager's recommendations. Maintains good public relations with community and park residents.

MANUFACTURED HOUSING INSTITUTE

15-6 Many skills and personal qualities are needed to run a mobile home park.

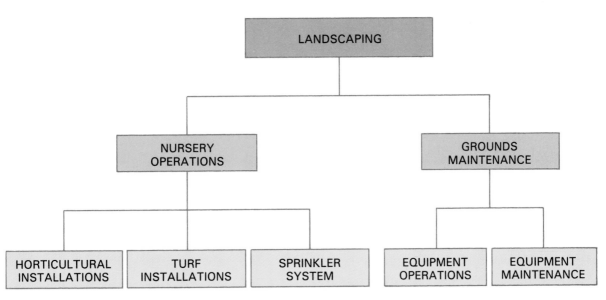

15-7 All jobs in this career cluster are related to landscaping.

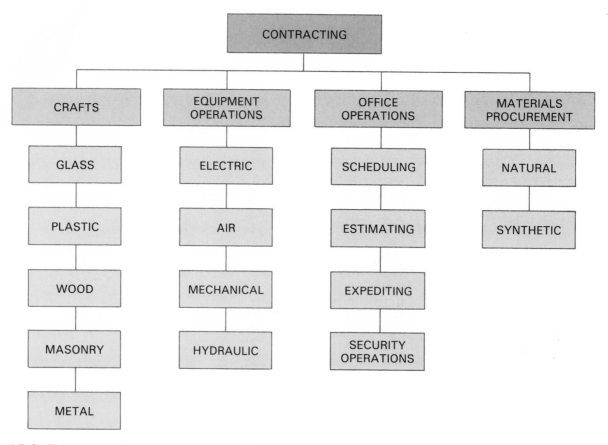

15-8 The career cluster of contracting has a wide variety of job opportunities.

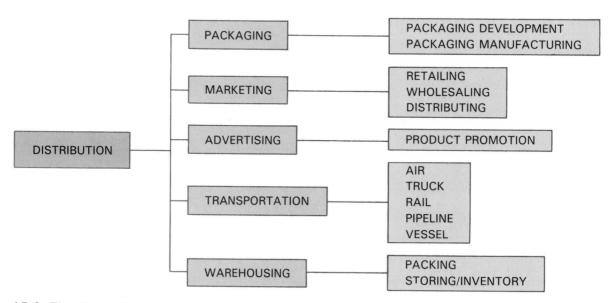

15-9 The distribution of manufactured products for housing offers many types of positions.

15-10 Drafters make precise, detailed drawings to specify the kind of work that will need to be done as a building is constructed.

Landscape architects

Landscape architects work with organizations, committees, governments, private firms, and individuals to beautify the land surrounding structures. Their work entails planning the placement of trees, shrubs, walkways, parking lots, and open areas around buildings. They usually study four or five years in college. Required courses include surveying, sketching, horticulture, landscape construction, botany, science, and mathematics. About half the states require licensing.

Drafters

From an architect's sketches and instructions, a drafter prepares the detailed *working drawings* used by the builder. See 15-10. These drawings tell what materials to use, give exact dimensions, and what and how much work is to be done by the contractor or builder.

Drafters must be able to produce neat and accurate drawings using compasses, dividers, and other drafting equipment. A knowledge of construction is needed as are patience, good eyesight, and a steady hand. Some drafting is also done with computers. In order to do computer drawings, a drafter must have knowledge of and experience with computers.

Drafters may specialize in certain aspects of the job. One such specialist is the architectural illustrator. He or she prepares the presentations and renderings that are used in brochures or shown to clients who want to know how the finished structure will look.

Modelmakers

To help clients visualize large projects, an architect may have a scale model of the project built. See 15-11. A modelmaker will be hired to do this. Most modelmakers are self-employed. Necessary skills include being able to read and interpret blueprints, to use scales, to visualize drawings in three dimensions, and to do precision work while shaping materials in miniature.

15-11 Modelmakers build three-dimensional models from an architect's drawings.

Surveyors

Using various tools, the surveyor locates corners and boundaries of tracts of land. Instrument findings are used to draw a map of the surveyed area.

Assisting the surveyor are other workers. *Instrument workers* adjust and operate the surveying instruments. *Chain workers* measure distances between survey points. *Rod workers* use a level rod and range pole to help measure distance and angles. Surveying involves outdoor work with much walking while carrying heavy instruments. Knowledge of mathematics is essential.

Engineers

Engineers are educated in programs leading to bachelor of science degrees. Engineers whose work is related to housing take courses in mathematics, blueprint reading, drafting, computer science, physics, humanities, and English. Four or five years might be spent in preparation, depending on the school.

In many cases, the architect may assume the tasks of determining the ability of the building to withstand stresses. But as structures become larger and more complex, the *structural engineer* is asked to advise the architect on design for safety and strength. This person estimates the weight the building must carry, the pressure of air movement against the sides and roof, pressures against the foundation, and extraordinary pressures from earth tremors. Many structural engineers are self-employed; others are employed by large engineering or architectural firms.

Mechanical engineers are concerned with the design of equipment for plumbing, heating, ventilating, and air conditioning. They plan the way this equipment will be used in buildings and oversee its installment.

Civil engineers are responsible for preparing the site. They level the land, design drainage and sewer systems, and lay out streets, driveways, and sidewalks. Another part of their work is to study the soil of the site. They must know how much weight it will support without settling. Many civil engineers work for federal, state, and local governments. Others are employed by housing developers.

Electrical engineers plan the electrical services needed for the operation of household appliances such as ranges, washers, dryers, air conditioners, and furnaces. Their calculations are included in the working drawings supplied to the builder.

Construction careers

A variety of skilled people work on building an average dwelling. These people include estimators, masons, carpenters, plumbers, plasterers, electricians, drywallers, roofers, and flooring specialists. Training is obtained on the job, in vocational schools, or in apprenticeship progams. Many are employed by builders and contractors. Others have their own businesses.

Estimators study the working drawings and determine how much the building will cost in materials, labor, and overhead. In large construction projects, this person may be an expert in the engineering field. In such cases, he or she is called a *construction cost engineer* or a *cost analysis engineer.* Estimators must know about materials, methods, and costs of construction. Some estimators have a background in construction work. Others enter the field after training programs beyond high school.

Masons and *cement workers* set up forms for footings, foundation walls, patios, and floors. See 15-12. They place concrete and use various hand and power tools to smooth and finish it. They must know the materials. They also must be familiar with cement additives which speed or retard the setting of concrete.

Bricklayers and *stonemasons* build walls, partitions, fireplaces, and other structures. They use brick, block, and stone as well as other natural or manufactured materials. They work with hand tools for the most part. Reading working drawings and making careful measurements are among the important skills they must master. Bricklayers must also be able to construct various bonds (patterns). They must be able to use accepted construction methods for safety and reinforcement and to work rapidly and neatly.

Carpenters put up the wooden framework in buildings, 15-13. They install windows, doors, cabinets, stairs, and paneling. They also lay hardwood floors, asphalt, and other types of rigid flooring materials. Some specialize. Rough carpenters build only the framework or set up the concrete forms. Finish carpenters install millwork, cabinets, stairs, etc. Some carpenters learn their work on the job. Others prepare through special vocational programs.

Electricians are people who install wiring in new constructions and make repairs on older wiring systems. The electrician must know how to read the electrical diagrams in the builder's working drawing. In addition, a knowledge of electrical codes and electrical loads is essential. See 15-14.

ASSOCIATED GENERAL CONTRACTORS OF AMERICA

15-12 Cement workers may build footings, walls, or a whole framework of concrete.

GEORGIA-PACIFIC CORP.

15-13 These carpenters are putting up the framework for a house.

Floor covering installers put down or replace resilient tile, vinyl flooring, and carpeting. Their work may include removing an old covering and sanding and cleaning the surface to be covered. They must be able to read architectural drawings and to measure, mark, and cut accurately.

Painters apply paints, varnishes, and other finishes to decorate and protect surfaces. Painting involves surface preparation by scraping, burning with a torch, sanding, washing, priming, and sealing. Then a new painted surface is applied with brushes, rollers, pads, and sprayers.

Paperhangers attach decorative paper or cloth to walls and ceilings. Sometimes they must first remove old wallpaper by soaking or steaming it, and sometimes minor patching of plaster is done. Then they prepare the wall surface by cleaning it and applying sizing. The sizing makes the surface less porous. Workers measure, cut, and hang materials, applying paste as needed.

Roofers apply shingles and other protective materials to make roofs weatherproof. They may also apply waterproofing to walls and other parts of the building. Roofers use a variety of materials including wood or asphalt shingles, hot tar and gravel, slate, tile, aluminum, copper, or steel.

Plumbers and *pipe fitters* install pipe systems that carry water, steam, air, or other liquids and gases. They also install plumbing fixtures, appliances, and heating, or refrigeration units. They will install piping between walls and under floors during early stages of construction. Then they will return during final construction stages to attach fixtures and install appliances.

Plasterers and *drywall installers* finish the framed walls with plaster or with smooth sheets of plaster-like material. Their methods differ, but their results are much alike. Plasterers apply wet, cement-like material to the wall in successive coats using trowels and other hand tools to smooth it.

Installing drywall is a task that is done in two steps. Installers attach large sheets of drywall to the walls and ceilings of rooms and nail or glue them in place. Finishers then apply mastics

15-14 This electrician is wiring a circuit breaker panel in a large, multifamily structure.

15-15 These drywall finishers are concealing nail heads and joints in walls and ceilings.

and perforated tape to conceal joints and nail heads after the drywall is attached, 15-15.

Construction machinery operators

Handling dirt or heavy construction units would be difficult, if not impossible, without heavy machines to lift and carry them. These machines are controlled by skilled workers who are often called "operating engineers." They are at the controls of cranes, 15-16; bulldozers; backhoes; forklifts; pavers; and trucks. Good eyesight and coordination are required. Unless carefully controlled, such equipment could endanger the lives of other construction workers.

Real estate

Careers in real estate include many kinds of tasks such as renting and managing property for clients, making appraisals on property, developing new building projects, and arranging loans for home buyers.

The most common career in the field of real estate is the real estate agent, 15-17. He or she helps people buy, sell, rent, and lease property. Real estate agents must be familiar with their communities, with real estate laws, with banking laws, and with building codes. A license is required by all states and is issued only after successful completion of a written test. Most real estate agents have a college background although it is not a requirement. Needed personality traits include a pleasant disposition, honesty, neatness, tact, enthusiasm, and maturity. A good memory for names, faces, and facts is helpful.

Interior designers

Interior designers plan and supervise the design and arrangement of building interiors and furnishings. They work from blueprints to make floor plans to scale and to prepare elevation drawings. Their drawings help clients visualize how the rooms will look.

Interior designers must have knowledge of basic housing principles. But they should also have a creative, artistic flair. Designers must be good at evaluating clients' needs and tastes and designing rooms that fulfill the clients' wishes.

AMERICAN PLYWOOD ASSOC.

15-16 A crane operator must work carefully to avoid damage to this building module or injury to other workers.

CENTURY 21

15-17 Real estate agents must know many facts about the housing they show to clients.

Interior designers work for either individual clients or for firms which sell furnishings, or for planning and designing services. They select and estimate costs of furniture, floor, and wall coverings and accessories, 15-18. When plans are approved, the designer may arrange the purchase of furnishings and hire and supervise various workers.

Three or four years of training in a professional school are required. Courses include principles of design, history of art, freehand and mechanical drawing, painting, furniture design, and textiles. A knowledge of antiques, art pieces, and furnishings is also needed.

Salespersons and consultants

Retailers of building materials, appliances, and home furnishings hire persons with a background in housing and furnishings. Their job is to demonstrate and sell their employer's products.

Some firms hire consultants who will help customers select the right furnishings, equipment, or materials. They also advise customers on installation and use of the products. Such personnel need to understand design, materials, and methods.

Secretaries and computer operators

No business could operate efficiently without the assistance of office workers, 15-19 and 15-20. The smaller the firm, the more their duties vary.

Work might include typing, filing, filling out reports, taking dictation, handling visitors and phone calls, scheduling appointments, bookkeeping, and operating duplicating equipment and blueprinters. Many secretaries function as special assistants to architects, engineers, builders, and contractors.

Computers have become important in the housing industry. They are used in every career

JOHNSON WAX

15-18 Interior designers plan interiors for clients from layout plans to construction and decoration. Decorators can help with decisions about draperies, upholstery, carpeting, furniture, and accessories.

15-19 This office worker is employed by an architectural firm. One of her tasks is to operate a blueprint machine.

DAVE KNOX

15-20 Office workers in smaller companies are called upon to do a variety of jobs.

cluster and at all levels. Because of this, computer operators are needed to assist many people in the housing industry, such as architects, engineers, interior designers, and real estate agents.

Occupations with utility companies

Utility companies that supply electricity, gas, and telephone services offer job opportunities related to housing. Gas and electric companies, for example, employ consultants who advise consumers on appliances. This requires not only knowledge of the product but sales ability as well. Department stores and large chain stores often have a public relations department in which people prepare materials on proper selection, use, and care of furnishings and appliances.

Service persons are hired by private firms or utility companies to repair and adjust appliances. Telephone companies employ *phone installers* and *line workers* to install equipment and lines and to keep them in repair.

The list of job descriptions becomes even longer when you consider the many other areas related to housing. Is there a position that appeals to you? Do you know the qualifications? Can you become qualified?

CAREER LEVELS

You can see that career opportunities related to housing are many and varied. They do not all carry the same amount of responsibility nor require the same qualifications. Career opportunities can be divided into three levels:
1. The professional level.
2. The mid level.
3. The entry level.

Professional level positions

Some of the people who help provide housing work on a *professional* level. Generally a college degree is required for these jobs. Special training and experience may be needed in addition to a degree.

Those in professional careers related to housing influence the quality of life for themselves and others. They make decisions that affect the lives of individuals, families, and whole communities.

Architects, engineers, and interior designers are a few of the people with professional level positions. Land use planners are also professionals. They work in both urban and rural areas. Wherever they are, they consider the needs and priorities of people using land. They

Careers in housing 317

also consider those who are affected by the way land is used. Will a certain use of the land pollute the environment? If so, what effect will the pollution have on those using the land or what is built on the land? How will those living nearby be affected? Will it make a difference to those who pass by? How will it affect future generations? These and other questions will be considered as decisions are made by land use planners.

Mid level positions

Professionals are key people because they make decisions that affect the work of others. But they need others to support them in their choices. The people who help carry out decisions that have been made are called *supportive personnel*.

People in mid level positions are often supportive of professionals. But their work sometimes involves supervising people in positions that carry less responsibility, 15-21.

For example, housing construction supervisors oversee the work of others. They usually do not do the wiring, plumbing, or roofing.

TOM KIRBY ADVERTISING FOR BULLOCK CO.

15-21 People who supervise assembly line employees are in mid level positions.

However, they need to know how to do these things to determine if others are doing their jobs correctly.

The mid level of career opportunities is very broad, and it has many sublevels. Thus, many people who work under a supervisor are also in mid level positions. Others include carpenters and lighting specialists. The fact that they are supervised does not make their work any less important.

Those in mid level positions are expected to have schooling beyond high school. It may be through a special class or by service as an *apprentice*. An apprentice is one who is going through an organized program of job training that is coupled with vocational classes.

Entry level positions

People in *entry level* positions are supportive of those in both professional and mid level positions. The qualifications for entry level positions are not high. You can enter a career area and be successful with less preparation than at the other levels. You are likely to learn much of what you need to know on the job. There is often opportunity to move up if you do your job well.

Some of the entry level positions related to housing include helpers. They might help a mover, an upholsterer, or a carpenter, as shown in 15-22. There are entry level jobs in every career area.

A few entry level positions still do not require a high school education. However, you are more likely to be sure of securing a position if you finish high school. Some courses related to housing careers are identified in 15-23.

Does your school have a program in *cooperative education?* (These offer opportunities to work part-time and attend classes part-time.) You may be able to secure a job through this kind of program. It will probably be an entry level position. You will receive training on the job. You will also receive help from a teacher in your school.

Career ladders

When the jobs in a career cluster are "stacked" according to the qualifications they

15-22 Entry level workers may have specific jobs such as cutting and placing lumber that has been marked by another carpenter.

COURSES RELATED TO HOUSING

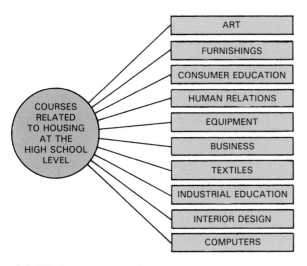

15-23 How many of these courses are offered in your school? Are there others related to housing?

require, they form a *career ladder* or a *career lattice.*

A career ladder shows the steps from entry level jobs to mid level or professional level ones. You can climb a career ladder by gaining more knowledge and experience. Study the career ladders that are shown in 15-24 and 15-25.

A *career lattice,* 15-26, shows that you can move in more than one direction as you change jobs within a career cluster. You can move either up or across the lattice. You may even be able to move at an angle—both up and across at the same time.

The terms *open entry* and *open exit* are sometimes used to describe moving on a career lattice. They mean that you can enter at any level for which you are qualified and that you can move across to any other position for which you are qualified.

BECOMING A SPECIALIST IN
ELECTRICAL HOUSEHOLD APPLIANCES

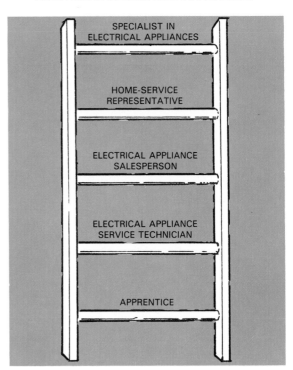

15-24 This career ladder shows the steps to take from an entry level position to a mid level position.

Careers in housing 319

QUALITIES FOR SUCCESS

Did you notice the magic word that determines your place on a career ladder or lattice? It is the word *qualified*. You become qualified by learning *job skills*.

Job skills

Any job you do requires some skills. If you are *competent* on a job, you can perform each skill well.

Suppose you own a lawn mower and take a job mowing lawns. Some of the job skills you will need to perform include:
- Moving large objects out of the way.
- Adjusting the mower to the desired height.
- Refueling the mower engine.
- Starting the mower engine.
- Mowing the grass evenly.
- Shutting off the mower engine.
- Catching or raking the grass clippings.

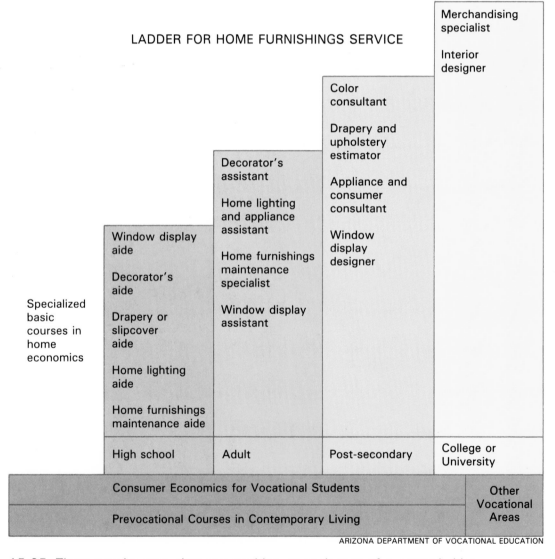

LADDER FOR HOME FURNISHINGS SERVICE

Specialized basic courses in home economics			
Window display aide Decorator's aide Drapery or slipcover aide Home lighting aide Home furnishings maintenance aide	Decorator's assistant Home lighting and appliance assistant Home furnishings maintenance specialist Window display assistant	Color consultant Drapery and upholstery estimator Appliance and consumer consultant Window display designer	Merchandising specialist Interior designer
High school	Adult	Post-secondary	College or University
Consumer Economics for Vocational Students			Other Vocational Areas
Prevocational Courses in Contemporary Living			

ARIZONA DEPARTMENT OF VOCATIONAL EDUCATION

15-25 There may be more than one position on each step of a career ladder. Education can help you climb a career ladder.

- Trimming and edging grass.
- Disposing of trash.

Each of these tasks involves detailed steps that are often taken in a certain order. If you were *task detailing* or listing the details for refueling the mower engine, what would you list first? Can you list the details in the order they should be done? Try listing the detailed steps for other tasks listed.

You can learn job skills by working with someone else on the job. This is especially true of entry-level jobs. Other places to learn job skills are in school and training programs.

Personal qualifications

You need to have an interst in your job. Sometimes a special interest helps to make you qualified for a position. If you like art and have

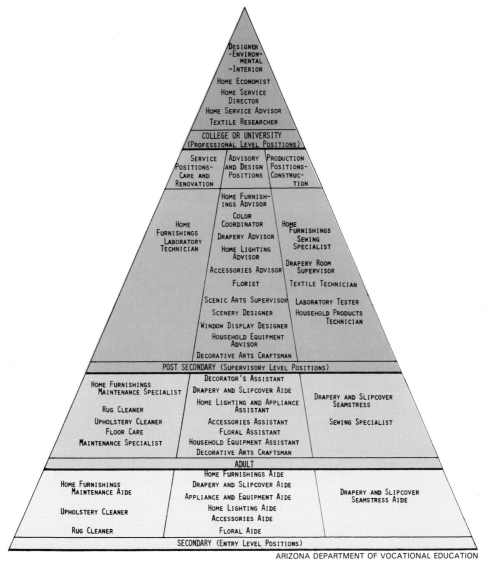

ARIZONA DEPARTMENT OF VOCATIONAL EDUCATION

15-26 The career lattice shows horizontal and vertical changes you can make within a career cluster.

Careers in housing 321

a special talent for it, you may qualify for a job that requires artistic abilities.

Many housing careers require artistic ability. Architects, landscape architects, furniture designers, and textile designers work with art.

Your personal *preferences* or what you like help to determine your qualifications. Do you like to work alone? Or do you prefer to work with someone else? Examine the career clusters in this chapter and find positions in which you would probably work alone much of the time. Then find ones in which you would work with others. Which ones appeal to you more?

Do you enjoy being outdoors? Or would you rather stay inside? What kind of life-style appeals to you? Do you like to sleep late in the morning? Can you work best during the day or during the night? Will your career choice let you spend as much time away from work as you would like? Are you work-oriented? Do you want your career to be the focal point of your life? Are you willing to work evenings and weekends?

Working conditions

When you are looking for a job, you will want to know about the working conditions. Then you will know what to expect. Some of the conditions that you should find out about include the following:

- Physical surroundings. Where will you be working? Is the place clean and safe?
- Work schedule. What are your working hours and days?
- Pay scale. How much will you be paid? Does everyone doing the job you are doing get the same pay? On what is the pay increase based?
- Advancement. Is there opportunity for advancement? How soon and how often can you expect to move up the ladder? Are there special expectations of you before you advance?
- Fringe benefits. Are there insurance benefits? How much sick leave is granted during the year? Does it accumulate? Is there personal or emergency leave? Are training programs provided? Is there a credit union?

- Dues and fees. Will you be expected to join a union or other organization? If so, what are the costs? Will it require some of your time?

You may also want to find out about public transportation to and from work. Or if you drive, where will you park your car? Are there eating facilities nearby? Are rest breaks provided? The conditions under which you work have a great affect on the amount of enjoyment you receive from your job.

to Know

apprentice . . . career cluster . . . career ladder . . . career lattice . . . career levels . . . career web . . . competent . . . cooperative edcucation . . . entry level positions . . . fringe benefits . . . job descriptions . . . job skills . . . mid level positions . . . personal qualifications . . . professional level positions . . . subclusters . . . supportive personnel . . . task detailing . . . working conditions

to Review

Write your answers on a separate sheet of paper.

1. (True or False) People who work in the building industry provide all that is needed for a good housing environment.

2. Define a career cluster.

3. List three sources of career information.

4. Name four career areas related to housing.

5. Write a job description for a position in a career related to housing.

6. Name one position in each of the career levels:
   a. Professional level.
   b. Mid level.
   c. Entry level.

7. People who help carry out decisions that have been made by higher authorities are called _____ _____.

8. Define the term apprentice.

9. What is the difference between a career ladder and a career lattice?

10. _____ _____ are the abilities you need to perform well on a job; _____ _____ include interest, natural talents, and personal preferences.

11. List five facts you should know about working conditions before you decide to take a job.

to Do

1. Find descriptions of several jobs related to housing and arrange them into career clusters. Use current editions of *Dictionary of Occupational Titles* and *Occupational Outlook Handbook* to find job descriptions.

2. Examine telephone directories to identify businesses that are related to housing.

3. Look through the classified advertising section of your newspaper. Find ads that are seeking employees in positions that help provide housing.

4. Make a collage using advertisements, pictures, and news articles about careers related to housing.

5. Choose a career related to housing that interests you. Research it further, and report to your class on it.

6. Draw a career ladder in the area of your interest. Begin with an entry level position and progress to a professional level position.

7. List the courses in your school that help prepare students for housing careers.

8. Ask your school counselor to give you an aptitude test. Determine which types of housing careers offer the best chances for you to succeed.

9. Write a feature article for your school or local newspaper telling about a career related to housing.

10. Write, call, or visit a local firm that employs people in housing careers. Find out employer expectations and working conditions.

11. Interview persons who have jobs related to housing. Find out what they like and dislike about their jobs.

12. Have a class dicsussion about attitudes in the "world of work." Determine which attitudes lead to success on the job and which do not.

13. Visit a local employment service to find out what careers related to housing are available in your area and across the nation.

Appendix
Energy-saving tips

Americans use more energy per person than any other people in the world. We have only six percent of the world's population, but we use about one-third of all the energy consumed on this globe.

Where does all this energy go? Industry takes about 36 percent. Commerce uses about 11 percent for enterprises including stores, offices, schools, and hospitals. Transportation accounts for about 27 percent. And residences take about 26 percent.

Where does residential energy go? Most of it, 70 percent, is used to heat and cool homes. An additional 20 percent goes for heating water. The remaining 10 percent goes into lighting, cooking, and running household appliances.

Americans can cut energy use and living costs by making homes energy efficient, even if they have to spend some money to do it. The money spent now will be returned through lower utility bills month after month.

PROTECT YOUR HOME FROM OUTSIDE HEAT AND COLD

Approximately 40 million single-family homes in the United States are not adequately protected from outside weather, according to Department of Energy estimates. (Utility companies will make an energy check of your home for a small fee.) Here are some tips to make sure yours is not one of them.

Insulation
- Find out if your home needs insulation. Your needs will depend on the climate in which you live and the amount of insulation, if any, you already have.
- Find out about R-values before you buy your insulation material. Then buy the thickness of insulation that will give you the R-value you need. R-values or numbers are insulation efficiency ratings. The "R" stands for resistance to winter heat loss or summer heat gain. The higher the R-number, the more effective the insulating capability. The numbers should appear on packages of all insulation materials.
- Insulate or increase the amount of insulation in your attic floor or top floor ceiling to the recommended R-values for your climate. Check the insulating qualities (R-values) of the floor coverings, draperies, etc.
- Don't insulate over eave vents or on top of recessed lighting fixtures or other heat-

producing equipment on the attic floor.
- Consider insulating exterior walls. This is an expensive measure that requires the service of a contractor, but it may be worth the cost if you live in a very hot or very cold climate.
- Insulate floors over unheated spaces such as crawl spaces and garages.

Windows and doors
- Test your windows and doors for air-tightness. Move a lighted candle around the frames and sashes of your windows. If the flame dances around, you need caulking and/or weatherstripping. Try slipping a quarter under your door. If it goes through easily, you need weatherstripping.
- Install storm windows and doors. Combination screen and storm windows and doors (triple-track glass combination) are the most convenient and energy efficient because they can be opened easily when there is no need to run heating or cooling equipment. Alternatives range from single-pane storm windows to clear plastic film which can be taped tightly to the inside of the window frames.

HEATING AND COOLING

To prevent wasting energy, follow these tips during both heating and cooling seasons.
- Close off unoccupied rooms and close their heat or air-conditioning vents. (This does not apply if you have a heat pump system. Leave it alone; closing vents could harm a heat pump.)
- Use kitchen, bath, and other ventilating fans sparingly.
- Keep your fireplace damper closed unless you have a fire going.
- Install ceiling fans that have a reverse switch so that air can be circulated whether you are heating or cooling your home.
- Clean or replace filters on furnaces and air conditioners as recommended by the manufacturer (usually at least once per month).
- Open and close drapes and shutters according to the time of the day and year to allow or prevent heat transfer.

Heating energy savers
- If you use electric furnace heating, consider a heat pump system. The heat pump uses thermal energy from outside air for both heating and cooling.
- If you plan to buy a new gas heating system, ask your gas utility or public service commission about the savings potential of electronic ignition. Ask also about possibilities for retrofitting the system you may already own.
- Consider the advantages of a clock thermostat for your heating system. The clock thermostat will turn the heat down for you automatically at a set hour before you retire and turn it up again before you wake.
- Consider buying a properly sized furnace that incorporates an automatic flue gas damper. This device reduces the loss of heat when the furnace is off.
- Lower your thermostat to 65 deg. F (18 deg. C) during the day and 55 deg. F (13 deg. C) at night (unless your physician advises you otherwise).
- Keep windows near your thermostat tightly closed. Otherwise, it will keep your furnace working after the rest of the room has reached a comfortable temperature.
- Install an insert in your fireplace. Some models allow you to retain the beauty of your fireplace yet are energy efficient.
- Have your oil furnace serviced as least once a year.
- Check the duct work for air leaks about once a year if you have a forced-air heating system. To do this, feel around the duct joints for escaping air when the fan is on. Relatively small leaks can be repaired simply by covering holes or cracks with duct tape. More stubborn problems may require caulking as well as taping.
- If you have oil heat, have someone check to see if the firing rate is correct.
- Don't let cold air seep into your home through the attic access door. Check the door to make sure it is well insulated and weatherstripped.
- Dust or vacuum radiator surfaces often. Dust and grime impede the flow of heat. And if

the radiators need painting, use flat paint, preferably black. It radiates heat better than glossy.
- Keep draperies and shades open in sunny windows; close them at night.
- For comfort in cooler indoor temperatures, use the best insulation of all—warm clothing.

Cooling energy savers
- If you need central air-conditioning, select a unit with the lowest suitable capacity and highest efficiency. A larger unit than you need not only costs more to run, but probably won't remove enough moisture from the air.
- Make sure the ducts in your air-conditioning system are properly insulated, especially those that pass through the attic or other uncooled spaces.
- If you don't need central air-conditioning, consider using individual units in rooms that need cooling from time to time.
- Install a whole-house ventilating fan in your attic or in an upstairs window to cool the house when it's cool outside, even if you have central air-conditioning. It will pay to use the fan rather than air-conditioning when the outside temperature is below 82 deg. F (28 deg. C). When windows in the house are open, the fan pulls cool air through the house and exhausts warm air through the attic.
- Set your thermostat at 78 deg. F (25 deg. C). This is a reasonably comfortable and energy-efficient indoor temperature.
- Don't set your thermostat at a colder setting than normal when you turn your air-conditioner on. It will not cool faster.
- Set the fan speed on high except in very humid weather. When it's humid, set the fan speed at low. You'll get less cooling, but more moisture will be removed from the air.
- Turn off your window air-conditioners when you leave a room for several hours.
- Consider using a fan with your window air-conditioner to spread the cooled air farther without greatly increasing your power use. But be sure the air-conditioner is strong enough to help cool the additional space.
- Don't place lamps or TV sets near your air-conditioning thermostat. Heat from these appliances is sensed by the thermostat and could cause the air-conditioner to run longer than necessary.
- Keep out daytime sun with outdoor awnings or indoor draperies or shades.
- Open the windows instead of using your air-conditioner or electric fan on cooler days and during cooler hours.
- If you don't use air-conditioning, be sure to keep windows and outside doors closed during the hottest hours of the day.
- Do your cooking and use other heat-generating appliances in the early morning and late evening hours when possible.
- Use vents and exhaust fans to pull heat and moisture from the attic, kitchen, and laundry directly to the outside.

HOT WATER ENERGY SAVERS

Heating water accounts for about 20 percent of all the energy used in homes. Don't waste it.
- Repair leaky faucets promptly.
- Do as much household cleaning as possible with cold water.
- Insulate your hot water storage tank and piping.
- Buy a water heater with thick insulation on the shell. While the initial cost may be more, the savings in energy costs will more than repay you.
- Add insulation around the water heater you now have if it's inadequately insulated, but be sure not to block off needed air vents. That would create a safety hazard.
- Check the temperature on your water heater. Most water heaters are set for 140 deg. F (60 deg. C) or higher, but you may not need water that hot unless you have a dishwasher. A setting of 120 deg. F (49 deg. C) can provide adequate hot water for most families.

ENERGY SAVERS IN THE KITCHEN, LAUNDRY, AND BATH

- Install an aerator in your kitchen sink faucet. By reducing the amount of water in the flow, you use less hot water and save energy.

- If you need to purchase a gas oven or range, look for one with an automatic (electronic) ignition system instead of pilot lights.
- If you have a gas stove, make sure the pilot light is burning efficiently—with a blue flame. A yellowish flame indicates an adjustment is needed.
- Never boil water in an open pan. Water will come to a boil faster and use less energy in a kettle or covered pan.
- Keep range-top burners and reflectors clean. They will reflect the heat better, and you will save energy.
- Match the size of pan to the heating element. More heat will get to the pan; less will be lost to surrounding air.
- If you cook with electricity, get in the habit of turning off the burners before the end of the allotted cooking time. The heating element will stay hot long enough to finish the cooking without using more electricity.
- When using the oven, cook more than one food at a time.
- Watch the clock or use a timer. Don't continually open the oven door to check food. Every time you open the door, heat escapes and more energy is used.
- Use small electric pans or ovens for small meals rather than the kitchen range or oven. They use less energy.
- Use pressure cookers and microwave or convection ovens if you have them. They can save energy by reducing cooking time.
- When cooking with a gas range-top burner, use moderate flame settings to save gas.
- When you have a choice, use the range-top or a countertop oven rather than the oven.
- When buying a dishwasher, look for a model with air-power and/or overnight dry settings. These features automatically turn off the dishwasher after the rinse cycle.
- If your dishwasher doesn't have an automatic air-dry switch, turn off the control knob after the final rinse. Prop the door open a little and let the dishes air dry.
- Be sure your dishwasher is full, but not overloaded, when you turn it on.
- Wash clothes in warm or cold water and rinse them in cold water. Use hot water only if absolutely necessary.
- Fill clothes washers and dryers, unless they have small-load attachments or variable water levels.
- Do not run the dryer longer than necessary to dry clothes.
- Separate drying loads into heavy and lightweight items. Since the lighter ones take less drying time, the dryer does not have to be on as long for these loads.
- Dry your clothes in consecutive loads. Once the dryer is warm, it cuts down on initial energy consumption.
- Save energy needed for ironing by hanging clothes in the bathroom while you're bathing or showering. The steam often removes the wrinkles for you.
- Take showers rather than tub baths, but limit your showering time and check the water flow if you want to save energy.
- Consider installing a flow restrictor in the pipe at the showerhead. These inexpensive, easy-to-install devices restrict the flow of water.

APPLIANCE ENERGY SAVERS

About eight percent of the energy that people use goes into running electrical home appliances, so appliance use and selection can make a considerable difference in home utility costs.

- Don't leave your appliances running when they're not in use.
- Keep appliances in good working order so they will last longer, work more efficiently, and use less energy.
- When buying appliances, read labels carefully. Compare energy use information and operating costs of similar models by the same and different manufacturers. Look for yellow and black "EnergyGuide" labels on the following major appliances: refrigerators, refrigerator-freezers, freezers, dishwashers, water heaters, clothes washers, air conditioners, and furnaces.
- Before buying new appliances with special features, find out how much energy they use compared with other models that may be less

convenient. A frost-free refrigerator, for example, uses more energy than one you have to defrost manually.

- Use appliances wisely. Use the one that takes the least amount of energy for the job. For example, toasting bread in an oven uses three times more energy than using a toaster.

LIGHTING ENERGY SAVERS

Most Americans overlight their homes, so lowering lighting levels is an easy conservation measure.

- Turn off lights in any room not being used.
- Light-zone your home and save electricity. Concentrate lighting in reading and working areas and where it's needed for safety (such as stairwells). Reduce lighting in other areas, but avoid very sharp contrasts.
- To reduce overall lighting in nonworking spaces, remove one bulb out of three in multiple light fixtures and replace it with a burned-out bulb for safety. Replace other bulbs throughout the house with bulbs of the next lower wattage.
- Consider installing solid state dimmers or hi-low switches when replacing light switches. They make it easy to reduce lighting intensity in a room and thus save energy.
- Use one large bulb instead of several small ones in areas where bright light is needed.

- Use long-life incandescent lamps only in hard-to-reach places. They are less energy efficient than ordinary bulbs.
- Turn three-way bulbs down to the lowest lighting level when watching television. You'll reduce the glare and save energy.
- Use fluorescent lights whenever you can. They give out more lumens per watt.
- Keep all lamps and lighting fixtures clean. Dirt absorbs light.
- Use outdoor lights only when and where they are needed. A photocell unit or timer will turn them on and off automatically.

YARD AND WORKSHOP ENERGY SAVERS

- Do not allow gasoline-powered yard equipment to idle for long periods.
- Use hand tools, hand lawn mowers, pruners, and clippers whenever possible.
- Maintain electrical tools in top operating condition. They should be clean and properly lubricated.
- Keep cutting edges sharp. A sharp bit or saw cuts more quickly and therefore uses less power.
- Buy power tools with the lowest horsepower adequate for the work you do.
- Remember to turn off shop lights, soldering irons, gluepots, and all bench heating devices right after use.

Glossary

A

absorbed light: light that is taken in, not reflected, by a surface.

abstract of title: a copy of all public records concerning a property. It shows the true legal owner and any debts that are held on the property.

accent lighting: sharp lighting used for decorative purposes, especially to focus on the point of emphasis in a room.

accessories: the "extras" or "added touches" in a design through which the designer expresses his or her personality; may be either functional (as ashtrays and lamps) or decorative (as pictures and figurines).

acoustical materials: materials that are used to reduce noise within a house.

acquisition: the act of getting something; one of the three major categories of housing decisions.

active solar system: a system which uses fans and pumps to move heated air or liquid from a solar collector to a storage area and then to where the heat is needed.

adobe: a building material consisting of sun-dried earth and straw; a structure built of adobe bricks.

aesthetics: the theory of the fine arts and of people's responses to them.

agreement of sale: a contract signed by the buyer and seller of property. It states all specific terms and conditions of the sale.

alcove: a recessed section of a room; a niche.

American Gas Association: the association which sets standards of safety, performance, and durability for gas appliances and tests the appliances.

analogous color harmony: a color harmony that combines three to five related colors.

antique: any object that is very old; term applied to objects made in a former period of time.

apartment: a suite of rooms in a multifamily dwelling which houses a living unit.

appraiser: someone who can give an expert estimate of the quality and value of a piece of property.

apprentice: one who is enrolled in an organized program of job training often supplemented with vocational classes; a beginner in an occupation.

apron: the part of a window below the sill.

architect: one who designs buildings and supervises their construction.

artificial light: light from sources other than the sun; produced light such as incandescent or fluorescent.

assign: to transfer the entire unexpired portion of a lease to someone else.

asymmetrical: a type of balance in which the two sides of a design are of equal importance but are not identical.

atmosphere: all the air surrounding the earth; also the general aesthetic effect produced by a design such as the mood created by the furnishings in a room.

attached homes: homes that are connected, usually by a common wall.

B

balance: a feeling of equilibrium; a principle of design.

balcony: a platform projecting from a building and enclosed by a balustrade. Balconies usually open onto an upper story.

basic life-style: a way of living that is concerned with only the basics or necessities of life.

basket weave: a variation of the plain weave in which two or more filling or warp yarns are woven as one.

behavioral environment: one's surroundings as affected by interaction among people.

belvadere: a small room on the roof of a house once used as a lookout.

bid: a statement of what a contractor would charge to build a specific dwelling.

blueprint: a photographic reproduction of an original floor plan showing exact structural details; often white on a blue background.

breach of contract: failure to meet all terms of a contract or agreement.

burl: a knot on some trees that produces an interesting, irregular grain pattern.

C

cabriole: a furniture leg with an "s-shaped" curve and decorative foot.

cafes: a window treatment made of fabric which covers part of a window. (More than one tier can be used to cover the entire window.) The top of each tier is joined to rings which slip over a curtain rod.

cantilever: a horizontal beam or member which extends beyond its support.

career: a profession or occupation.

career cluster (or career web): a group of several careers which are closely related.

career ladder: a progression of related careers, each one requiring more qualifications than the previous one.

career lattice: a chart showing related career opportunities organized in such a way that by moving up the chart, the careers require more qualifications, and by moving across the chart, the careers are in a slightly different subject area.

carpentry: the work or trade of a carpenter, one who builds or repairs wooden articles, buildings, etc.

carrying charges: the amounts, other than interest, added to the price of something that is bought on an installment plan.

central-satellite decisions: a group of decisions consisting of a major decision that is surrounded by related, but independent, decisions.

chain decisions: a sequence of decisions in which one decision triggers others. All decisions in the chain must be made to complete an action.

climate: prevailing weather conditions of a region as determined by the temperature and meteorological changes over a period of years.

closing costs: fees for settling the many legal and financial matters of buying and selling property.

cluster housing: the grouping of dwellings close together in order to save more land for shared areas such as public gardens and parks.

cluster units: modules which are combined to form a dwelling. The modules or units can be easily added or removed, depending on the spatial needs of the living unit.

code: a body of laws arranged systematically for easy reference, as a building code which regulates building materials and construction methods.

colonnade: a series of columns which support the extension of a roof.

color: an element of design; often the most noticed element.

color harmony (or color scheme): a pleasing combination of colors.

color wheel: a particular circular arrangement of primary, secondary, and intermediate colors; the basis for color relationships.

common storage: storage used by all members of a living unit.

community: a particular area that is smaller than a region, but larger than a neighborhood. Examples include cities, towns, villages. Also, the people living within a given area who have a common interest.

community life-style: a way of life in which a group of people combine their resources for the common good of all.

complementary color harmony: a color harmony based on a pair of complementary colors or hues.

complementary hues: hues which are direclty across from one another on the color wheel.

condominium: a type of ownership in which the buyer owns individual living space and also has an undivided interest in the common areas and facilities of the multi-unit project.

conservation: protection from loss or waste.

constructed environment: the result of interaction between the natural environment and human effort.

contact person: a person who enjoys being in contact with other people most of the time.

contemporary styles: styles (of furniture or buildings) of the present time; the very latest designs. They may or may not gain widespread acceptance.

contracting family: a family that is becoming smaller as children become adults and leave their parents' home.

contractor: a person who contracts or agrees to supply certain materials or to do certain work for a stipulated fee, especially one who contracts to build buildings.

cool colors (or receding colors): colors that are close to blue on the color wheel. They are relaxing colors.

cooperative: a type of ownership in which a property is owned by a corporation. Residents buy stock in the corporation which entitles them to occupy a certain living space. Each resident owns an undivided interest in the entire property.

cooperative education: schooling that includes work experience.

cornice: horizontal molding along the top of a building, wall, mantel, etc.; also a horizontal band used to conceal the tops of draperies.

cornice lighting: a type of structural lighting in which a row of fluorescent tubes is placed along a wall just below the ceiling. All the light is directed downward.

cost: the amount of human and nonhuman resources used to achieve something.

cove lighting: a type of structural lighting in which the light source is recessed in the upper part of a wall. The light is directed upward to the ceiling.

credit card: a card used instead of cash to buy goods and services. The company that offers the card is then payed for the cost of the product and possibly interest for the time between purchase and payment to the credit company.

crotchwood: a special wood grain formed where branches grow out from the trunk of a tree.

cultural heritage: the arts, skills, customs, and traits of a particular group of people which are passed down from one generation to another.

curtains: flat fabric panels used to cover windows. They have a pocket hem at the top which slips onto a curtain rod.

custom-designed house: a house which is designed to meet the needs, priorities, and life situations of a particular living unit and which is built according to the living unit's specifications.

D

decibel: a unit of measure for the volume of sound.

decision: the act of making up one's mind; a conclusion; a choice.

decision-making process: a series of three steps

that are taken in order to make a rational decision. The steps are: 1-problem identification; 2-seeking alternate solutions; 3-choosing one of the alternatives and taking action.

declaration of ownership: a document stating the conditions and restrictions of the sale, ownership, and use of property within a certain group of condominium units.

deed: the legal document by which a title of real property is transferred from one person to another.

dehumidifier: an appliance that removes excess humidity from the air.

design: the arrangement of parts that produces an artistic unit.

diffused light: light that is scattered over a large area. It has no glare.

direct lighting: lighting that shines directly toward the surface to be lit. Very little is reflected from other surfaces.

divan bed: a type of dual-purpose sleep furniture in which a mattress folds up inside the seat of the sofa.

dormer: a structure which projects through a sloping roof and contains a window.

double cylinder lock: a door lock which requires a key to be unlocked from the inside as well as the outside.

downlights: a type of structural lighting installed in ceilings. They may be recessed or surface-mounted.

down payment: initial payment made to secure a purchase when the rest of the amount owed will be paid in regular installments of a lesser amount.

draw draperies: pinch-pleated panels of fabric which can cover windows completely or be pulled to the sides.

duplex: two dwellings combined in a single structure.

dwelling: any type of structure in which people live.

E

earth sheltered housing: housing that is partially covered with soil.

eaves: the lower border of a roof which extends out beyond the wall.

eclectic: a type of decor based on a mixture of furniture styles.

ecology: the study of the relationship between living organisms and their surroundings.

economic: having to do with meeting the material needs of people or with the management of income, expenditures, etc.

economic level: a rank or status in society dependent upon the amount of money a person or family has to spend.

ecosystem: a community together with its environment in which each living thing—plant or animal—is indispensible to the life of every other living thing.

electronic air cleaner: an appliance used in homes, offices, and other buildings to remove particles in the air that cause air pollution.

elements of design: color, line, form, texture.

emphasis: a center of interest in a design; an object or area of special importance; a principle of design.

EnergyGuide label: a label designed to allow a consumer to compare average costs of operating similar appliances.

environment: surroundings; all the conditions, circumstances, and influences surrounding and affecting the development of a living organism.

equity: the money value of a house beyond what is owed on the house.

eviction: a legal procedure which forces a tenant to leave the property before the rental agreement expires.

expanding family: family in the process of growing; one of the stages of a family life cycle.

extended family: a living unit consisting of a nuclear family plus near relatives.

exterior: the outside structure of a building.

F

family life cycle: a series of stages through which a family passes during its lifetime.

fiber content: the type or types of fibers used

to make a textile item such as upholstery or carpeting.

finance: to provide credit to an individual or business.

finance charge: a fee paid for the privilege of using credit. It includes interest and carrying charges.

fixed income: an income which remains constant regardless of economic changes.

flat roof: roof with just enough slope to provide water drainage.

floor plan: a scale drawing showing the size and arrangement of rooms, halls, doors, etc. on one floor of a building.

fluorescent light: light produced as electricity activates mercury vapor within a sealed tube to create invisible ultraviolet rays. These rays are converted to visible light rays by a fluorescent material that coats the inside of the glass tube.

fluorocarbons: a group of chemicals which are in some aerosol sprays and can cause breathing problems.

footcandle: a unit of measure for illumination; the amount of light a standard candle throws onto a surface which is one foot away.

force cup: a plunger used to loosen clogs in drain pipes.

foreclosure: a legal preceeding in which a lending firm takes possession of the mortgaged property of a debtor who fails to live up to the terms of a contract.

form: the physical shape and structure of objects; one of the three major categories of housing decisions; one of the elements of design.

formal balance: symmetrical balance.

founding family: initial stage of family life cycle before children are born.

frame: the structure that encloses and supports a window.

free-standing home: A dwelling that stands alone and is not connected to any other structure.

fringe benefits: benefits other than wages that are provided by an employer to an employee, such as paid vacations, pension plans, and health insurance.

full warranty: a written agreement which allows a consumer to have a broken appliance repaired or replaced free of charge (at the warrantor's option).

G

gable roof: a roof that comes to a point in the center and slopes on both sides.

gambrel roof: a two-pitched roof with the lower slope steeper than the upper slope.

general lighting: soft, even lighting throughout a room or area.

general warranty deed: a deed which guarantees that the title is clear of any claims against it.

geothermal energy: energy coming from the heat of the earth's interior.

gingerbread: a term used to describe the excessive ornamentation found on Victorian style buildings.

goals of design: beauty, appropriateness, unity with variation.

gross income: total income before any deductions are made.

H

habitat: place where a person or thing is normally found.

habitual behavior: an action that is done as a matter of routine, without thought.

hardwood: wood from trees which lose their leaves.

heat pump: a mechanical device used for both heating and cooling buildings.

high tech: a high level of technology.

hip roof: a roof with sloping ends and sloping sides.

home: any place a person lives.

house: a free-standing, single-family dwelling.

housing: a dwelling together with all that is within it and near it; includes furnishings, yard, neighborhood, and community.

hue: the name of a color; the one thing that makes a color unique.

human ecology: the interdependence of people and their environment.

human resources: resources which are available from people. Examples include ability, knowledge, energy, attitude, health.

humidifier: an appliance that adds the desired amount of moisture to the air.

humidity: amount of moisture in the air; humidity levels in buildings can be controlled by humidifiers and dehumidifiers.

I

incandescent light: the light produced when electric current heats a tungsten filament inside a bulb so that it glows.

indirect lighting: lighting that is directed mainly toward walls and ceilngs. It is reflected from these surfaces to produce soft, general lighting for a room.

individualistic life-style: a way of life that is unique and that sets one apart from others.

individual life cycle: a series of stages through which a person passes during his or her lifetime.

influential life-style: a way of life that influences or affects others.

informal balance: asymmetrical balance.

initial acquisition: getting an object that a person has not had before.

inspector: someone who judges the construction and present condition of buildings.

installment buying: the process of buying something by making a series of payments during a given length of time.

insulation: limitation of transfer of heat or sound between the inside and outside of a structure or between parts of a structure; materials used to block such transfer.

integration: act of uniting; process of including persons from different backgrounds into a group or society as equals.

intensity: the brightness or dullness of a hue.

interest: the price paid for the use of borrowed money. It is usually stated as an annual percentage rate of the amount borrowed.

interior: the inside of a building.

intermediate colors (or tertiary colors): colors made by mixing equal amounts of a primary color and a secondary color.

J

Jacquard weave: an intricate method of weaving in which the warp threads are individually controlled. Elaborate designs can be made.

job description: a brief explanation of what a particular job is like: what duties it involves, what qualifications are needed, and what opportunities it offers.

job skills: the abilities needed to perform the tasks that a certain job demands.

K

kit house: a house which is partially completed in a factory.

knitted fabrics: fabrics made of interlooping yarns.

L

landlord (or lessor): the owner of property who leases or rents it to another person.

landscaping: changing the appearance of a site by altering the topography and adding decorative plantings.

lease: a legal document transferring the use of property from one person to another for a certain length of time in return for payment in the form of rent.

lein waver: a document which prevents a person from having to pay for items used by a contractor in remodeling if the contractor does not pay for them.

lessee: one who has signed a lease and pays rent to a lessor or landlord for the use of property.

life cycle: a series of stages through which an individual or a family passes during its lifetime.

life situations: circumstances which affect persons and the way they live; factors which determine the way persons interact with each other and with their housing.

life-style: a living pattern or way of life.

light fixture: a furnishing or structure that contains one or more light bulbs. It is usually permanently attached to a wall or ceiling.

light meter: a device used to measure amounts of light.

limited warranty: a written agreement which only obligates a warrantor to do certain kinds of repairs at no charge to the consumer or to replace the product under certain conditions.

line: an element of design. It gives a sense of motion and direction to a design.

living unit: people who share the same living quarters.

location: a place which every part of housing has, either inside or outside a dwelling; one of the three major categories of housing decisions.

long-term financing: financing for a major purchase such as a house which may take as long as 30 years to repay.

loss leader sale: a type of sale in which a store greatly reduces the prices on a few items hoping that customers will also buy items that are not on sale.

luminous ceiling: a ceiling made of translucent panels which cover recessed lights.

M

macroenvironment: your total surroundings.

maintenance fee: a fee paid by a condominium owner used for the repair and maintenance of the common areas of the condominium.

Mansard roof: a roof having two slopes on all sides with the lower one steeper than the upper one.

manufactured fibers: fibers made from chemicals. Examples include nylon, polyester, acrylic, olefin.

manufactured housing: housing that is built in factories and then moved in sections to the site.

masonry: construction of stone, brick, or concrete materials; also the work done by a mason who works with such materials.

median income: the middle income in a series of incomes.

microenvironment: a small part of your total surroundings; your housing environment.

migrant workers: seasonal workers who move from farm to farm as work becomes available. They are often forced to live in substandard housing.

minimum property standards (MPS): standards set by the Federal Housing Administration which regulate the sizes of lots.

minority group: part of a population that differs from the rest in some characteristics.

mobile home: a factory-built, single-family dwelling. It can be moved by attaching wheels to it.

modern styles: styles (of furniture or buildings) which have become popular in the recent past.

monochromatic color harmony: a color harmony based on a single color.

mortar: a mixture of cement or lime with sand and water that is used in masonry or plastering.

mortgage: a pledge of property as security for the payment of a debt.

motor home: an automotive vehicle equipped as a home.

multifamily home: a structure that provides housing for more than one living unit, such as an apartment building.

multipurpose rooms: rooms with sleeping or dressing space which also provide space for other activities.

N

natural environment: the environment as provided by nature. Resources of the natural environment are land, water, plants, and air.

natural fibers: fibers made from plant or animal sources. Examples include cotton, flax, wool, silk.

natural light: light from the sun.

neighborhood: a section of a community in which some similarities are usually found in the buildings and in the people.

net income: income after deductions such as social security and income tax have been made; take-home pay.

neutralized hues: hues which have been changed by the addition of white, gray, or black.

neutrals: black, white, and gray.

noise: unwanted sound; a form of pollution.

noncontact person: a person who enjoys being alone most of the time.

nonhuman resources: resources which are not directly supplied by people. Examples include property, money, public libraries, city parks, schools, stores.

nonwoven fabrics: textile items which are not woven or knitted. Used loosely, the term includes bonded fiber webs, needlepunched fabrics, vinyl, and leather.

normal value (of a hue): the value of a hue that is shown on the color wheel.

nuclear family: a living unit consisting of a husband and wife and their children; also, a childless married couple.

O

one-parent family: a family with only a mother or a father, not both.

open areas: areas in a house without walls as divisions.

ordinance: a statute enacted by a city government.

orientation: the placement of a dwelling in a specific location in order to take advantage of factors such as sunlight, wind direction, and scenery; adaptation to a situation or environment.

P

pane: the sheet of glass in a window.

partial wall: wall that does not go all the way up to the ceiling.

passive solar system: a system which includes any design or construction material that makes maximum use of sun, light, or wind for heating and cooling. This type of system has no working parts.

patio: an open area used for outdoor living. It may be adjacent to or surrounded by the dwelling.

pediment: an architectural decoration above a portico, window, or door; often triangular in shape.

pendant: an ornament hanging from a roof or ceiling.

penthouse: a dwelling located on the top of a building.

period furniture styles: furniture styles that first became popular during certain times in history.

personal priorities: the ideas, objects, and people that a person holds as important.

photo-voltaic system: a device which converts light to electricity.

physical neighborhood: the material aspects of a neighborhood; a neighborhood in which the land and buildings are used for similar purposes—either residential, commercial, or industrial.

pile weave: a variation of a basic weave in which additional yarn is located on the fabric's surface.

plain weave: a method of interlacing yarns in which each filling yarn passes over, then under, each warp yarn.

planned community: a community which is completely designed before the first building is built. Residences, schools, churches, shopping centers, health and public service facilities, and recreational facilities are all part of the design.

planned neighborhood: a neighborhood in which the size and layout of individual lots are determined before any houses are built. The types of homes which are built must fit into the overall plan.

plywood: a building material consisting of thin sheets or veneers of wood which are bonded together under pressure.

portico: an open space covered with a roof that is supported by columns; often found at the entrance of a building.

pressed wood: a board made by pressing together bits of sawdust.

primary colors: colors from which all other colors can be made; red, yellow, and blue.

primary needs (or basic needs): the most important needs of all humans.

principles of design: proportion, balance, emphasis, rhythm.

private zone: the part of the site hidden from public view. It provides space for recreation and relaxation.

process: the method used to accomplish a task.

property tax: money paid to the government for property one owns.

proportion: the ratio of one part to another part or to the whole; a principle of design.

public zone: the part of a site that can be seen from the street.

Q

qualified: having met certain conditions or requirements; having the necessary or desired characteristics.

quality of life: the degree of satisfaction obtained from life situations.

quiet area of home: the part of a dwelling that provides space for sleeping, resting, grooming, and dressing; includes bedrooms and bathrooms.

quitclaim deed: a deed that transfers whatever interest the seller has in the property.

R

radon: a natural radioactive gas found in the earth.

rational decision: a decision based on reasoning.

real estate firm: a business that deals with property in the form of land and buildings.

real property: land, together with anything attached to it, as buildings, fences, and plants.

recessed downlights: a type of structural lighting in which the light source is recessed into the ceiling.

recycle: to use again.

reflected light: light that bounces off a surface.

region: a specific part of the world, a country, or a state.

remodel: to rebuild; to change the structure of something.

rent: a stated amount paid at fixed intervals for the use of property such as a dwelling or land; also the act of holding property under an agreement to pay rent.

renter: one who rents property.

resident: one who lives in a place as distinguished from a visitor or transient.

residential: of or suitable for residences or homes.

resources: objects, qualities, or people that can be used to help meet needs and goals.

retrofitting: changing an existing structure to make it more energy efficient.

rhythm: a sense of movement in a natural flow from one part of a design to another; a principle of design.

rib weave: a variation of the plain weave in which the warp and filling yarns are unequal in size.

Roman shades: shades which form accordian folds as they are raised.

row houses: a continuous group of houses connected by common sidewalls.

rural poor: persons in rural areas who are forced to live in substandard housing because of economic reasons.

S

sash: the framework which surrounds the panes of glass in a window.

satin weave: a method of interlacing yarns in which each warp or filling yarn passes over several yarns and then under one yarn. The interlacings progress by two to either the right or left, creating a smooth fabric surface.

seasonal sale: a sale held at the end of a selling season to get rid of old items so that a store can make room for new items.

secondary colors: colors made by mixing equal amounts of two primary colors; green, violet, orange.

secondary needs: human needs that are of lower priority than primary needs.

security deposit: an amount paid by a renter to a landlord in addition to monthly payments. It insures the landlord against financial loss caused by the renter.

segregation: the process of setting apart; the isolation of a race, class, or ethnic group by voluntary or involuntary means.

self-actualization: the fulfillment of one's potential.

self-esteem: having a positive, confident attitude about oneself.

service zone: the part of the site that is used for necessary activities. Service zones include sidewalks, driveways, and garages.

shade: a value of a hue that is darker than the hue's normal value.

sill: the horizontal piece at the base of a window.

single-family home: a structure that provides housing for one living unit.

site (or lot): the piece of land on which a dwelling is built.

slum: a heavily populated area in which living conditions are extremely poor; an area in which most of the buildings are detrimental to health, safety, or morals.

social area of home: the part of a dwelling that provides space for recreation, entertaining, and dining; includes living room, family room, dining room.

social class: a rank or level in a particular society.

social neighborhood: a type of neighborhood determined by the people who live in it. Social neighborhoods may be either homogenous or heterogenous; low-density or high-density.

socioeconomic status: a term used to describe both the social class and economic level of a person or group.

sofa bed: a general term used to describe any type of dual-purpose sleep furniture; specifically, a sofa with a back that folds down to form a bed.

soffit lighting: a type of structural lighting which can be either attached to or recessed into a ceiling.

softwood: wood from evergreen trees.

solar collectors: special plates installed in the roof of a building to soak up the sun's heat.

solar energy: energy from the sun; the primary source of all energy forms.

solid wood furniture: furniture in which all exposed parts are made of whole pieces of wood.

spatial need: the need for space.

special warranty deed: a deed that guarantees that during the time the seller held title to the property, the seller did nothing which would impair the buyer's title.

specific lighting (or task lighting): lighting in a certain area that is bright enough to allow detailed tasks to be done comfortably. It is often used to supplement general lighting.

splat-back chair: a chair whose back consists of thin, flat, decorative pieces.

spur-of-the-moment decision: a decision that is made quickly, with little thought of the possible consequences.

status: position, rank, standing.

structural lighting: lighting that is part of the built-in design of a building.

stucco: a plaster-like material which, when applied to the exterior walls of a building, forms a hard covering.

studio couch: a type of dual-purpose sleep furniture consisting of an upholstered mattress on an upholstered frame. When the upper cushions are removed, it is much like a twin bed.

studio lounge: a type of dual-purpose sleep furniture consisting of a foam pad resting on flat springs.

sublet: to transfer part interest in a property to someone else.

suburb: a smaller community, often residential, within commuting distance of a larger community.

supportive life-style: a way of life that gives psychological, financial, or physical support to others.

supportive personnel: persons who help carry out the decisions made by their superiors.

symmetrical: a type of balance in which the two sides of a design are alike in size, shape, and relative position of parts.

T

task detailing: identifying each step that must be done to complete a task.

tenant: one who pays rent to occupy or use property.

tenement house: a building divided into apartments, especially one that is in a poor section of a community and is overcrowded and dirty.

texture: the surface characteristics of an object that appeal to the senses of sight and touch; an element of design.

tint: a value of a hue that is lighter than the hue's normal value.

title: a document that gives evidence of the rights of ownership and possession of a particular property.

title insurance: insurance against financial loss caused by errors in the abstract of title for a property.

topography: the physical features of land such as hills and rivers; the art of representing such features on maps and charts.

town house: a single-family dwelling that is connected to a similar house by a common sidewall.

track lighting: a type of structural lighting consisting of several fixtures mounted on a track.

traditional styles: styles (of furniture or buildings) which became popular during a certain period of history.

traffic patterns: the paths people follow as they move within a room or from one room to another.

triplex: a multifamily dwelling for three living units.

turret: a small tower.

twill weave: a method of interlacing yarns in which each warp or filling yarn passes over two or more yarns and then under one yarn. The interlacings progress by one to either the right or left to create a pattern of diagonal lines or wales.

U

Underwriters' Laboratories (UL) symbol: a symbol placed on appliances which meet UL standards for safety.

unfinished furniture: furniture having no finish or final coat, as of paint, stain, or varnish.

unity: an arrangement of parts that produces a single harmonious effect.

upholstered furniture: pieces of furniture which have springs, padding, and a fabric covering.

urban: of, in, or relating to a city or town.

utility: something useful to the public, as the service of gas, water, electricity.

V

valance lighting: a type of structural lighting used over windows. A row of fluorescent tubes directs light both upward and downward.

value (of a hue): the lightness or darkness of a hue.

value scale: a representation of the full range of values for a hue, from tints to shades.

veneered wood (or plywood): wood made by bonding several thin layers of wood together at right angles to each other. Fine wood is often used for the top layer.

ventilation: the circulation of air; a means of providing fresh air.

visual pollution: the destruction of beauty in natural and constructed environments.

W

wall bed (or Murphy bed): a bed that is stored against the wall when it is not being used.

wall bracket lighting: a type of structural lighting in which a row of fluorescent tubes on a wall directs light both upward and downward.

wall washers: a type of structural lighting installed in ceilings. They direct a uniform amount of light onto a wall.

warm colors (or advancing colors): colors close to red on the color wheel. They are stimulating colors, and they draw attention.

warranty: a written guarantee of a product's performance and of the maker's responsibilities concerning defective parts.

watt: a unit of measure for electric power.

well-being: the state of being healthy, happy,

and content.

windbreak: that which provides shelter from wind, especially a hedge or row of trees.

wood grain: the natural decorative characteristics of wood. Pattern depends to a great extent on how wood is cut from the log.

work area of home: the parts of a dwelling that are needed to maintain and service other areas; includes kitchen, utility room, workshop.

working conditions: the physical and financial aspects of a job; the surroundings, pay scale, fringe benefits.

work triangle: the triangle formed within a kitchen by drawing an imaginary line from the refrigerator to the range to the sink.

woven fabrics: fabrics made by interlacing sets of yarns.

Z

zoning rules: city regulations which determine the way real property may be used.

Acknowledgments

The author wishes to thank Lettie Cale, Hazel Coatsworth, Willie Mae Coombs, Mary Alice Davis, Amy Jean Knorr, Dolores Watkins, and Madeline Minchin for their assistance in developing the framework for the content of this book. Appreciation is also extended to Peggy Brown and Milton Lewis for reading and commenting on the chapters; to colleagues and members of her family for their support and encouragement; to Robert Lewis for his help in preparing the glossary; to Janet Dearing for her help in developing the instructor's guide; to Sylvia Gillis for typing the manuscript; and to Philip Bartholomew for help with photography and the use of illustrations from his interior design collection.

Index

A

Abstract of title, 106
Accessories,
  bargains in, 243, 244
  decorative, 206, 207
  functional, 206, 207
Acquiring housing, 91-113
  cost, 92, 93
  process, 91-93
Acquisition, 64
Adjustable rate mortgage, 107
Agreement of sale, 105
Air,
  satisfying needs and personal
    priorities, 16-19
  reducing inside pollution, 225
Analogous color harmony, 145-148
Architects, 308
Artificial light, 176-179
Assigning a lease, 100
Automatic washers, 219-221

B

Backgrounds, 156-165, 239-241
  bargains in, 239-241
  ceilings, 164, 165
  floors, 156-161
  walls, 161-164
Bargains,
  home decorating and design, 235-254
  redecorating, 244, 245
  remodeling, 249-254

Basic life-style, 42-44
Beauty, satisfying needs and personal
    priorities, 26, 27
Blinds, 171
Blueprint, 118, 120
Bonded wood, 191, 192
Breach of contract, renting housing,
    100, 101
Built-in storage units, 132, 133
Burglars, security from, 21, 228-230
Buying a home, 101-112
  building a house, 102
  condominium ownership, 110, 111
  cooperative ownership, 111, 112
  estimating housing costs, 101, 102
  new house, 102, 103
  steps in, 105-112
  "used" house, 103, 104

C

Career clusters, 306-308
Career information, 308
Careers in housing, 305-323
Careers, job descriptions, 308-317
Career ladders, 318, 319
Career levels, 317-319
  entry, 318
  mid level positions, 318
  professional, 317, 318
Career web, 306, 307
Carpets and rugs, 159-161